CONTEMPORARY ISSUES IN CORPORATE RESTRUCTURING

CONTEMPORARY ISSUES IN CORPORATE RESTRUCTURING

Edited by
Prof. S.L. Gupta
Chairman
Department of Management
Kurukshetra University
Kurukshetra

ANMOL PUBLICATIONS PVT. LTD.
NEW DELHI - 110 002 (INDIA)

ANMOL PUBLICATIONS PVT. LTD.
4374/4B, Ansari Road, Daryaganj
New Delhi - 110 002

Contemporary Issues in Corporate Restructuring

First Edition, 2001

ISBN 81-261-0728-6

PRINTED IN INDIA

Published by J.L. Kumar for Anmol Publications Pvt. Ltd., New Delhi - 110 002 and Printed at Mehra Offset Press, Delhi.

CONTENTS

SECTION - I

INTRODUCTION & GENERAL ISSUES

SECTION - II

STRATEGIES

SECTION - III

FINANCIAL RESTRUCTURING

SECTION - IV

RESTRUCTURING: ORGANISATION & HRD

SECTION - V

CORPORATE GOVERNANCE

FOREWORD

All of us are now exposed to the trinity of the words: Liberalisation, Privatisation and Globalisation. Globalisation has not only gained universal currency, it has also developed a highly volatile, complex and unpredictable business environment. In fact, it has provided a new dimension in shape of both great challenges and lucrative rewards. Consequently, it has brought about a radical shift in the structure and functioning of the business sector all over the world.

Since globalisation agenda has been adopted by nearly all the countries, leading to the emergence of a global village, now revamping of economies through restructuring to usher in markets is noticeable. No one can overcome the new challenges with the old and conventional techniques. Essentially, restructuring is the need of the day in all the spheres, and Indian corporate sector in this respect is not the exception.

The basic objective of corporate restructuring is to consolidate all the business activities and operations by a corporations by a corporate unit in order to meet the emerging challenges and enhancing value of the firm. In other words, restructuring is realignment of the major instrumentalities of management for greater effectiveness and creating value through every possible means. The important forms of corporate restructuring include expansion, contraction, divestment and change in ownership and organisational control. The emerging issues pertaining to corporate restructuring in India are manifold, i.e. organisational restructuring, financial restructuring, market restructuring, strategies for corporate restructuring, etc.

The present book exhibits a valuable information on the contemporary trends and issues relating to corporate restructuring. The edited book contains a sizeable number of papers written by various experts from different fields. The subject matter of the above book is well selected and presented in a logical manner. Anybody who is keen to know about this latest theme of corporate restructuring can straightway refer to this book, and need not, thereafter, turn the pages of any other book.

Prof. S.L. Gupta, the editor of this book, with many years of experience and expertise, here presents a very meaningful and timely contribution to such an important field of study. The treatment and clarity on the subject matter is praiseworthy. I strongly believe that it will provide a means of reliable guidance for the teachers, researchers, students and business executives.

R.S. Chaudhry
IAS (Retd)
Vice-Chancellor,
Kurukshetra University, Kurukshetra.

PREFACE

Today, numerous events are taking place at the fast rate all over the world. The rapid technological developments, liberalisation of trade and economies, intense competition and integration of financial markets across the globe have resulted into more changes in the business world in the last decade than in the previous fifty years. So, it has become mandatory for the business enterprises to restructure themselves so as to effectively cope up with emerging challenges ahead and to remain competitive, profitable and efficient. Recently, major giant multinational corporates of the world have undergone drastic changes and have restructured themselves.

For the continuous existence, ongoing developments and for gaining competitiveness edge, corporate restructuring has become essential, even compulsory for business enterprises, which may occur in the organisational structure, operational activities, control and ownership pattern. One has to be alive and alert to the environment and make changes as one goes along. For restructuring, there are no set principles and no specific prescription of the way to go ahead. Each unit has to restructure itself and invent a model of management based on its own premises and values. All this requires not only minds that are alive and fertile but also attitude receptive to change.

Liberalisation and the process of globalisation of the Indian economy, initiated in the 1990s, have threatened the control, if not the survival of many Indian business enterprises. They have to go to beyond palliatives of short term protection from the government, to face competition in a global environment. There is no going back on the road that we have taken. Control and restrictions show the path of competition and free trade, and rationalisation and reorganisation indicate towards necessary concomitant. Moreover, business combinations, mergers, acquisitions divestitutes, demergers are becoming normal corporate activities which co-exist without any contradictions and legal restrictions. The seeds of restructuring were shown in USA and UK after the World War II. Major petroleum giants like Mobile & Royal Dutch Shell initiated exercise of consolidations and demergers in the early 1950s. Mergers and Industrial restructuring have raised important issues both for business decisions and for public policy formulation. No firm is regarded safe from takeover possibility.

This book presents an overall view of corporate restructuring alongwith contemporary issues relating to it. The volume has been split into five sections, namely Introduction & General Issues, Strategies, Financial Restructuring, Organisational & Human Resource Development, and finally, Corporate Governance. The first section includes such papers as deal with the conceptual & general issues of corporate restructuring. Important among them are contemporary issues of corporate restructuring in India, need of corporate restructuring in the new millennium, corporate objectives from Indian value systems, restructuring in the era of e-commerce, corporate restructuring in Indian perspective.

Certain aspects relating to strategies of corporate restructuring like re-engineering management, market restructuring, structuring as a value added strategy for business growth, military strategies, restructuring a viable option for public sector undertaking have been stated in the second section. Papers on corporate restructuring relating to financial issues, named in this book as Financial Restructuring, have been presented in the third section. A few aspects of financial restructuring like equity carve-out, retrospection of Indian capital market, mergers & takeovers, synergy of combination, intellectual capital as a key to financial restructuring are presented in this section.

Fourth section of this book concentrates on organisational and human resource development restructuring. Important issues like redundancy, need for emotionally intelligent leaders, HRD strategy, challenges for HR professional, total employee involvement and transformational leadership driven management have been incorporated in this section. The emerging issues on corporate governance and their impact on corporate restructuring have been presented in the fifth section of this book. Important issues like restructuring of company liquidation process, restructuring corporate governance in India, changing horizon of corporate governance, internal restructuring and corporate governance, etc have been included in this section.

This book is mainly based upon the papers which were presented in the National Seminar on Contemporary Issues in Corporate Restructuring in India in the New Millennium organised by the Department of Management, Kurukshetra University under the directorship of the undersigned. I am short of words to express my profound sense of gratitude to Honorable Shri R.S. Chaudhry, Vice-Chancellor, Kurukshetra University for his inspiring idea to bring out this publication and writing for Foreward Note to this book. His indispensable help, affection and guidance have been a source of constant inspiration and stimulation for me.

I express my deep sense of gratitude to Prof. Hoshiar Singh Pro-Vice Chancellor of Kurukshetra University for his scholary advice. I am also indebted to Dr. Hawa Singh, Registrar, Kurukshetra University, Dr. L.C. Gupta, Director, Directorate of Correspondence Courses, Kurukshetra University, Prof. V.K. Bhalla, Delhi University, Mr. J.L. Kumar, Managing Director, Anmol Publications Pvt. Ltd., New Delhi and my wife Shashi Gupta for their cooperation and suggestions. I express my sincere thanks to all the contributors for their valuable articles which present an adequate material on the topic discussed therein.

Prof. S.L. Gupta

Section-I

INTRODUCTION & GENERAL ISSUES

1

CORPORATE RESTRUCTURING IN INDIA: AN OVERVIEW

*Prof. S.L. Gupta**

In the era of rapid technological development, globalization of trade and economies, intense competition and integration of financial markets across the globe, it has become mandatory for the business organization to restructure themselves so as to effectively cope up with the emerging challenges. Indian corporate have to be internationally competitive otherwise they may not be able to survive in this era. Restructuring corporations is vital: it is vital to remain competitive, remain profitable, remain efficient. Major corporation in the world have gone through ups and downs e.g. IBM has gone through ups and downs. But they have always restructured, always changed. There are no set principles, there is no prescription that this is the way it shall be done. There is no standardized formula for a management that these are the systems and that this is missing. You cannot write an Indian version of a prescription for management. One has to alive and alert to the environment and makes changes as one goes along.

But the need to restructure Indian corporations is very important today. There is no going back on the road that we have taken. All products would have to find their place in a more competitive

* Chairman, Dept. of Management, Kurukshetra University.

world. All this requires not only minds that are alive and fertile and receptive to change but organizations, which are receptive to change.

Organizational restructuring is modern response to above cited challenges. Organizations are redesigning themselves for the various reasons, which may be reducing the costs of operations, or consolidating the various human and financial resources of organization's subsidiaries. *The quest is to cut the fat but not the muscle.*

Merchant banking has transformed with a paradigm shift in the portfolio investment. IT & Pharmaceuticals shares are fastly replacing the shares of traditional heavy weight industries like cement, petrochemicals and steel. Mutual fund industry has suddenly revived with many money grcwth schemes mopping up a large chunk of public savings.

Spate of mergers and acquisition deals in telecom, IT and banking industry has vigorously initiated the process of financial restructuring of the resultant unit. With stock markets rising in USA and India, *equity component is fastly replacing the debt part.* New instruments like derivatives interest rates swaps and foreign currency swaps have offered new avenues to the financial managers to channelize their funds.

The legal and judicial issues are also gaining importance in the era of corporate restructuring. The Government is chalking out a fresh agenda for corporate restructuring involving legal formalities. Department of company affairs secretary has advocated setting up of a separate authority to deal with the mergers, de-mergers, and corporate restructuring matters in order to expedite approvals and decisions and improving the corporate efficiency. A separate entity to deal with the mergers and acquisitions is required because the laws related to these issues are very complicated and processing procedure is very time consuming.

Top management of Blue Chip Corporations is actively involved in chalking out new strategies for corporate sizing, change of ownership, closures, privatization of public sector enterprises are the various strategies being adopted by the govt. as well as private owned companies.

Mergers, takeovers, restructuring and corporate control have become central public and corporate policy issues. To some, Mergers and Acquisitions, restructuring and corporate control activities represent a new industrial force that will lead the corporate world to new heights of creativity and productivity.

The Changing Business Environment in India

The underlying framework of India's post-independence policy regime was constructed during the 1930's. However, few of the architects of this inward-oriented trade regime could have anticipated the depth and breadth of state controls which were progressively introduced from the 1950's to the 1970s. These controls regulated not only the transactions between the Indian economy and the outside world, but also the activities of companies in India.

From the time of the Second Five-Year Plan (1956-61), the government's economic development programme was built around the principle of self-reliance. Protection was achieved by a combination of tariffs, non-tariff barriers (NTBs) and restrictions on import channels. During the course of the 1960s and 1970s, the Indian economy became progressively more inward-oriented. By 1980, the modal tariff rate was 100 per cent on non-durable consumer goods, 60 per cent on consumer durables and intermediates, and 40 per cent on capital goods. In addition, import licenses were used to curb the imports of all but a few consumer goods, and those goods whose import was allowed were generally products for which likely produced equivalents were not available.

The inward orientation of the Indian economy was further accentuated by restriction on foreign direct investment (FDI) and import of technology. The Foreign Exchange Regulation Act (FERA), 1974, obliged foreign companies to reduce their equity participation in joint ventures to below 40 per cent.

Technology licensing agreements were designed to promote and protect indigenous technological capability between indigenous firms and overseas technology licensers.

Controls over trade and inward investment were a common feature of import substitution industrialization strategies in developing countries. Much less common were controls over domestic industry. These were developed extensively by the Indian states. The Industries (Development and Regulation) Act, 1951, reserved the sectors for state ownership. The state was to control the commanding heighten of the economy, although there were considerable ambiguities and get-out clauses concerning what the private sector could and could not do in sectors mainly reserved for state activity. Key sectors and firms not directly under the control of the state were regulated by the licensing system. Approval was required from the concerned ministry by companies which wished to establish new plants, produce new goods, increase production by more than 10 per cent, or change location. Control over larger enterprises was further extended by the Monopolies and Restrictive Trade Practices Act (MRTP) in 1969.

However, from the early 1980s, what had been a remarkably stable policy regime began to change in rather fundamental ways. The first reforms to the system of economic control took place in the period 1981-87, affecting both industry policy and trade policy. Licensing restrictions were relaxed and in 1985 a system of 'broad-banding' was introduced, which freed up firms to shift product mixes and switch capacity to related items. In addition, controls on large companies and foreign corporations were relaxed. The number of firms subjected to MRTP rules was also reduced, and the focus of the MRTP shifted from control of the business houses towards control of specific restrictive practices.

Some relaxation of control over linkages with the outside

world was also introduced at this time. The 40 per cent limit on equity participation by foreign companies was raised to 51 per cent in cases leading to technology transfer or improved exports, and the control of the state import houses over trade was reduced. Quantitative restrictions on imports were reduced, and most outright ban on imports of products were abandoned. Import restrictions on capital goods which had no Indian source of supply and intermediate goods were reduced in order to increase the industry's efficiency.

These policy changes, which were timid in comparison with those introduced in many other developing countries, certainly increased competition within the economy. However, minor policy changes came only with the liberalization programme initiated in 1991. In the course of the 1990s, tariff levels were reduced significantly, quantitative restrictions on imports were largely abandoned, foreign direct investment freed up, exchange controls simplified, the industrial licensing system abolished, reservation of economic activities for the state reduced in scope, and restrictions on large companies relaxed. These policy changes had an enormous impact on the competitive environment. Competition between enterprises in India was stimulated, and the combination of trade liberalization and investment liberalization opened up the economy to external pressures. A growing inflow of FDI, though in no way comparable to the capital inflows in China or indeed Brazil, represented a significant change from the previous decades. While there was opposition to these processes of liberalization in both the domestic economy and in the regulation of external relations, there was nevertheless a sufficiently robust coalition supporting this radical change in policy regime to ensure that it was sustained, despite changes in governments.

From the vantage point of the mid-1990s, firms struggling to meet the challenges increasingly posed by liberalization found themselves operating in an environment which was characterized by three distinctive features:

The rate of industrial growth (as well as the growth in GDP and thus in purchasing power) which had only averaged 3.3% per annum during the period just before liberalization, rose rapidly thereafter.

Unlike many other low-income economies which had also begun to liberalize during the 1980s and change in the Indian policy regime was largely driven by internal interest groups. This meant that policy makers were able to control the pace of liberalization (especially in the external trade regime) and were thereby able to prevent the high rates of de-industrialization and rapid restructuring which have frequently characterized economies following a more rapid path of liberalization, for example, Argentina. Tariff protection was maintained, especially in the consumer goods sectors, leading to frequent conflicts with external trading partners such as the European Union.

Despite a significant freeing up in many products and factor markets, there remained significant barriers to exit, particularly with regard to the displacement of labour, where most of the existing labour legislation was left intact. Associated with this was a strong trade union movement and a pattern of industrial relations characterized by frequent conflict, sometimes not just between management and labour, but also between different unions.

FORMS OF CORPORATE RESTRUCTURING

Mergers and acquisitions

From a legal standpoint, there are many distinctions between various types of mergers and combinations. Most generally, mergers mean any transaction that forms one economic unit from two or more previous ones. A horizontal merger involves two firms operating in the same kind of business activity. Thus, a merger between two steel firms would represent a horizontal merger. Vertical mergers involve different stages of production operations. In the oil industry distinctions are made between exploration and production activity, refining operations, and marketing to the ultimate consumer. In the pharmaceutical industry one could distinguish between research and development of new drugs, the production of drug, and the marketing drug products through retail drug stores. Conglomerate mergers involve firms engaged in unrelated types of business activity. Among conglomerate mergers, three types have been distinguished; product extension mergers broaden the product lines of firms. Finally a pure conglomerate merger involves unrelated business activities that would not qualify as either product extension or market extension mergers.

Two major forms of combination have been recognized in compiling data mergers and acquisitions. Infact the departmentation of investment banking firms engaged in providing advice on this activities is usually referred to as the mergers and acquisitions department.

If one firm wishes to gain control over another, it typically seeks approval for the merger from the other firm's management and Board of Directors. An alternative approach is the "bear hug." In this approach, a company mails a letter to the directors of the takeover target announcing the acquisition proposal and requiring the directors to make a quick decision on the bid. If approval cannot be obtained, the acquiring company can appeal directly to the stockholders by means of the tender offer, unless the management and the directors of the target firm hold enough stock to retain control. If the shareholders respond favourably to the tender offer, the acquiring company will gain control and have the power to replace the directors who have not cooperated in the takeover effort. (This is referred to as a *hostile takeover.*) The target firm may seek to avoid being acquired or may seek to join with another firm with which it would rather be associated. The target firm, therefore, may seek to elicit an offer from a partner it considers more desirable. Or the target firm may engage in a form of restructuring such as offering to pay shareholders a large cash dividend financed by debt. This restructuring may be preferred by shareholders to the outside offer and the restructuring may make the target less attractive to the bidder.

Based on Profitability, mergers are four types:

(1) merger between two profitable companies;

(2) merger between two losing companies;

(3) merger between one profitable and one losing company wherein the acquiring company is profitable and the target is losing;

(4) merger between one profitable and one losing company wherein the acquiring company is losing and the target is profitable.

Mergers between Parke-Davis India Ltd. And Warner Hindustan Ltd is of Type 1; merger between Alembic Chemical Works Ltd and Neomer Ltd of type 2; merger between D.C.W. Ltd and Plastic Resins and Chemicals Ltd is of Type 3; and merger Spundish Engineers Ltd. and Tractors India Ltd is of type 4.

In addition to the benefits derived by way of merging horizontally, vertically, concentric and conglomerate fashion, merger between two losing companies or merger of profitable company with losing company has been designed to reap tax advantage. And therefore Types 2, 3 and 4 stated above are often earmarked as tax benefit merger. Income Tax Act, 1961 allow carry forward of some absorbed expenses/allowances of the amalgamating companies by the amalgamated company. The Amalgamated company is entitled to claim the unabsorbed Allowance under section 32 A (6), unabsorbed development allowance under Section 33a (5), unabsorbed expenditure on acquisition of patent right and copyright under Section 35A(b) and unabsorbed preliminary expenses under Section 35d(5). By virtue of Section 72 A the amalgamated company is allowed to carry forward unabsorbed depreciation and business losses of the amalgamating company on recommendation of the Specified Authority and on approval of the Central Government. However, the tax benefit under section 72 A can be availed of pursuing a revival program for the losing amalgamating company. And such persuasion of revival program is subject to rigid scrutiny by the specified Authority mentioned in the Income Tax Act. In India, the merger cases between one profitable and another losing Company were mostly directed to reap the tax benefit offered in Section 72 a. However, in some cases of merger between one profitable and another losing company wherein approval under Section 72 A could not be obtained or wherein it was believed to be too difficult to pursue the conditions stated therein, the companies in the fray merged in a reverse fashion to avail of carry foreward facilities available under Section 72. Section 72 of Income Tax Act facilities carry forward of unabsorbed depreciation and business loss of a company for setting of in future periods (for business loss within eight years and for unabsorbed depreciation without time restriction), if the company remains in operation for sometimes in the year of such setting-off, Thus it requires the survival of the losing company to avail the carry forward facility so wherein approval under section 72A could not be obtained or wherein the parties in merger dislike to records to Section 72A, they may merge in a recoveries fashion keeping the losing alive. Tractors India Ltd. merged with Spunmdish Engineers Ltd. and Oriental Carbon and Chemicals Ltd. merged with Dharuhera Chemicals Ltd. in reverse fashion to avail of tax benefit under Section 72. Even in case of merger between tow losing companies tax benefit can be availed of by way of merger. In case of merger of Neomer Ltd. with Alembic Chemicals Worked company Ltd., the acquiring company became profitable in the post-merger period and availed of the carry forward facility. Thus merger classification based on profitability facilitates the identification of tax benefit mergers excepting Type I, all other three types essentially indicate the cases of tax benefit merger. And subsequently we shall explore that tax benefit provides sufficient impetus for corporate merger in India.

Merger Procedure

By virtuc of Section 39 A of the Companies Act, 1956 the High court is empowered to sanction scheme of amalgamation where application is being made under section 391. While sanctioning the scheme of amalgamation the High Court may make provision for the following:

(i) The transfer of property and liabilities of the amalgamating company to the amalgamated company;

(ii) Means of payment to shareholders of the amalgamating companies;

(iii) The continuation by or against the amalgamated company of any legal proceedings by or against the amalgamating company;

(iv) The dissolution (without winding up) of the amalgamating company;

(v) The provision to be made for any person as the Court may direct or decent from the compromise or arrangement;

(vi) Any other incidental consequential and supplementary matters.

If the affairs of the amalgamating company are conducted in a manner which are prejudicial to the public interest and to the interest of member, the Court would not accord sanction to the scheme of amalgamation. In all such cases the Court is guided by the report of official liquidation of the amalgamating company.

The parties in merger are requested to submit the order of the Court granting sanction to the scheme of amalgamation to the Registrar of companies for registration within thirty days. For the purpose of amalgamation the amalgamated company must be a company within the meaning of the Section 3 of the companies Act, 1956, however, the amalgamating

Companies may be anybody corporate whether it is a company within the meaning of the Section 3 or not.

The companies in merger should be authorized by the object clause of the Memorandum to go for merger, otherwise it will ultra wise the Memorandum and the Court cannot grant dissection touch 'scheme of amalgamation' [Jalpaiguri Tea Company Ltd(1974), company Cases 335]. A contrary opinion is also there, the Calcutta High court in Marybong and kyel Tata Tea Estates Ltd 1977, 47 company cases 82, observed that Section 394 gives jurisdiction to the court to sanction an arrangement, even though there may be no power vested in the company through object clause of its Memorandum. It is argued that were there is a statutory provision dealing with amalgamating of companies no special power in object clause is necessary for amalgamating with another company. Also in any scheme of amalgamation, all the companies in merger should comply with the formalities specified in Section 391 and Section 394 of the Companies Act. It is not enough if only one party of the merger fulfills the requirement [Union Service Private Ltd (1973), Company cases 319]. The creditors of the company has no say in the scheme of amalgamating

The term creditors include the Government and financial Institutions to which moneys are due from the company for various reasons. In the case of Union of India vs. Asia Udyog Pvt. LTD (1974) 95, I.T.R.299, Delhi High court pointed out the lacuna of the law and suggested to correct the situation by amendment to the law.

Even if the schemes of amalgamating is recommended by the Board of Directors and approved by the shareholders, still it is not obligatory for the court to sanction the scheme. Only if the schemes is reasonable and fair to all the parties concerned then the court has the discretion or power to sanction the scheme (Corron Tea Co. Ltd (1966) 2, Company Law Journal 278).

The scheme of amalgamating should be approved by the

Board of Directors and recommended to the shareholders. The shareholders in turn should adopt and approve such scheme in a meeting convened for the purpose by three-fourth majority. Under Section 394 A, the Central Government has the right to get notice of every application made to the court under Sections 391 and 394 of the Companies Act and give representation on scheme of amalgamation. In the case of Breadsell Company Ltd (1968), [Company Law Journal 261], the Madras High court made it clear that the court should send only the scheme of amalgamation to the Central Government for its remarks or objection before the Court takes decision on the scheme of merger. The powers and functions of the Central Government under Section 394 A are exercised by the Company Law Board through its Regional directs.

The amalgamated company has to discharge the claims of the dissenting shareholders as per Section 395. Lastly, the central Government has the power to order amalgamation in the national interest under Section 396 of the Companies Act.

Joint ventures involve the intersection of only a small fraction of the activities of the companies involved and usually for a limited duration of ten to fifteen years or less. They may represent a separate entity in which each of the parties makes cash and other forms of investments.

Sell-Off

The literature describes several kinds of sell-off. The two major types are spin-offs and divestitures. A spin-off creates a separate new legal entity; its shares are distributed on a pro rata basis to existing shareholders of the parent company. Thus, existing stockholders have the same proportion of ownership in the new entity as in the original firm. There is, however, a separation of control, and eventually the new entity as a separate decision-making unit may develop policies and strategies different from those of the original parent. Note that no cash is received by the original parent. In a sense, a spin-off is the split-off, in which a portion of existing shareholders receives stock in a subsidiary in exchange for parent company stock. Still a different variation of the spin-off is a split-up, in which the entire firm is broken up in a series of spin-offs, so that the parent no longer exists and only the new offspring survive.

In contrast to the class of spin-offs in which only shares are transferred or exchanged is another group of transactions in which cash comes into the firm-divestitures. Basically, a divestiture involves the sale of a portion of the firm to an outside third party. Cash or equivalent consideration is received by the divesting firm. Typically, the buyer is an existing firm, so that no legal entity results. It simply represents a form of expansion on the part of the buying firm.

A variation on divestiture is the equity carve-out. An equity carve-out involves the sale of a portion of the firm via equity offering to outsiders. In other words, new shares of equity are sold to outsiders which give them ownership of a portion of the previously existing firm. A new legal entity is created. The equity holders in the new entity need not be the same as the equity holders in the original seller. A new control group is immediately created.

The distinctions between these various forms of spin-offs are somewhat arbitrary, and some writers view them all as simply various forms of stock dividends, except for transactions that involve the sale of shares to parties other than existing shareholders.

Corporate Control

The third grouping of activities can be put as "corporate control." Premium buy-backs represent the repurchase of a substantial stock-holder's ownership interest at a premium above the market price (called green-mail). Often in competition with such buy-backs, a standstill agreement is written. This represents a voluntary contract in which the stockholder who is bought out agrees not to make further attempts to take over the company in the future. When a standstill agreement is made without a buy-back, the substantial stockholders simply agrees not to increase his or her ownership which presumably would put him or her in an effective control position.

Anti-takeover amendments are changes in the corporate bye-laws to make an acquisition of the company more difficult or more expansive. These include (1) supermajority voting provisions requiring a high percentage (For example, 80 per cent) of stockholders to approve a merger, (2) staggered terms for directors which can delay change of control for a number of years, and (3) golden parachutes which award large termination payments to existing management if control of the firm is changed and management is terminated.

In a proxy contest and outside group seeks to obtain representation on the firm's board of directors. The outsiders are referred to as "dissidents" or "insurgents" who seek to reduce the control position of a firm often has effective control of the board of directors, proxy contests are usually regarded as directed against the existing management.

Changes in Ownership Structure

Changes in ownership structure represent the fourth group of restructuring activities one form is through exchange offers, which may be the exchange of debt or preferred stock for common stock, or conversely, of common stock for the more senior claims. Exchanging debt for common stock increases leverage; exchanging common stock for debt decreases leverage.

A second form is share repurchase, which simply means that the corporation buys back some fraction of its outstanding shares of common stock. Tender offers may be made for share repurchase. The percentage of shares purchased may be small or substantial

In a going-private transaction, the entire equity interest in a previously public corporation is purchased by a small group of investors. The firm is no longer subject to the regulation of the Securities and Exchange Commission, whose purpose is to protect public investors. Going-Private transactions typically include members of the incumbent management group who obtain a substantial proportion of the equity ownership of the newly private company. When the transaction is initiated by the incumbent management, it is referred to as a management buy-out (MBO). Usually, a small group of outside investors provides funds and, typically, secures representation on the private company's board of directors. These outside investors also arrange other financing from third-party investors. When financing from third parties involves substantial borrowing by the private company, such transactions are referred to as leveraged buy-outs (LBOs).

Issues Raised by Restructuring

These activities have stirred much controversy. Are they good or bad for the economic health of the nation? Do they divert the energies of managers from bona fide economic activity to financial manipulation? Do they use up financial resources which otherwise would be employed in "real" investment activities? Why has such heightened merger activity been a phenomenon of the last 20 years?

The seeds of corporate restructuring were sown in USA and UK after the World War II. Major petroleum giants like Mobile and Royal Dutch Shell initiated exercise of consolidations and demergers in the early 1950s. Mergers and Industrial restructuring have raised important issues both for business decisions and for public policy formulation. No firm is regarded safe from take over possibility. On the more positive side merger and acquisitions may be critical for healthy expansion of business firms as they evolve through successive stages of growth and development. In India also the public sector disinvestment programme and mergers of various private sector companies has initiated the process of corporate restructuring.

Corporate restructuring whereas yields super normal profits to corporate has also attached to psychological implications. Are these mergers and acquisition activities are good or bad for the economic health of the nation? Do they divert the energies of managers from bona fide economic activity to financial manipulation? Certain issues like people rendered jobless as a result of retrenchment and lay off, small companies being swallowed by large companies etc., that need to be addressed. This may create socio-economic imbalances in the developing countries like India. The technology oriented merger lead to creation of more capital intensive industrial giants rendering labour-intensive industries in doldrums. This has special significance for economies of over-populated countries having surplus pools of unskilled labour like India.

To curb the threat of hostile takeovers a code of conduct has to be evolved which can check the insider trading aimed at artificially manipulating the prices of shares of the company to be acquired, fund syphoning etc. Some view the restructuring activity with a great alarm. They hold that competition will be decreased, efficiency reduced and financial instability increased. Other see Restructuring exercise as a natural expression of market forces. Any code of conduct of corporate governance ignoring these opposite views would prove to be counter productive to the interests of the economy as a whole.

The code of corporate governance is being rewritten by the sudden spate of merger and acquisition deals. The expectations of shareholders of merged entity is growing exponentially which is posing a major challenge to the modern managers. There is a great demand for simplification, greater accountability and transparency necessitated by increased inventor awareness and competitive market forces.

REFERENCES

Ranjit Kumar Mandal, Corporate Mergers in India, (objectives and effectiveness) Karishna Publishers Distributers, 1995.

Corporate Restructuring. John Humphrey, Raphael & Prasad, Response Braus (Safe) 1998.

J. Fred Weston, K wang S. Chung & Susan, *Mergers, Restructuring and Corporate Control*, Practice Hall of India (P) Ltd., New Delhi 1996.

S. Shiva Ramu,*Corporate Growth through Mergers & Acquisitions*, Response Braus (Safe) 1998.

Economic Times, (6.6.2000).

Foreign Trade Review, Vol. XXXV No. 1 .... June 2000).

R.B.I. Bulletin, Volume L IV No. 10 (Oct. 2000).

Mishra, R.K. (1998), "Corporate Governance in Public Enterprises: A New Framework", ASCI Formal of Management.

Human Development in South Asia - Report - (1999)

Productivity - Jan. - Mar. 2000 (vol. 40, no. 4)

OECD code o Corporate Governance

Supplement on Corporate Governance, Financial Lines (March 19, 1999)

Report of the Kumar Manglam Birla Committee on Corporate Governance appointed in SEBI.

The Corporate Restructuring of the 1980s and Its Import for the 1990s by Gorden Doneldson in Donald H. Chew.

2

RECENT ISSUES IN CORPORATE RESTRUCTURING IN THE NEW MILLENNIUM

*J.D. Aggarwal**

With the dawn of the new millennium corporate India stands on the threshold of hope and history. The only way to describe India today is that it is one of the most happening countries in the world. Over the last few years India has shed its traditional image of being a protected and confirmed state. For the first time ever in its entire existence, India has embarked upon a systematic and comprehensive program of structural adjustment that is leaving virtually no sector untouched.

The national and international economic environment is changing swiftly, indicating a radical change in the way business is conducted. The emerging trends are expected to radically change in the process and content of management of organisation. It is now incumbent upon the managers to critically appreciate the causes and consequences of paradigm shifts in economic environment. The ability of a manager to comprehend the dynamics of such changes and adapt accordingly will determine the growth and success of his organization. In this background corporate restructuring naturally assumes overriding importance.

Of late restructuring has become a buzz word. There is

---

* Director, Indian Institute of Finance, New Delhi.

restructuring all around. Business are restructuring, industries are restructuring and even countries are restructuring. In search of excellence and competitive edge, companies are experimenting with a lot of new tools and ideas. But no initiatives will deliver results unless a proper restructuring exercise is undertaken. Thus, the act of restructuring should precede all other activities aimed at achieving growth.

The pace of change has never been so fast. In order to ensure survival and attain effectiveness corporate need to realign their endowment to meet the challenges of future. And this alignment is brought about by corporate restructuring. Restructuring involves abandoning outmoded ways of running an organisation and embracing new ones. It requires that organizations keep on adapting in response to internal and external changes. Restructuring is usually embarked upon either to address significant external change such as liberalization or a major internal change such as organizational failure. It can also be resorted to if the management decides a change in corporate philosophy, core value or management style. But in India corporate restructuring followed the liberalization measures initiated in 1991. As 1994 study of 92 public and private sector corporations reveals that 81 had almost completed their restructuring process the same year. An early 1999 Business world report indicates that a large number of nation's largest 200 companies are seriously engaged with restructuring exercise.

There has been much thinking on the part of researchers, academicians, consultants and corporate managers on the objectives of corporate restructuring. In this connection issues involved in restructuring naturally gains importance. In my opinion placing culture on exalted pedestal while carrying out corporate restructuring is of utmost importance. Thus there should be a cultural approach towards corporate restructuring i.e. culture specific restructuring. While carrying out restructuring the whole gamut of culture should be treated with deference. Some of the points that should be kept in mind while it is on are: values, leader norms and reaction to critical incidences, criteria for rewarding, recruitment, selection, promotion, and transfer. These apart, other factors which can have significant bearing on the outcome restructuring are: Organizational design and structure, organizational systems and procedures, and formal statement on organizational philosophy, creed and charter.

In the new era of liberalization and globalisation some of issues constituting the basis of restructuring are:

Higher Earning

Trends indicate that delivering of higher earning and creation of corporate value are the two basic goals of corporate restructuring. Recent stock market boom has shown that there is a scramble for companies registering higher growth and disdain for average performing company. Ability to generate enough cash largely determine value creation.

Core Competence

One of the vital components of restructuring is focus. This is the age of specialization. The concept of learning organisation is gaining momentum. Therefore emphasis should be laid on exploiting the rise on learning curve. Reasonable mileage can be derived out of such experiences only when companies focus on core competencies. Dabling in too many areas would diffuse focus as management attention would be distracted.

The best way to provide good returns for investors, is to concentrate on what one knows best. In order sustain the onslaught of competition enterprises need to be more focused.

Divestiture and Networking

Companies should directly oversee the critical aspects of their business but exit from peripherals. It is not that companies should completely abandon peripherals. They can still play important role through a joint venture or strategic alliance.

Vision, Strategy and Structure

Corporate restructuring should be properly adjusted to vision, strategy and structure. Companies should be very clear about what heights they want to scale, by when and how. Answers to these questions will immensely influence the success or failure of restructuring program. The vision should be properly aligned to the set of values that the company nurtures.

Proactive Leadership

Leadership has been one of the most talked about subjects in management circles. Management style can influence restructuring process to a great extent. All the successful companies have demonstrated clearly leadership style wherein managers have been able to relate on a one-to-one level with employees.

Empowerment

Empowerment can go a long way in ensuring the success of a restructuring exercise. Without proper delegation no restructuring can be said to be complete. In view of changing socio-economic scenario it is very important that companies decentralized decision making. In the new milieu a change over to SBUs-type lines of business structure form a functional structure would be more appropriate. There should be considerable investment in manpower to strengthen their capability and empower them. Empowerement should be concomitant to responsibility and accountability. Delegation is effective when good decisions are made; and good decision require an effective management information system. Therefore while dealing with empowerment MIS should not be given a short-shrift.

Reengineering Process

Improving processes and aligning a company's resources only will lead to the success of restructuring. Redesigning business process should be attached high priority in corporate restructuring exercise.

Issues of privatization and deregulation are also important in the exercise of restructuring. Decision on downsizing will go a long way in shaping corporate restructuring.

Capacity to adapt to fast changing environment distinguishes a successful organisation from a run of the mill organization an this capacity can come about only through a well thought out corporate restructuring.

In spite of rules and regulations aimed at weakening the shackles of red tapism, current provisions do not augur well for the perfect blossoming of corporate India. In order to infuse the much needed element of viability into Indian Corporate system it needs to emerge out of confines and penetrate the overseas market with confidence and conviction. For this Indian companies will have to set up plants and trading offices in other countries. The challenge posed by MNCs can be dealt with by becoming one. If we want to go global, we will have to review the restrictive bottlenecks in our current alliances and joint ventures and restructure the whole system. There is an urgent need for easing the process of acquisitions and mergers.

The process of restructuring faces the choice of building technologies or buying them. Buying technologies is no solution, building them is. The buying of technology involves various sorts of handicaps. The process of restructuring will be complete only when there is focus on Research and Development efforts. Forming alliances can certainly be helpful but there is no better substitute to building strong Research and Development base. Research and Development projects should have clear link of strategy and be according to the customer needs.

The way we think also forms a crucial part of our restructuring exercise. The concern of maximizing shareholder value should not cloud our thinking. All the shareholders should be accorded proper importance. The lack of harmony and balance can jeopardize restructuring plans.

Corporate restructuring, denotes major re-orientation, reorganization or realignment of the assets, investment and liability structure of any company through well thought out management actions with view to significantly change the quality and quantity for the future cash flow statements. This includes mergers, acquisitions, divestitures, spin-offs and all other internal management upgradations to cover the possible types of redesigns for company. The idea of corporate restructuring gains importance in the wake of intensifying competition, globalisation and technological changes. It has been found that majority of the diversified multi-product companies are restructuring their corporate operations to gain efficiency and synergy in operations. This involves transfer of business units from one company to the other or breaking up of a larger group into smaller ones. Smaller companies, on the other hand, are forming alliances and joint ventures for their survival and growth. The exercise ensures that there is change in ownership and control to comply with a variety of business laws.

Some of the basic components of restructuring are: expansion, diversification,.collaboration, spinning off, hiding off, Mergers and acquisitions,

Acquisition of companies and business units or mergers with other companies has been in practice for the last one decade. Acquisition of companies should ideally be friendly and peaceful but at times it turns hostile. In the context of India merger is used for consolidating separate entities into one through a statutory process of amalgamation. A host of reasons may be cited as to why companies or groups resort to mergers and acquisitions aggressively. But a closer look reveals that most of them are not aimed at enhancing shareholder value. And here lies the reason for the success or failure of any corporate restructuring. Certainly excessive concern for shareholder value is not justified as there are other areas as well which require attention but shareholder value should certainly be at the top of the mind of managers. Shareholder value oriented restructuring programs stand the chance of better success rate. Mergers and Acquisitions become imperative because of speedy growth and expansion of capacity. Cut throat competition may be cited as yet another cause for undertaking expansion. In recent times there has been a plethora of mergers and acquisitions in the corporate world. In such cases emerging companies control the market share by facing the competition head on.

Quick and low risk entry into news market is yet another reason for this. Such arrangement help companies establishes their control over the market without much difficulty. In such cases companies get to use already functioning distribution channels and other facilities. Other reason for mergers and acquisitions may be strategic control over backward and forward linkages. A study conducted by Wyatt Worldwide cites three reasons for merger and acquisition deals. These are gaining market share, increasing access to new markets and achieving competitiveness.

The main impetus for most of the mergers is the concept of synergistic operating economies. Since ordinarily the existing undertakings are assumed to be operating below their optimal level, it is envisaged of two undertaking together with a resultant reduction in operating costs producing better results. The resultant economy is regarded as synergistic economy.

It also helps in cutting competition between both the companies.

Merger are also guided by the objective of diversification of activities. Such amalgamations generally create conglomerate undertaking. Mergers are often welcomed by the managerial staff in view of the imminent benefits. The party which acquires usually offers benefits to the staff in order to gain and strengthen managerial support.

With mergers hopes of attaining enhanced efficiency, market power and of course profit. The premise behind merger, in almost all the cases, is the desire to acquire and sustain growth. The development and nurturing of a new and virgin undertaken is much more costly, risky time consuming and problematic than the acquiring of an existing company in a growth sector even though the acquisition may be at a premium. The surviving company may, infact, acquire only such assets of the merging company as are likely to serve the purpose of growth better. Both the business and the shareholders gain from mergers and takeovers. Business gains by having centralized administration which results in improved operations. The shareholders, on the other hand, benefit from the premium.

Shareholders gain from mergers in a number of ways.. Mergers generally provide impetus to growth of economy, diversification of product line, realization of greater profit etc.

Mergers certainly offer many advantages but such restructuring exercise should not be viewed as totally risk free. In the entire exercise counsel from certain specialized agencies, like solicitors and finance professionals should be sought whenever necessary. Accommodation of legal and commercial side in the process of transaction is very important. Solicitors should be involved in the negotiations between the parties at as early a stage as possible. It helps in protecting individual interests of the merging undertaking and ensures that his client does not enter any self destructive deal. The solicitor, if appraise at appropriate time can help suggest the most beneficial and effective tax model.

As the wave of merger and acquisition is sweeping across the corporate landscape so is doing its flip side. Though de-mergers and spin-off do not hold so much attention but they are a reality and with certain advantages of course. De-mergers and spin-offs help in enhancing the growth of the economy. The undertakings may demerge in order to delineate businesses and to form up the concomitant responsibilities, liabilities and management so as to derive improved results from each of the newly emerged branches of the original undertaking. It would be in the interest of business to dispose off the loss making branch and invest the assets and efforts, that were being expended in the loss making branch, to the rest of the business. Conditions may crop up when the source of funding insists upon the disposal of that part of the undertaking which represent a risk so as to ensure a greater surety of returns.

Mergers and de-mergers are both concept of high utility and if used property, would go a long way in improving our economy. The division that would come out of de-mergers would lead to greater expertise and more intensive supervision. The trend of mergers and de-mergers should not be tampered with. It should be nurtured for the long term benefits.

Industry representatives had been suggesting extension of tax benefit to demerged companies. They think demerged companies should also be given the benefit of tax concession on the lines of merged companies. The Finance Minister even accepted their suggestion in the last budget. In demerger, the transfer of undertakings should be made by the transfer of company in such a manner that all the properties of the undertaking become the properties of the transferee company, all the liabilities relateable to the undertaking become the liabilities of the transferee company and the transfer of the above properties and liabilities is made at the value appearing in the books of the transferror company.

The various concessions granted under the Income Tax Act will certainly facilitate the process of demerger. It will be noticed that the tax concessions relate to exemption from capital gains.

In recent times there has been a spate of activities aimed at encouraging staff and workers to participate in the ownership and management of the company. The process of empowering staff is accomplished by offering them with stock option. This also is a new concept which is being adopted by many companies in our country.

In the restructuring exercise portfolio restructuring forms a vital component. Though empirical evidence does not support this, the motive behind portfolio restructuring is to achieve industry specialization. But it has been seen that portfolio restructuring impacts Research and Development efforts of a firm. In that related- constrained diversified firms spend more funds on Research and Development after restructuring compared to other types of firms.

Financial restructuring is a part of corporate restructuring. The most popular method of financial restructuring is equity carve out to generate cash for investment. This is mostly done through issuing shares of subsidiaries to the public. This pattern is also used in many developed countries. However India presents a mixed scenario. While some companies have used equity carve out in subsidiaries, some have done this for their holding companies. Indian Conglomerates face quite a different set of problems. These business houses have very little equity in their promoted companies with the change in scenario they are facing hostile takeovers bids from foreign investors. In order to deal with the situation, they have resorted to equity carve-in method. Various forms are adopted to increase shareholding. The Tata group, for instance, has adopted both equity carve-out and equity carve-in methods.

Strategy and structure are crucially lined to each other in any organisation. Any mismatch could prove detrimental to the welfare of the organisation and, therefore, calls for organizational restructuring. The nature of relationship between strategy and structure has an implication on the performance of a firm. The decision to go for organizational restructuring depends on many factor. One such factor can be cited as organizational misfit with strategy. The other factor which influences organization restructuring is the nature of the Board of Directors. This significantly influences the restructuring decision of an organisation.

Financial Reengineering and Corporate Restructuring

The globalisatoin of the Indian economy has brought about radical changes in the field of finance. Finance as such is a very dynamic field and has passed through various turbutent phases, Initially finance was considered as a poor cousin of economics and it was not given any importance. But soon its presence was felt in every segment of the system and it was given the title of life blood of an organization. This fast phase of dynamism in the field of finance made it essential for all the organization to come up with new and fresh ideas to be able to face the cut throat competition,. And as it is rightly said, "Necessity is the mother of innovation"' it has led to the birth of a new discipline called "financial engineering or innovations.".

It is very difficult to describe in a sentence or two what actually is meant by term " Financial Reengineering", but broadly speaking all the new revolutionary products, trades strategies and major financing deals can be considered to form a part of it. It involves the design, the development and the implementation of innovative financial instruments and processes. It can also be interpreted as the formulation of creative solutions to problem in finance. In fact a lot of creativity and zeal of being innovative is involved in this discipline. At times, it involves a slight twist to old ideas or piecing together of the existing products and processes to fit a particular set of circumstances. Thus, the principle does not oppose slight modifications in existing instruments but strongly advocates that old instruments/ methods which have become obsolete should be thrown away. New principles should be developed that are commensurate to the present day requirements.

Financial innovation is not limited to corporate and institutional applications. Many of the creative financial innovation in recent years have been directed in retail finance. These include adjustable rate mortgages, cash management accounts, Noki accounts, IRAs and various new forms of life insurance. In corporate finance new instruments are developed to secure the funds necessary for operations of large scale business. Mergers and Acquisitions, bridge financing to secure the funds necessary for takeover and leveraged buyouts, junk bonds are the recent innovations. In the field of investment and money management new instrument such as high yield mutual funds, money market mutual funds, sweeps systems, repo markets etc. have been developed. In order to convert high risk investment instrument to low risk investment instruments ingenious devices as repackaging and collaterilization have also been resorted to . Similarly in securities and derivatives product trading and risk management such innovations have taken place. Many of the innovative new products trading in capital markets today originated as solution to a particular clients needs. Sometimes solutions created are one of a kind and have little recyclability but at other times they have much wider applicability and can be productized.

Tremendous growth in this field can be attributed to a number of factors that affect the firm. These factors can be divided into two categories.

1) Environmental factors

2) Intrafirm factors.

The environmental factors may be regarded as the factors that are external to the firm and over which the firm has no control but which are of great concern to the firm due to their impact on the performance of the firm,. They include increased price volatility, a general globalisation of industry and financial market, tax asymmetries, technological advances, advances in financial theory, regulatory change., increased competition and transaction costs.

The second group consists of those factors that are internal to the firm and over which the firm has atleast some control- the intrafirm factors. This include liquidity needs, risk aversion among managers and owners, agency cost, greater level of quantity sophistication among investment mangers and more formal training of senior level personnel, sophistication among investment managers and more formal training of senior level personnel.

Financial Reengineering, is its initial stage at present but if we look back we find that innovations have been taking place ever since finance has developed. The integration of the worlds capitals market coupled with the economic expansion and increased emphasis on assets allocation strategies by portfolio managers has led to an enormous increase in the volume of cross border securities transactions. This has placed a great strain on almost all institutions all over the world to upgrade, innovate and standardize their offerings. The pressure becomes all the more severe when we realize the fact that one of the negative effects of globalisation weakening the hands of the monetary authority is controlling any major upset in the economy. So we see that the need for financial innovation has already become prominent and will become more pronounced in the years to come.

3

EFFECTIVE CORPORATE RESTRUCTURING
The Need of the New Millennium

M.S. Turan & B.S. Bodla***

Introduction

As we enter the Twenty-first century and bid good-bye to the last decade of the Twentieth Century, we find the world milieu a total contrast to what was obtaining ten years ago. This decade has seen the globalisation of business with intense competition against domestic as well as the international players. Globalisation of Indian economy is creating both opportunities and challenges for the industry and trade. With economic reforms in the ninth year, Indian business is gradually becoming stronger and there is hope and excitement for developing new and more profitable international markets. At the same time in the make of this development, some of the internationally well established and competitive companies which are entering into Indian market are putting pressure on Indian companies to cut costs, improve quality and modernize management systems. Private and public sector enterprises as well as governmental institutions are facing new challenges of the market environment.(Kaura & Pull, 1995)

* Chairman Dept. of Business Management, G.J.U., Hisar.

** Reader, Dept. of Business Management, G.J.U., Hisar.

To create a truly great corporate advantage, Indian enterprises/organizations are now required to re-think about business strategies, structures and processes, renew and re-position themselves to effectively serve the needs of emerging competitive market and the society. Hence, the aspects of restructing and re-engineering of the corporate have become more relevant and important in the emerging scenario. These restructuring activities are driven by commercial factors and the buzzwords are shareholder value creation"- be it concentrating on core competencies or shedding smaller or loss making units (Bhavana Doshi,1999).

Corporate Restructuring: An overview

Corporate restructuring leads to radical transformation. It focuses on transforming the business as a whole with the objective of bringing better customer focus, enhanced competitiveness, quicker response and greater clarity of structure, rules and accountability. The object of corporate restructuring is efficient and competitive business operations by increasing the market share, brand power and synergies. Therefore, many of the diversified multi-product companies are restructuring their corporate operations into more homogenous units to increase profitability and future growth. This is the process of shedding the unviable units and consolidate business portfolio in their respective areas of strengths, competitive advantage and core competence.

Accordingly the restructuring at the enterprise is looked up more as re-organization of the existing structure, regrouping of business including reallocations, alliances and mergers etc. To derive the advantages of core competence and market potential in the globalised environment. Infact, restructuring tries to improve upon what already exists. This may or may not bring a fundamental change and drastic improvements. Restructuring may be in the form of Re-organization, Automation, Upsizing, Downsizing and Outsourcing. On the other hand, Re-engineering focus on building all together a new business process keeping the customer in mind. Michael Hammer (1995) the founding father of Re-engineering defined it as, "Fundamental re-thinking and radical re-design of business process to achieve dramatic improvements in critical, contemporary measure of performance such as cost, quality, service and speed."

Hence, corporate restructuring is the comprehensive process, by which a company can consolidate its business operations and strengthen its position for achieving desired objectives. Corporate restructuring involves three major aspects - business portfolio restructuring, capital/financial restructuring and organizational restructuring.

The corporate have choices in the way restructuring is endeavoured. The top management may plan and execute restructuring by the top management with or without the participation of other stakeholders. It can be attempted all at one go, a comprehensive re-engineering, so to speak, or in phased manner over a relatively long period of time. It may be attempted with or without the expert advice of consultants. Restructuring may be attempted as an execution of a preconceived blueprint or in an evolutionary manner. It can be imitative, that is, conform to what some leading organization has done, or it can be innovative, with experimentation and improvisation.

Corporate Restructuring: A US Experience

According to extensive surveys undertaken in USA, restructuring is one of the most controversial management techniques. In USA a number of companies have derived dramatic improvements in there business performance as a result of restructuring. However, we do have adequate evidences which indicate that a number of such attempts were either abandoned half way or found to be unsuccessful. (Khader and Suryanarayanana 1998). It is revealed by the surveys that intra-organizational communication is vital to the success of restructuring attempt alongwith the committed top leadership behind it (Burke and Pepard, 1995). Generally, the following are reasons for the resistance to corporate restructuring exercise:

- It questions traditions and long held values.
- It strives to revise the behavior habits.
- Restructuring cuts across the mental models of all as it is too radical a change.
- It requires decentralisation
- Attempts to shed many jobs.
- It shakes the people from the current comfortable positions by challenging inertia.

In fact, the restructuring has become like a cult movement. Most segments of society in USA seems questioning its popularity and credibility. Studies reveal that about 70 percent of the attempts have resulted in either failures or abandonment halfway. The main causes of this include inadequate attention to human face by equating re-structuring with downsizing, application at lower stages without establishing its strategic relevance, and absence of increased commitment and involvement by the top management.

Corporate Restructuring in India

The canvas of massive economic restructuring in India initiated in the eighties and accelerated in 1991 covered a wide range from delicensing and decontrol to globalization. The continuing economic process is putting profound impact on the style of management and operational structure of corporate sector. Indian organizations are now forced to unlearn the traditional way of doing business, and adopt new approaches by fundamentally rethinking the way they need to operate and meet the current challenges of emerging market oriented economy and survive. It is simply because of this the corporate restructuring in India is currently hot. A 1994 study of 92 public and private sector corporations found that 81 had been restructured or were undergoing or planning restructuring. The most common restructuring changes were gaining greater customer focus through greater decentralization and delaying, more focused human resources development and staff redeployment, and revamping of the functions of production, personnel, finance, research and development, marketing and MIS. A Business world' report in early 1999 indicated that most of the nation's largest 200 companies had undergone or were undergoing restructuring (Khandawala, 1999).

The emerging era of globalization, hyper-competition and technological turbulance have made the major corporate change a must. The corporate India needs for more professionalism, greater concern for customer, greater investment in HRD, better MIS, increased decenteralization, rightsizing, more attention to value driving processes, a better understanding of international management practices, etc. In this context most of the large business houses like Tatas, Birlas, Singhanias, Thapars, State Bank of India, ONGC, SAIL, Bharat Petroleum, L&T, Hindustan Lever, Dabur, BILT, Godrej Soaps have engaged world renowned consultants like Arthus D.Little, Andersen Consulting, A.T. Kearney, Booz, Allen & Hamilton, Boston Consulting Group, KPMG, Mckinsey and Price Waterhouse, to restructure their total business so as to reposition themselves in the domestic and global environment.

A recent study conducted in the area of restructuring in the Indian context brought out that four components of business operations, namely business strategy, business process, technology and human resources, need immediate restructuring to cope with the opportunities and challenges posed by liberalization (Shah,1996). Further it is established through studies in some Indian entreprises as well as surveys conducted in U.S.A., that the restructuring process needs to be attempted properly and carefully with the commitment of the top management.

Fundamentals of Effective Corporate Restructuring

The spirit of accepting fundamental and radical change is yet to be inculcated in the thinking process of Indian managers. This is primarily so because of culture-specific issues and for fear of adverse impact on human resource. In India, the dominating focus while restructuring is the end result, rather than the process. Moreover, there are doubts about the benefits of restructuring made on the advice of international management consultants. Nadir Godrej has reportedly said, "I feel that consultants tend to have the habit of borrowing your watch in order to tell you the time". This statement seems more true about international management consultants as these consultants, as assumed, lack familiarity about Indian operating conditions, culture, values and constraints. Vikram Thapar of BILT reportedly commented, "Nobody takes consultants at face value. They definitely make mistakes". Since the international management consultants are mostly US or UK based, where massive downsizing resorted to quite often the staff suffers retrenchment on hiring of consultants and this demotivates the staff. As stated already the popularity and credibility of corporate restructuring processes are increasingly questioned because of no guarantee of obtaining success in this expensive task. In this context, it becomes essential for the academicians, researchers and consultants to identify the ways and means to succeed in restructuring. A survey (Coulson Thomas, 1994) undertaken in the west identifies the following ways to succeed with re-engineering:

- Setting aggressive Re-engineering performance target.
- Comprehensive Review of Customer needs and market trends.
- Comprehensive prototyping/pilot-project of redesign.
- Earmarking additional senior executives for implementation.

Let us further examine some of the important recent cases of restructuring so as to pin-point the bases for a successful restructuring exercise.

HCL-Hewlett Packard (now two separate entities)

At HCL- HP, the restructuring was attempted with the objective of cutting time to design a new product down to three months; launching a new product in six months; and to kill it and launch a replacement over the next three months. In order to achieve the said objective, the company restructured the process of information flow from the marketing team to R&D and manufacturing teams. At weekly meeting of cross-functional teams for the marketing, manufacturing and research departments, the marketing team's suggestions are mapped on the spot to the available technologies, which are tracked by a special team. Problems with product designs initiated earlier are also thrashed out. So, at any point of time, several product designs are in various stages of completion, ensuring a continous stream of new product into the market. It is reported that new products are being introduced at intervals of four months.

Philips

The Netherlands based electrical and electronics conglomerate, Philips initiated a major restructuring program in 1996 as a result of disappointing profitability and the need to make the organization more flexible to react adequately to changing market conditions. The program led to an ongoing process of restructuring and discontinuance of underperforming or non core activities in 1996, 1997 and 1998.

All of the underperforming and non-strategic business identified during portfolio analysis were discontinued or sold to a great extent. The main loss making operations that have been restructured or eliminated over the past two years included Grunding, Philips Media, the Data Communication activities of Industrial Electronics. Business that have also been sold include Polygram, Philips Car Systems, Optoelectronics and a number of. Of Components business, Consumer Electronics retail and rental activities in Australia and sundry activities such as Philips travel agency.

The Philips group also initiated various projects to improve the performance of its operations, including such measures as the closure of factories, shift of production facilities to low-waged areas, consolidation of production centres and realignment of sales organizations. The total restructuring charges recorded against income from operations in 1998 was guilders 726 million, principally for the sectors of consumer products and Components.

In the footstep of the parent company, Philips India is also undertaking a major restructuring exercise that should see the company re-emerge as a favourite with investors. It also started divesting business in non-core areas and concentrating in core areas which is likely result in a higher profitability in the current financial year. Its lighting division achieved significantly higher growth in 1998 in comparison with the industry, resulting in improved market share in all segments maps, luminaries, lighting electronics and gear. The company has recently added a new activity to this division, automotive lighting and it is the sole supplier of lamps for the Indica car.

Ballarpur Industries Limited (BILT)

Billarpur Industries Limited (BILT), the flagship of the L.M. Thapar group, was in tatters two years ago. The management hired McKinsey to restructure the company. BILT was highly diversified into paper, chemicals, glass, edible oils, leather, ingots, castings, etc. This spread of products was serviced by some 14 divisions. Its core businesses, paper and chemicals, were not doing well; interest burden was high; and there was overstaffing. There was also apparently some bad blood between the family representatives of the Thapars in BILT' top management. Under McKinsey's advice, the 14 divisions were restructured into four divisions that became autonomous SBUs. All other business except paper were hived off to another group company. Diversification was put on hold although expansion of paper capacity at minimal additional cost was planned to reap economics of scale. There was sharp cost cutting and economizing, involving cost reduction at the corporate headquarters through reducing office space and salaries, and economizing on operations. A foreign technological joint venture in industrial paper was being planned. A net profit of Rs. 160 million on a turnover of Rs. 7,000 million was expected for the year 1998-99. The prices of BILT share rose from around Rs. 13 in 1997 to Rs. 43.50 on 7th March, 2000.

Siemens Nixdorf (SNI)

In the early nineties Siemens nixdorf (SNI), producer of data processing equipment including mainframes and PCs, software, and infotech services, was a huge corporation with nearly 40,000 staff and DM 12,000 million annual revenues. It was operating in a hyper-competitive environment. It was a bit rigid and engineering oriented in a very dynamic, customer dominated industry. It lost DM 350 million in 1993-94. A new CEO took official charge in late 1994. But even before taking charge, for three months he spent time at SNI talking to managers, thousands of employees, customers, and other stakeholders about SNI' problems and seeking suggestions. Upon taking charge, one of his first acts was to call in three persons he judged were effective change agents, namely, the heads of corporate communications, corporate strategy, and human resource management. Their brief was to identify 30 other live wires in the company who also could act as change agents. This core change agent team of 30 developed a 19-point programme of action that emphasized mind-set change and behavioural change along 30 dimensions. The team availed of the help of a professor from Babson College to develop a framework and agenda for massive change towards an entrepreneurial culture. To bring about culture change, the 30 core team members in turn recruited another 2,000 opinion leaders from round the company. These 2,000 were sent to the US for a 13-week course, during which they visited American companies that were restructuring, several Silicon Valley companies to imbibe their entrepreneurial culture, and got formal training in some aspects of professional management. Despite its financial problems, the company spent some $ 10,000 per person for this course.

A schedule of change spread over four quarters was developed and published. Each quarter, change was kicked off by a workshop at Honover, Germany. Each workshop culminated with an agreed upon list of actions to be implemented. A large number of cross-functional project teams were formed to implement these. The achievements of these project teams were displayed at a Results Fair in May, 1995, attended by over 12,000 employees. Town meetings were conducted by senior managers all over the plants to discuss the company's problems with the workforce and to elicit their ideas and suggestions.

Moreover, the company was broken up into some 250 units, and each of them was headed by an entrepreneurial type with considerable operating autonomy. Delayering resulted in the number of layers between managers and customers being reduced to three. To bring in more focus, SNI divested 22 business but also added 10 new ones.

To drive productivity, each manager identified key yield points to improve processes and also the non-financials. Change tools like cost-benefit analysis and various problem solving techniques were made available to decision makers in pocket guide form. To motivate employees, they were given the freedom to choose from a list the criteria on which they could be evaluated, and thus become eligible for reward on exceeding targets on these self-chosen criteria. The top management, played more of a catalytic role than a directive role. The company changed profoundly.

The widespread change apparently worked: after the heavy loss of 1993-94, the company broke even in 1995-96, and posted a DM 550 million profit in 1996-97.

In the light of the above discussions, some fundamentals for effective restructuring in India have been developed. These corner stones of a successful restructuring attempt are as follows:

Focus and Core Competence

An important component of effective re-structuring is sharp focus. A management consultant (Start Saint) has rightly said,"one fundamental drive which companies ought to make is to work out what they are going to concentrate on. In many companies business has tended to be a little haphazard and this has created a cluster of activities which diverted management attention and use financial resources which are generally scarce and can be more effectively applied to the company's business".

Another fundamental to successful restructuring is to identify and stay on its kay business or core competencies. This will provide a competitive advantage to the restructing firm over its existing as well as new competitors. The principles of core competence is that a company should stay in business where it has built up core skills over a number of years and acquired added advantage. In India TATAs present a typical example of Business Portfolio Restructuring:

(a) The decision to sell TOMCO to HINDUSTAN LEVER

(b) TISCO, shedding non-core assets such as cement

(c) TATA have exited from soap making and entered Telecom.

(d) TATA industries have withdrawn from TCS's joint venture with IBM.

The ongoing restructuring process in case of Tata group of companies have resulted into an encouraging performance (*The Economic Times*, Feb. 18, 2000). The third quarter performance has reflected that while the aggregate sales of 20 key Tata group companies were up 21 percent to Rs. 6690 crore, aggregate net profits jumped 88 percent to Rs. 385 crore in the quarter ended December 31, 1999.

Selectives Divestiture

Given the importance of focus and core competence corporate should exit from peripheral, low priority non-core competence activities. As Stuart Saint of Arthur D. Little management consultancy firm declared. We have been working with a number of companies.... to determine what are the critical aspects of their business which they must own and manage through a third party." Divestiture need not mean complete exit; the company can still have an involvement with an activity or business through a joint venture or strategic as Saint explained,"If we look at the moves of the industry over the last 20 to 30 years, they have progressively focused or required that what really matters is where they create value. They still undertake a number of activities within the company which support rather than add true value... What really does add value within the company is putting the activities that support it more on a joint venture or a partnership basis." Leo Puri, too called for strategic partnership as well as outsourcing to add value. Actually, the strategy alliances can provide complementary capabilities, improve economics, lower risk and add value.

Clear Vision and Strategy

The companies need to be clear on what peak they want to scale, by when, how, and how they would measure progress. The vision is generaed out of values in terms of what one stands for and a set of views of the future. Nicholas Bloy of Boston consulting group advised management to ask some right questions given below:

* What is the corporate vision for 2005 AD(e.g. To be a multinational company of choice, creating value through growth and continuours improvement)?
* What quantitative objectives would indicate vision achievement ?
* Given the vision what strategies need to be implemented to achieve it ?

* What are the key valule-driving processes in the company's businesses and how to improve them?
* What is to be done next?

Proactive Leadership

Most management consultants encourage a proactive, firm (though not necessarily authoritarian) leadership. All restructuring has to be sustailned. Here the critical aspect is obviously the management style to realise the restructuring successes. Experience tells us that in companies where this has been successful, there was a clear leadership style that which is prepared to take charge at the top, and demonstrate commitment to the process. Leadership includes empowerment, counselling and encouragement.

Empowerment

Empowerment can take several forms: delegation of operating authority, skilling, better information for decision making, etc. Leo Puri of McKinsey called for mobilisation of power through greater delegation to the frontline but with sharper performance accountability. Actually delegation is one of the seven pillars of restructuring wisdom. Effective restructuring calls for change from centralised decision making to decentralised decision making.

Effective MIS

The delegation and skilling is not enough for successful restructuring. For effectives decision making, needed information should be quickly made available to manager. This requires an effectives MIS. David Moore of Arther Anderson consulting group called for upgradation of information for decision making. This indicates the need for wider use of infotech.

Re-engineering Processes

A high performance business is one which satisfies its shareholders by improving its processes and aligning its organisation and resources. It means that the business process redesign is an important component of the whole restructuring exercise. Hence processes involved in the valule-creation chain need to be identified and revamped.

Deregulation and Privatisation

For restructuring public enterprises there is a need for having a clearly defined deregulation path. Plans should be laid out, with a time-table of when exactly each path of the deregulation is going to happen. Translating that into company profits becomes much easier for equilty analysts. Carol Bell of J.P. Morgan opined that the lower the government ownershihp the better as far as market valaluation was concerned. Many management experts also feels that the truly effective companies are finding that they can compete more effectively if they are in private hands.

Right sizing

As long as there is a big growth market for products, the market is prepared to accept and be more forgiving of having large labour forcees than it would otherwise be. To add vallue, YPF, the Argentinian national oil company shed over 44,000 of its 50,000 employees as part of its restructuring. As Bloy commented on YPF's restructuring, "Its transformation was painful but the end appears to justify the means". Once downsizing becomes socially and politically acceptable in India, it could quickly become a major plank of the restructuring strategies. Saini wrote : "The story of YPF is perhaps of particular relevance to the siltulation in India".

REFERENCES

Kaura, M.N. and S. Pulle (1995), "Restructuring of Banks: An evaluation of Key Issues in Implementation", *ASCI Journal of Management,* 24(2), pp. 86-94.

Krishnan, B. (1994), "An Agenda for Restructuring", *Business Today*, Aug. 7-21, pp. 154-155.

Bhavana Doshi (1999), "Restructuring Amalmagating Taxes". *The Chartered Accountant,* September, pp. 19

Hammer, Michacl (1995) "The Re-engineering Revolution: *The Handbook*", Harper Collin Publishers, London, pp. 336.

Khader, S.A. and Suryanaryanan K. (1998), "Restructuring and Re-engineering in India: Choice or Compulsion", *Productivity*, Vol. 39, No 1, April-June p. 2

Burke, G. And Peppard J. (1995), *Examining Business Process Re-engineering,* Kegan Page Ltd., London, p. 320.

Khandwalla N. Pradip (1999), "Restructuring: WIMC Vs Self-Help", *The Chartered Accountant,* August, P.12

Coulson-Thomas, C. (1994), "Business Process Re-engineering: Myth and Reality", (Ed.), Kagan Page, London, p. 254.

Rai N. Janardhan (1999), "Philips N V-Illuminating Success", *Chartered Financial Analyst,* June, p. 55 and p.57.

The Economic Times, "Restructuring Pays", Feb. 18, 2000.

4

CORPORATE RESTRUCTURING: AN INDIAN PERSPECTIVE

S.L. Gupta & Pardeep Gupta***

Introduction

In India, restructuring of corporation started in the mid - 1990s. Many organizations try to find a 'fit' between strategy and structure. The rule of the game have changed with the new economic policy. Earlier with controlled and protected markets, many businesses diversified their activities. This led to uneconomic capacities and unrelated business portfolios. In the wake of economic liberalization and globalization, Indian companies are in the process of large scale restructuring. They are seeking to confine their business to the core area of their competence.

Restructuring is indicative of the fact that more and more industries will move from diffidence to confidence and that will make the industrial scenario succeed. The Restructuring process covers hiring off unremunerative and unrelated activities, a hang-over of the license-permit raj; mergers, amalgamation, acquisition, expansions, closure, demergers etc. To inject synergy in the business operations.

A glance at the business news will demonstrate that a great many mergers and acquisitions are currently in works. The pace

* Chairman, Dept. of Management, Kurukshetra University, Kurukshetra.

** Lecturer, Dept. of Business Management, Guru Jambheshwar University, Hisar.

of business combination has been high over the past few years and is showing no signs of a let up. Mergers and Acquisitions are taking place at an unprecedented pace in India. Crossborder Mergers and acquisitions have been growing over the last few years. The cause for this phenomenon is the realisation among corporate that it is possible for them to survive in an increasingly complex globalising economy only by joining hands with those who have similar interests.

Objective of the Paper

The world is in a state of flux, being influenced by the forces of globalisation and as a consequences is facing intense competition. As a coping strategy, organizations are going in for corporate restructuring. This paper tries to put across the various manifestations of corporate restructuring and attempts to delineate the trends in India. It concludes by examining mergers and acquisitions related sections of the companies and Income Tax Acts* so that Indian companies can become internationally competitive without any loss of time.

Restructuring Calibration

The alliance in India are taking in various forms such as Marketing tie-ups; operations handling; joint ventures; technology licensing; manufacturing; memorandum of understandings; services ;supply; setting up a new business, mergers and acquisition etc.

With mergers and acquisitions becoming the new norm for growth, strategic alliances have become quite common in recent years. While the acquirers sought an entry into new areas, to consolidate positions within an industry or bring related businesses under a single company, the sellers were keen to focus on their core competencies or to exit unuable businesses.

The cement industry which got mauled in the recession was easily the star attraction in the M & A arena. It was an eventful year for Grasim with Indian Rayon's Cement division being transferred to it. Grasim's acquisition of Digvijay Cements- having a capacity of one million tonnes- not only earned it a slot in the top three cement companies in the country, but also spread its reach across the land.

Another acquisition in the cement industry was that of Narmada Cements. The company, with a capacity of 1.2 million tonne, was acquired by Larsen and Toubro adding to its then existing capacity of four million tonnes.

In intra- group restructuring, The Sanjay Lalbhai Group merged Arvind Intex, Arvind Cotspin and Arvind Polycot with Arvind Products, a subsidiary of Arvind Mills, as Arvind Mills has exposures in these companies and also had business dealings with them.

A spate of consolidation was also been in the Tata Group. Tisco sold its cement plant to Lafarge and also bought out the cold- rolling mill of Tata SSL. Engineering services and material handling systems companies, Tata Technodyne, and Tata Material Handling Systems were merged with Tata Refractories(TRF), fitting well with the latter's business profile.

In beverages, consolidated coffee merged Asian Coffee, Coffee lands and two other plantation companies with itself.

The effects of these M& A activity will be evident this year as corporate performance has begin to look up. Aiding growth will be the recent internal restructuring being undertaken by corporate.

Internal Restructuring: Faced with uncontrollable external factors that were threatening performance, companies were also forced to look inwards.

On the shopfloor, introducing better processes to improve productivity gained currency. This was imperative as competition was not only coming from new domestic players, but also from overseas markets, which had more efficient production facilities. To complete effectively, Indian companies had to lower their costs. Industries like cement , steel, aluminum, paper and chemicals which had had a horrendous time started discovering inefficiencies that were previously ignore.

Original Equipment Manufactured were squeezing their vendors with lower rates and lower credit periods. These vendors in turn ,squeezes their vendors and thus passed the buck, the players with the least bargaining power bearing the burnt.

Another major and social challenging process was that of Voluntary Retirement Schemes (VRS).

Table 1
Industry-wise Distribution of Strategic Alliances

S.No.	*Industry*	*Number*	*Percentage*
1.	Automobiles	21	16.3
2.	Petrichemicals	13	10
3.	Pharmaceuticals	13	10
4.	Software	11	8.5
5.	Consumer Product	10	7.8
6.	Electronics	8	6.2
7.	Telecom	7	5.4
8.	Electrical Equipment	6	4.6
9.	Power	6	4.6
10.	Finance	6	4.6
11.	Services	6	4.6
12.	Metals	5	3.8
13.	Chemicals	4	3
14.	Agribusiness	4	3
15.	Cement	2	1.6
16.	Advertising	2	1.6
17.	Office Automation	1	0.7
18.	Courier	1	0.7
19.	Rubber	1	0.7
20.	Healthcare	1	0.7
21.	Hotels	1	0.7

Source: Publications by Centre for Monitoring Indian Economy

The benefits of this exercise are evident in the performance of many corporate in the current year.

Table 1 depicts the industry-wise data for 129 strategic alliances for the period of 1998-99.

From the above table, one finds that most of the alliances are taking place in the area of automobiles followed by petro-chemicals and Pharmaceuticals. This is probably because of good number of companies have set up their operations in India like Mercedes, Honda, Mitsubishi, Ford, BMW, Daewoo etc. All these are vying for a market in the upper segment and striving hard to mange the costs. There is definitely an attempt to indigenice the operations and there are number of tie-ups with Indian manufacturers for supplying different components..

Legal framework

Creating shareholder values through corporate restructuring took precedence over everything else in 1998-1999, as companies pushed hard to win back investors, confidence. The ensuing paragraphs discuss the ways the government can facilitate and encourage the process of restructuring by making necessary changes in the Companies Act, Income Tax Act and other related laws.

While a number of the measures aimed at making amalgamations, demergers and sales tax neutrality were introduced in the last budget, there are a few inadequacies which need to be addressed in the forthcoming budget.

It is essential to recast Section 72 A of the Income Tax Act to support corporate mergers and acquisitions. Permission and uncertainties surrounding this section has been a major hurdle. It would be better if all tax allowances of the sick merging company like unabsorbed depreciation and business loss, should be allowed for carry forward/ adjustment by the merged company without having to obtain specific permission from the prescribed authority.

In the present scenario of takeovers, acquisitions of 51% of paid up capital are enough to have a control on the management. However, to avail of any tax benefit it has to acquire at least 75% of the shares. Thus the investment by bidding company effectively has no tax benefit. To encourage bidding and to pass on some tax benefits, the profit or loss of subsidiary companies should be allowed to be added or deducted from the holding company on the basis of proportionate holding, if the total holding exceeds 51%.

Restructuring transactions for corporate should be outside the purviews of Section 269 of the Income Tax Act approval to avoid unnecessary administrative delays to the restructuring process.

In the case of amalgamation, the benefits of the 'Carry forward' and the 'set off' of accumulated losses and unabsorbed depreciation of the amalgamating companies is presently available to the amalgamated company on condition that 75 per cent in the value of the assets of the amalgamating company are retained by the amalgamated company carries on the business of the amalgamating company for at least five years from the date of amalgamation. These two conditions do not facilitate amalgamation. In fact they defeat the objective of amalgamation.

The requirement that the amalgamated company should continue the same business of the amalgamated company for a minimum period of five years should be dispensed with.

Demergers at present can be effected through Section 391 to 394 of the Companies Act. This cause delay because of the involvement of the court. It is desirable that demergers should be made possible under Section293 of the Companies Act and brought within the powers of Board of Directors. Also, under the present law all the property (assets of the undertaking) being transferred by the demerged company, immediately before the demerger, becomes the property of the Resulting Company by virtue of the demerger. This provision discourages demerger. The assets and Liabilites reliable to the undertakings, which are mutually agreed upon for transfer, should alone be required to be transferred and not all the assets and liabilities of the undertaking.

The transfer of all assets may not be possible because of certain legal and contractual restrictions. Similarly the transfer of all liabilities relatable to the undertaking is not practical and feasible. The resulting company should be allowed to pay the consideration partly by way of debt instruments to the equity shareholders (not preference shareholders) of the demerged company. The demerged company should also be eligible to receive the consideration.

The requirement of resulting company issuing only shares to the shareholders of the demerged company in consideration of the demerger is rather harsh. Also, the condition that shareholders holding not less than three-fourth in value of shares in the demerged company shall become shareholders of the resulting company by virtue of the demerger is incongruous with section 391 of the companies Act, which provides that the Scheme of Arrangement is applicable and binding on all shareholders once it is approved by three fourths in value of shareholders and sanctioned by court. Also, the linking cost of acquisition of the shares in the resulting company with the proportion of net book value of the assets transfer to the net worth of the demerged company is uncalled for as it would result in practical difficulties and unnecessary complications.

Concluding Remarks

In India, liberalization of the economy since 1991 has changed the environment for business houses. There is pressure from foreign investors on the Indian business houses, who are faced with the threat of takeovers. Faced with this threat and global competition, Indian companies are now realizing the need to restructure their operations. To survive in the global market, companies are realizing the need to cut down on the number of activities and specialize in certain select areas. The two pertinent factors for corporate restructuring are conscious attempt at cutting costs and using mergers and acquisitions to unlock shareholder value.

REFERENCES

1. *The Hindustan Times,* 14 February 2000.
2. Verma, V.,"Strategic Alliances- An Indian Perspective" *Management and Change,* Vol. 3, Number 2 (July-December 1999).
3. Vamsi, A.K.'"Corporate Consolidation"' The Chartered Accountant, May 1999.
4. Shiva Ramu, S., *Restructuring and Break-ups.* Response Book, New Delhi.
5. Ananthanarayanan, R., *Business Standard,* February 2000 pp. 30-34.

5

CORPORATE OBJECTIVES FROM INDIAN VALUE SYSTEM

M.M.Goel & Ashok Kumar***

In the present times of economic and corporate restructuring, where on one side we see the emergence of concepts like core competence being lean, thin and globally competitive and on the other side, we are a witness to unimaginable mergers, takeovers and acquisitions. The development and expansion of a wired economy is further adding to the complexities, turmoil, stress and strain in the existing system. This calls for not only to cope up with but also for bringing a qualitative active change in the environment with a better value system. This essay derives corporate objectives from Indian value system.

This approach can enrich the corporate excellence in providing more sound theoretical base not only for motivation but also for corporate governance. We can derive guidelines and recommendations for the corporate executives to develop personal ethics and an Indian value system so that he can prepare himself to devise appropriate corporate restructuring strategies to meet the challenges of change. These guidelines have been derived primarily from four objectives of life—dharma, artha, kama, moksha—and five debts (rins)—bhuta, deva,[1] pitra, rishi

* Reader, Dept. of Economics, Kurukshetra University, Kurukshetra.

** Lecturer, Dept. of Economics, Kurukshetra University, Kurukshetra.

and nari which form the core of Indian value system. Although all of us are greatly indebted to four major strands—the Tagorean, the Vivekanandian, the Gandhian and the Aurobindovian, and the Srimad Bhagvad Gita without which it is just impossible to understand the Indian Value System.

Values

Value refers to the worth or excellence or degree of worth ascribed to an object or a class of objects. It is an enduring conviction—that a specific mode of conduct or end state of existence is personally or socially perferable to the alternative mode of conduct or end state of existence. Thus values can mean both 'end state values', as well as 'values as means'. End state organizational values like productivity, profitability, market share, innovation, growth and like are hardly liable to dispute. It is in the case of values as means that the normative stance can no longer be ignored. Our concern here is not on what is valued, but rather about how one goes about achieving what is valued. Economic or political success cannot be the yardstick to measure value as means. Rather, the former has to submit to the test of the latter for each person.

As soon as the value is internalized, it becomes, consciously or unconsciously, a standard or criterion for guiding the action of an individual, developing and maintaining his attitudes towards relevant objects and situations, justifying his own and others actions and attitudes, morally justifying himself and others and comparing himself with others. It contains a moral flavor and thus, carries an individuals ideas to what is right, good or desirable.Our thesis is that the subjective is the cause, the objective the effect. The external millieu, with all its net works and artifacts, is in truth a projection of man's internal millieu; individually and collectively. Another assumption which is proposed in this article is that the organizational values always derive from the individual values - especially those of the founding features and of the very top executives. The value is the cause and the behaviour is the effect. In individual and corporate personality (if we conceive it in abstract), the values lie at the core. Following diagram illustrates it.

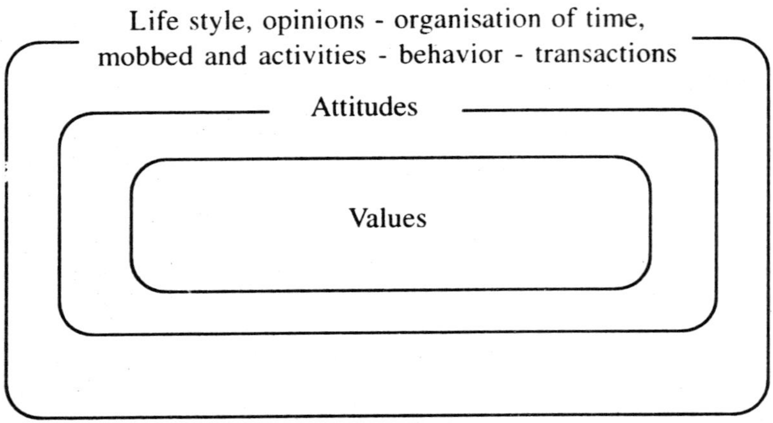

The core of the personality (Individual or organizational) containing the values is not fixed but changes very slowly. The middle part i.e. attitudes can be modified more easily; and the peripheral personality shows changes more quickly. Culture is a source of values. In Indian culture, peace, cooperation, harmony, equity, democracy and allied social values are considered desirable. The American culture promotes achievement and success, activity and involvement, efficiency and practicality, professionalism, progress, material comfort, individualism, freedom, autonomy, equality, pleasure, humanitarianism, youthfulness and fitness and health.

Indian organizations disply a mixed set of values, characteristics of both Western and Eastern societies (i.e. belief in Attachment vs. Materialistic orientation, Collectivism vs. Individualism, humanism vs. Power orientation). Among Indian managers factors affecting personal values include humanism composed of forgiveness, service and harmony; dharma (sense of duty); detachment; compliance to authority and self interest. The universal values in Indian organizations are outcome of orientation, materialistic orientation, power orientation, work motivation, work commitment and uncertainty avoidance.

The Value System

There may be a set of values which form a value system for each individual or organization. It can have three dimensions - basic set of values, degree or level of values and the hierarchy of dominance of values. Allport, Vermon and Lindzey identified six types of values:

1. Theoretical - discovery of truth through a critical and rational approach i.e. *Satyam*
2. Economic - useful and practical i.e. *Shivam.*
3. Aesthetic - form and harmony i.e. *Sundram.*
4. Social - love of people by Service (Lokseva, Karseva)
5. Political - acquisition of power and influence like adoption of some philosophy e.g. Marxism, Hinduism etc.
6. Religious - unity of experience and understanding of cosmos as a whole.

THE VALUE SYSTEM

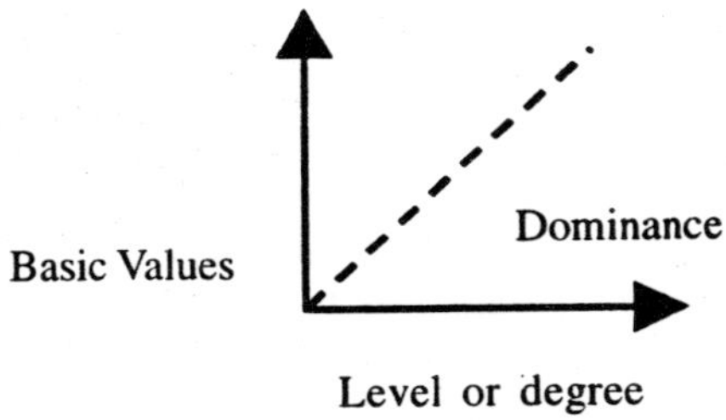

Graves identified seven levels of values given below:-

1. Reactive - Unaware, reacts to basic needs.
2. Tribalistic - Shows high dependence and influenced by tradition.

3. Egocentrism - Rugged individualism, aggressive and selfish.
4. Conformity - Low tolerance for ambiguity; difficulty in accepting divergent views.
5. Manipulative - Goal achievement by manipulation, status seeker, materialistic.
6. Sociometric - seeks social relationships, affiliation and hates materialism, Competition.
7. Existential - High tolerance for ambiguity, divergent views; outspoken on inflexible systems, restrictive policies, status symbols and arbitrary use of authority; seeks full expression of growth and self- fulfillment needs through work.

To survive, sustain and develop in 21st century the corporate professionals need to be made existential through Retention, Respect and Responsibility (3R of Human Resource Management). To make corporate professionals Existential Goel has developed 'ASK' Model of existence.

A - Abilities of head & heart

S - Skills

K - Knowledge

According to the ASK model of existence the corporate manpower must have complete, full, up to date, accurate knowledge of the profession. Also the corporate manpower needs to be self-accountable and must establish their credibility through ethice of morality. The last (but not the least) attribute of ASK model of existence is the abilities of head & heart to form the positive attitude for becoming in the profession through enthusiastic endeavor with patience, confidence and intelligence.

Among Indian managers humanism, individualism, power and self orientation (furtherance of self interest and money making), planning, tact, work orientation, commitment, and compliance values have been found more dominant. Indian managers attach high importance to personalism, egoistic concerns, prestige, dignity, security and job satisfaction.

Goel suggested that we need sincere, dedicated and enthusiastic manpower for which we need the 'SHE' model for values given below:

S - Spiritualistic

H - Humanistic

E - Existential

In the widely read book on Japanese management by Pascale and Athose, the following list of values in force in Matsushita Electric Co. is cited :

1. National service through industry;
2. fairness
3. harmony and cooperation
4. struggle for betterment
5. courtesy and humility
6. adjustment and assimilation
7. gratitude

In an equally well-known contemporary book 'In Search of Excellence' by Peters and Waterman following crystallized list is furnished:

1. a belief in being the best.
2. a belief in the importance of details of execution.
3. a belief in the importance of people as individuals.
4. a belief in superior quality and service.
5. a belief that most members of organisation should be innovators.
6. a belief in importance of informality to enhance communication.

7. explicit belief in and recognition of the importance of economic growth and profits.

The Indian Value System and Corporate Objectives

The values rooted in the deep structure of Indian culture and society are summarized below as researched by S.K.Chakraborty:

1. The individual must be respected : As the divine enshrined in him/her, whether good or bad, older or younger, rich or poor.
2. Cooperation and trust : As the divine inner being in all is a Unity - deception/deprivation of others is depreciation/ deception of oneself.
3. Jealousy is harmful for Mental health.
4. Chitta-Shudhi or Purification of Mind : The all noble thoughts (bhavnas) of compassion, friendliness , humility, gratitude, etc. lead to a refined and accurate perception of human relationships, contributing to sounder decisions.
5. Top quality Product/services: which is a function of the quality of mind or consciousness of the doer.
6. Work is worship: As the best way to approach the divine is to offer each piece of work mentally in as complete , perfect, humble, and pure in form and spirit to him. See sloke (B.G.: 18:46) which confirms that man can attain him by worshipping through work.
7. Containment of greed.
8. Ethico-moral soundness: As every karma or action is a cause for subsequent effect.
9. Self-discipline and self restraint: As they conserve energy, strengthen will power, create trust and confer dignity.
10. Customer satisfaction: As he is the divine came as human being to us.

11. Creativity: As human creativity is an extension of cosmic creativity.
12. Inspiration to give: As giving is more fulfilling, dignifying and to retire the rins(debts)
13. Renunciation and detachment: Not of or from duties, but of/from selfish rewards & egoistic demands in the work-place.

Four objectives—Dharma, Artha, Kama and Moksha

According to Vedic literature each individual has four object for his life span namely - Dharma, Artha, Kama and Moksha, which he has to strive for . The word dharma is different from its English equivalent religion. The Dharma is derived from the Sanskrit verb dhri(or dhru) which has two meanings - one to wear or to put on and two, to keep in order. This indicates that dharma means a set of rules or special behaviour which one put on to keep oneself disciplined or in order. Another meaning of dharma is sense of duty which can be derived from phrases like kshatra-dharma(duty of a warrior) or pitra-dharma(duty of a father). A third meaning of dharma can be derived from the phrases like jala-dharma(property of water) and it is property or characteristic. All these meanings suggest that dharma is a sense of duty which decides the behavior and norms of an individual arising due to his innate nature or prakrity. The following sloke explains,

Sreyan swadharma viguna pardharmart swanusthitat,
Swabhavniyatam karm Kurvan na aapnoti kilibisham.

(B.G.: 18:47)

Far superior is own duty even if lowly,
Than other's with glamour and glory.
Duty that is by swadharm decreed
Is sacred if done as an hones deed.

For a corporate entity its dharma is its basic purpose embedded in the explicit mission, reflected in its philosphy in abstract generally and in its motto, logo, insignia or monogram specifically.

The second object is *artha*. It includes earning money or liquidity (drvaya in Indian ethos) and all capital productive assets. The corporate objective similar to this can be growth in terms of investment, assets, sales, distribution channels, manpower; profatibility in terms of effectiveness and efficiency of operations. The corporations can not afford to be stable, either they have to grow or they have to fall with present value system. It the corporations do not grow, the morale and motivational levels of the employees can not be sustained for long. We also know that logically it is not possible to have infinite growth for all organizations. Hence, the concepts of contentment, satisfaction and limiting the desires automatically emerge. The growth alone is thus a narrow objective, rather sustainable growth and development(includes effectiveness, efficiency) as objectives are possible as a part of Vedic corporate set of objectives. The following sloke condemns the actions full of greed,

Yaya tu dharmkamarthan dhritya dharyate Arjuna,
Prsangen phalakankshi dhriti as parth rajsi.

(B.G.:18:34)

What to pursuit of dharm, kam, arth,
O Arjun, commits for all one's worth.
Gives attachment, for fruit yearning,
Is trust mundane to the discerning.

The third object is kama. In its limited sense it means sex, but in broad sense this stands for all kind of wordly desires or kamnas. It is advised as that kama should be nurtured as a duty of dharma by the mortals(B.G.:07:11). In Measlows need hierarchy it can be equated with set of physiological, safety, social, and esteem needs. For a corporate entity the objectives of kama can be satisfying the aspirations of major groups i.e. customers, employees, shareholders, suppliers and publics. The kama is also a need to survive, perpetuate, evolve, associate and flourish. The organizations have to change themselves continuously to evaluate and to survive, and they do so by positioning and repositioning of their brands. The kama without moksha and dharma is not advised (B.G.:03:41), (B.G.:16:21). Following two slokas explain the consequences of kama of a man of unequamanity,

Dhyayata vishyan punsa sanga teshu upjayate,
Sangaat sanjayate kama kamat krodha abhijayate.
(B.G.:02:62)

Krodhat bhavti samamoh, sammohat samritivibhrama,
Samritibhranshat budhinasha budhinashat pranashati
.(B.G.:02:63)

In receptive minds casual whims lodge,
Imagination nurtures what mere fancy was.
Attachment plants grow with lust flowers,
Frustration bears anger to turn all sour.
Anger judgment and discretion clouds,
Agitation covers memory in a shroud.
Wasted memory one's intelligence ends,
Lost intelligence deathward sends.

The fourth object is moksha. Other similar concepts to moksha are achievement of Brahma in Vedic literature and nirvana in Buddhist literature. The word moksha means freedom from the cycle of birth and rebirth. Gautam Buddha concluded that there is need to achieve nirvana(moksha) because the world is full of sorrows, which come in life due to desires and their non-fulfillment. He also suggested the *Asthamarg* (Eight fold path) to get freedom from the desires. The astha-marg seems to be in conflict with four objects *(dharma, artha, kama* and *moksha).* But a close analysis shows that this a middle path of materialism and spiritualism. The Vedic literature also gives equal importance to dharma and moksha on one side and kama and artha on the other side. The moksha is not about freedom from duty(karma) rather it is fulfilling the duty without being trapped in the chains of karma created by the time or kala. For a corporate entity the concept of moksha can mean achievement of such an ideal state in the society when all kinds of conflicts(causes of sorrows) are eliminated. This is possible only when the organisation is working with awareness and vitality in total harmony with social, cultural, political, legal, physical and technological environments. Meaning of the moksha for organizations can be derived from following sloka,

Yadichhalabhasantushta davandateet vimatsara,
Sama siddho asiddho cha kritva api na nibdhyate.

(B.G.: 04:22)

The word davandanteet means free from all kinds of resistances and conflicts. Such an organizations has to produce only those goods and services which are desirable in the society(B.G.:03:20). The Gita also suggest that anything should be done with single reason that it is worst doing (B.G.:18:09) and (B.G.:18:05). This state of equilibrium is the moksha or the eternal station where the organizations is accountable only to itself. And this is the ultimate corporate objectives,

Tam ev sharnam gachh sarvbhaven Bharat,
tatprasadat param shantim sthanam prapayasi shasvatam.

(B.G.:18:62)

or

You ought to seek refuge in Him alone,
O Arjun , by every device to you known.
By His grace the unattainable peace,
A station eternal will be in your reach.

The following diagram summarizes the derivations from four life objectives.

Vedic objects	Corporate derivatives Dharma
Dharma	Purpose, Mission, Philosphy
Artha	Profitability , Effectiveness, Efficiency
Kama	Survival, Safety, Image, VitalityMoksha Noksha Total Equilibrium and zero resistance with external and internal environments with self accountability and self actualization

It needs to be noted that the period of consciousness has already started and will be the name of the game in the 21st century. To ensure spirituality among the corporate professionals, it has been advocated as below:

Ananya chintyanto mam ye janah paryu pasate
Tesam nitya bhiyutanam yoga-ksemam Vahamyaham.

(B.G.: 09:22)

Who set their minds on one supreme?
And make me their worship theme,
As yogis of equanimity well qualify,
I aid them and there needs supply.

Meaning thereby, those who always worship me with exclusive devotion, meditating on my transcendental form-to them I carry what they lack, and I preserve what they have. Infact, spiritually guided materialism is the synthesis of all the four objects. It needs to be understood and propagated and calls for moving from wants based economy to needs based economy. Spirituality is essential for the removal of stress and strain as well as the social and economic health of the society for all times to come.

Emergence of societal marketing, green marketing and ethical marketing concepts shows a tendency to decrease the conflict between social and corporate world, Business can be consumer friendly and socially beneficial only if undertaken in accordance with NAW approach. Here, NAW stands for Need, Affordability and Worth of the product. The pertinenet questions before the consumer are:-

Does(he) Need the product, which has been so glamorously advertised?

Is the product Affordable?

Is the product Worth its price?

I would like to take this opportunity to point out that a product would be popular only it it satisfy the essential need of the consumers, creates employment and is utilitarian. Glamour alone cannot be a substitute for the basic requirement of Need, Affordability and Worst (NAW) of the product.

It is very much clear that life objectives described in Vedic literature guide all human beings and organizations very vividly about their aims which are of highest order i.e. existential in nature. Corporations suffering from short term aims of profitability and sales maximization generally do so at the cost of major aim i.e. survival and sustainable development.

Indian value system also provides set of areas towards which one has to perform his duties in terms of concept of indebtedness (rins). Each human being has these five debts(Rin)- Nature(Bhuta), Juman(Nar), Deva (Gods), Rishi (Learned) and Pitra (Ancestors)- and he has to perform all his duties to get rid of this indebtedness.

1. *Bhuta rin*—Indebtedness to countless members of subhuman species like the trees, birds, insects, animals and their incalculable gifts to ourselves. This suggests all organizations have a duty to preserve and save flora and fauna.

2. *Nar rin*—Indebtedness to humanity at large, to countless people, known and unknown, seen and unseen, remembered and forgotten, great and small- who have consistently done their bit, all converging to make each moment

of our existence a reality. We observe that putting people first at work place, customer delight in the markets, vendor development and small investor protection themes are the base lines now a days in corporate world. But the question is how many of us live to this philosophy humbly in reality? Without being humanistic, we cannot and will not be able to perform our duties properly. Therefore, humanistic approach needs to be accepted as a panacea for understanding the duties of any corporate professional. For this essential attribute we need to follow completely and absolutely sloke number 15 of chapter 17 of Bhagvad Gita given below:-

Anudvega-karam Vakyam Satyam Priyahitam Ca Yat
Svadhyayabhya Sanam Caive Vakmayam Tap Ucyate
(B.G.:17:15)

"Words that neither hurt nor provoke,
Truthfully to benefit other are spoke,
Or in process of self study pronounced,
O Arjun, to penance of speech amount"

Meaning thereby, meditative communion with one's own true self and uttering words that cause no agitation and that are truthful, pleasant and beneficial, are called the austerity of speech. Thus, the manager needs to be objective, dependable to know or to tell the truth by becoming humanistic.

3. *Deva rin*—Indebtedness to supra-human powers like earth, air, fire, water, sun, Moon, India etc. This set has two subsets-one includes basic elements and other includes the heavenly bodies. I don't understand what kind of duties we can perform towards Sun and Moon. But Vedic literature suggested to perform Yjana and Havan to keep the astrobodies in peace. Ohm Shantihi is still a aprt of innumerable mantras. I am sure that when many persons together prayer for peace for others, themselves and even for heavenly bodies- it definitely has a collective impact over their psyches and their expectations actually mate-

rialize. Our duties to first set- earth, air , water and fire- are explicitly a strong advocacy to save the environment and energy(fire) conservation. These powers should be used by the organizations with great prudence. Emergence of ISO-14000 shows a paradigm shift in the thinking that if we use the resources optimally only then environmental damage can be minimized.

4. *Rishi rin*—Indebtedness to the sages (Learned and men of knowledge) who by leading the lives of self-denial realized the highest truths and left them for us a priceless heritage. This rin suggests that corporate world should disseminate its skills and knowledge to other section of society by investing in human resource development programs, adopting schools and colleges and by providing on-the-job training to business students. The corporate sector should adopt its potential manpower in the beginning of the professional courses. The trend in favor of intellectual Property Rights is in tune with this debt, as it suggests to give the due of the sages.

5. *Pitra rin*—Indebtedness to parents and ancestors for that cumulative contributions to our present standing. An individual can pay of this debt partly by serving his parents and partly by upbringing his off spring and making them good citizen. Corporate entity can pay off this debt by suppurating other new organizations. The concept of intrapreneurship is an example of this value.

DUTIES FORM FIVE DEBTS

Indebtedness	initiates Corporate Duties to Save, Preserve, and Enhance
Bhuta Rin	Flora and fauna
Nar Rin	Humanity as a whole
Deva Rin	Physical Environment- air, earth, water
Rishi Rin	Knowledge
Pitra Rin	Heritage, Parents, Future Generations

The working climate has to be shifted from holiday culture to Holy days culture in the organization. Indian value system provides a philosophy which motivates the managers not by providing monetary and non-monetary incentives taken from Maslow's need hierarchy or Herzberg. Two factor theory, but by the fact that one has to work as he is indebted and the debt has to be retired. The manager's attitude towards his social existence, if inspired by the above indebtedness orientation will naturally shift towards duties, obligations and sacrifice from covetousness and selfishness. The trusteeship shall grow and distributive justice will be more securely founded. Indeed this systematic approach beckons the manager to be honorable to so live intake society that as many as of these inescapable debts as possible are liquidated before departure from this world. This will help the manager to transcend to spiritual status even while living within the society.

Tagore has written,"It can not be asserted that man shall have no independence, but that he shall not be selfish. For oneself there must be something of one's own; everything else should be for others."

Radhakrishnan has translated a sloka (B.G.:03:14) from the Gita which justifies, "From food creatures come into being;from rain is the birth of food; from sacrifice(Yajna or Havan) rain comes into being and the sacrifice is born of work." This framework leaves no doubt that the manager has to become a karmyogi by performing his duties in accordance to his Dharma remaining Nishkama. This is also a key to perfection and a way to change the destiny. As Dr. Dharamveer Bharti writes in his play Andha Yug. Krishna explains to Arjuna-

"Jab bhi koi anasakt ho kar
chunoti deta hai itihas ko
usi kshan nakshtron ki disha badal jati hai.
Niyati nahin hai purva-nirdharit
manav nirnay use har kṣhan banata hai mitata hai."

Means, whenever someone without greed challenges the history, the movement of planets change (However unfavorable) immediately. The destiny is not pre-decided , it is the human decision which decide the it every moment. The sacred objectives are the key to survival and sustainable growth as clearly stated below,

"Urdhwam gachhanti satvavastha madhaye tishthati rajsa,
jaghanyagunavritistha agha gachhanti tamsa."

(B.G.: 14:18)

Men of virtues to heaven go,
Earthy remain who mundaneness show.
Those who evil propensities display,
Parth, of base temper, downward stray.

The present corporate scenario is analogous to very first day of battle of *Mahabharata,* where our Corporate Manager is feeling like Arjuna. Doubt, dismay, fear, anxiety and weakness have affected his decision-making ability. *Srimad Bhagvad Gita* in the strictest sense not a book of religion is most clear and perceptible manifestation of Indian Value system. Authored by Vyas, *Mahabharata* runs into a hundred thousand couplets. With only seven hundred of these. The Gita is its better known portion. This gospel of reason and citadel of knowledge is a treatise on human psychology, metaphysics and spiritual upliftment. The whole phenomenon is a complete systematic and theoretical approach to motivation. Krishna, the universal consciousness presents his argument to his friend Arjuna in favour of a fight. At the end of this discourse, Arjuna refunds his vigor and enthusiasm to wage a war that brings victory.

To sum up, I wish to emphasize that for every ill of Indian Corporate World in 21st Century there are Vedic pills and *Bhagvad* Gita is the panacea.

REFERENCES

1. Ajhar Kajmi, *Business Policy.*
2. Jitendra, *Dialogue Divine.*
3. John A. Pearce II, Richard B. Robinson Jr.- *Strategic Management.*
4. Muriel James, Dorothy Jongeward, *Born to Win.*
5. Philip Kotler, Gary Armstrong, *Principles of Marketing.*
6. R.S. Dwivedi, *Human Relations and Organizational Behaviors.*
7. S.K. Chakraborty, *Management by Values.*
8. *Srimad Bhagvad Gita*

Articles

1. Chaman dhanda, Gita: *A Motivational Approach*
2. M.M.Goel, *Feminisation of Media and Advertisement*

6

CONTEMPORARY ISSUES FOR CORPORATE RESTRUCTURING IN THE ERA OF E-COMMERCE

Usha Arora & Ms. Varuna Godara***

Sky is no longer the limit for the E-companies: E-business transactions are set for spiralling growth in India as the Internet culture spreads. A survey by the NASS COM estimates that e-business will exponentially grow to touch Rs. 100 billion by 2002, up from a meagre Rs. 1.31 billion in 1998-99, and the demand for e-commerce professionals will reach 2,00,000 by 2002.

India has a tremendous potential in the area of IT-enabled services as well as other services like engineering, finance, law, academics and administrative services. Not only in services, India can do well in products also. Question in front of Indian companies is not whether they can afford E-commerce or not. But the question is - "can they afford to neglect E-commerce". Increasing competition among product and service providers and increasing expectations of customers locally or worldwide, will be key reasons for the growth of E-commerce in India.

But businesses have to adapt to the pressing demands of e-commerce with a restructuring of traditional corporate organizational model. E-business is much more than simply opening

* Reader, Dept of Business, G. J. University, Hisar.

** Research Scholar, Department of Business, G.J. University, Hisar.

up a new, on-line sales channel. It's about using technology to streamline the organizational model, cutting expenditures and increasing efficiency. It's about lowering costs and establishing closer, more responsive relationships with your customers, suppliers and partners. In an interactive age, competition will not be inter companies but inter alliances, Mergers and takeovers are currently in trend. We can not go back from globalisation. Corporate strategy should focus on two things: (1) Flow of money, and (2) Flow of information. These two are not new to the business. Even in the ancient times in barter system also, information about the people in need of particular products was needed.

Only then products were exchanged in mutual interests. In the changing competitive global scenario business basics are the same but technology is different. Mutual interests of both parties are matched as earlier which can only be done by getting information, then a deal can be made. Information has emerged as the most decisive, valuable and critical resource for individual customers, entrepreneurs, societies and countries. Customers need information about speedy response, consistency, reliability, multiplicity and accuracy of product. Companies want information for how to gain maximum sales and maximum recognition worldwide. Both of them by demolishing barriers to trade and travel, globalising economy and making instantaneous communication.

The success or failure of an organisation depends to a large extent on the perception, belief and attitude of the chief executive. Most of the chiefs of large and medium organizations have changed their way and already have recognized the need and importance of E-commerce. If a company is unable to adopt E-business, it will not be possible to survive in the long run. But small business houses should also show their presence on the net. They can start on-line business for as little as $50, whereas medium companies are likely to play thousands of dollars for e-commerce systems that meet their needs. Large, complex organizations typically need e-commerce systems that cost US $

100,000 or more. On-line commerce has significant benefits not must for customers and large established retailers but it also opens a world of opportunity for local artisans and small entrepreneurs. The internet is rewriting business rules in every sense. Companies are born overnight, grow to dizzy heights and start threatening established companies. For example Amazon.com, the internet book store could grow bigger than the entire publishing industry in US and threaten the dominance of the 175-year old book store giant Barnes & Noble in less than five years. According to one Marketer's report, every 1.7 seconds one new user- that is, one new potential customer joins the Internet at a rate of 52000 users per day. Corporate can restructure and tap the vast market.

Information is the lifeblood of one's business. But that information may be scattered across, in various departments, networks and IT systems. In the changing scenario of e-commerce, companies need restructuring to be able to access, leverage and exploit that information system as a competitive advantage for them. Many technical and non-technical issues are indulged in success or failure of restructuring. The most important key to success is the information. But a lot many information technologies tools - like ERP (Enterprise Resource planning), Internet,Intranets, electronic data Interchange, internet based Home banking, Internet payment systems, Data Mining, Client/Server Technology, Biometric Technology or Artificial Intelligence, Interface Technologies, Smart Cards, Device Based Transactions and E-commerce are needed to collect and process the information. Information may be about

(1) Product

(2) Price

(3) Advertising

(4) Customer convenience

(5) Customer satisfaction

(6) The total cost of business

(7) Employees

(8) Security aspects

(9) Tax and legal implications.

Increasing global competition and crashing product prices are forming businesses to find new ways of achieving more from less. Speed and quick adjustment to new market conditions, streamlining of supply-chains and customer satisfaction are new mantras which every chief information officer (CIO) must chant to meet their objectives. To make task easier companies must use data-ware housing which is also an enable for e-business. Its most common use is for traditional financial and cost management, where a company can analyze the profitability of each customer through data warehousing. Enterprise resource planning and brand new enterprise resource management techniques can be used for product selection, material requirement planning for product and source production, manufacturing, resource planning engineering, finance, human resources, project management etc.

Role of EDP manager must be taken over by CIO. CIO must be assigned duty of technology gatekeeper. Business plan of making investment in information technology, greater expectations of end-users, growing mobility of professionals are the factors that have combined to make a CIO's role tougher and more challenging. They must be more generalists than specialists to deal with technological changes, staff, a variety of demands of computers users and simultaneously participate in corporate planning.

Gone are the days when profit and losses, capital structure and other financial information served the purpose. Today corporate strategy needs to give much importance to flow of information rather than flow of money. While CFO is responsible for flow of information because nowadays flow of information includes flow of money. The importance of including CIO in corporate planning must be realized.

Since information holds the key to success of future products, understanding information needs and wants of customers is necessary. Corporate should design their information system with the help of data warehousing to get knowledge about customer habits, beliefs, values, culture, tastes and so on. Corporate need to develop globally differentiated and variety products and services for different customers. E-customers want product of their choice and they have option to click over to other mails. So to a large extent customers must be allowed to design and fabricate the products. The consumers who buy goods on-line are arguably more informed and affluent than other customers. Though the needs of these on-line customers is the same as everyone else's, yet they are different because they can click through and compare the price and quality of products within seconds. Monopoly of corporate in a nation have come to an end in the era of E-business. Any net based company can compete with them, so today's pricing policy should be competitive not monopolistic. Corporate restructuring requires much stress upon the strong information system that give idea about competitors and keep their steps watching. Pricing policy must be based globally, rather than on national level.

After product formulation and pricing, corporates need to communicate to the target customers about their products. Corporate need to change media on which they advertise. In 1997 a debate swirled around (a) whether on-line advertising was viable whether we could come up with standards to make it all tenable. But now every body needs to understand that these are very simple and viable advertising methods on the web, like e-mail ads, exchanges Banner exechanges work best when they are a within an industry (b) backed by sophisticated targeting technology. Randomly placing ads is not the best way to drive traffic. Link exchanges, on the other hand, add more value to the surfer and therefore, make more sense. If we go to a web site selling air conditioning systems, it might be nice to see a page of linkages to installers, repair shops, water treatment systems etc. Things which are symbiotic and useful.

E-mail ads are proving to be very powerful in as much as they are very tightly targeted. The audience of a news litter is and excellent target because their interests are so narrow. So while restructuring, corporate must change advertising media, Agencies and even presentation of messages.

The ball revolves around the same point i.e. the customer. The foremost aim of the companies is to take care of convenience and satisfaction of customers. Information must be collected about all the parameters which affect their behaviour and opinion. But during the process:

(1) Tell people what information you are collecting and what you are going to do with it.

(2) Allow them to participate if they choose.

(3) Allow them to review the information you have about them to correct mis-information and

(4) Provide security to ensure that their information is safe from other prying eyes. All of the above may sound draconian, but it really boils down to good marketing. For100% customer satisfaction follow these rules. Thus one will be treating his customer with the respect they deserve. CRM or Customer Relationship Management can also be done with the help of data warehousing. It is a way by which corporate can focus on customers and find out what they can do to get more customers and retain existing ones. It is data warehousing that helps companies to identify these key customers and help them build target market programs for customer acquisition and customer retention. It is not only important in service based companies, but also in others as well.

One of the contemporary issues to be discussed here is to manage internal customers who sell their services in return of money to accept change. So there is no need to surprise if we call employees as customers. These customers must also be satisfied in order to reach the Goals.They find e-commerce uncomfortable and there is a tendency to try to go back to doing things the old way. They have a lot of queries while restructuring process is going on. They must be assured that the new technology will enhance their skills and improve productivity. Management academy can be set up to explore the hidden competencies of the employees.

Today, three is desktop on every desk. From the secretary in the front office to the CEO to the CA in the back-office. E-business percolates down to the entire organisation. The success of the transformation depends on how well the crew understands and implements e-commerce. Training the people in the e-business concepts and skills is thus critical in make a smooth transition to an e-business.

Aligning peoples skills to organizational objectives is critical for corporate. Assessing the training needs of the employees and ensuring they get relevant, effective training on time is the key to the evolution of a learning organisation. The analysis may include:

— Correlating technology usage with business value.

— Defining training objectives vis-à-vis organizational objectives.

— Identifying associated functions and employees.

— Chalking a training strategy.

Organizations face a number of challenging obstacles in trying to provide high quality and timely IT training. Finding result-oriented training programs on new technologies all the time. Imparting the same quality of training to people spread across the country. Training people in as less time as possible without compromising on productivity. Determining the effectiveness of information technology training. Finding qualified and skilled information technology instructions. Finding high quality vendors and suppliers of information technology training.

However, proper training of employee can make old employees do 90% of the work.

There is an urgent need of information safely locked. When corporate restructuring has been done and one takes pride in having implemented the latest ERP and E-commerce which enables his customers to log orders, reduce cycle time and ensure better productivity, he must take care of hackers and crackers. One has lot of information, out of which he may not like to share confidential business information. A security policy should be made for this purpose which may comprise of:

(1) Classification and labeling of information (e.g.company confidential, private, non-confidential information)

(2) Confidentially and non-disclosure agreements with employees, private suppliers and partners.

(3) Physical and environment security to prevent unauthorized access, damage, etc.

(4) Computer and network management procedures (e.g. capacity planning, virus protection, network security parameters etc.)

(5) Systems access control (when, how and by whom information would be accessed).

(6) Business continuity planning (disaster recovery plan).

(7) Interment security.

Tax implications of e-commerce have a relevance to be discussed here. Internet poses many peculiar technological problems which makes it difficult to formulate a sound taxation policy 1) Internet has no physical location. It is difficult to monitor or prevent transmissions of information or electronic cash. (2) Person's location and identity is necessary for tax purposes. Corporate must force Govt. To make legal and taxation policies for the e-commerce.

Business success requires the ability to see the trees in the proverbial forest. It is easy to get carried away by sheer novelty of internet technology, and many sites reflect this initial enthusiasm. But just placing corporate reports and sales catalogues on the Internet and declaring that one has restructured his organisation and proclaiming success is not enough. Incorporating the Internet as an integral component of one's business strategy now, and in future, requires careful planning, alignment and perseverance. Otherwise future of an organisation is in dark.

Section II

STRATEGIES

7

CORPORATE RESTRUCTURING: A VALUE ADDED STRATEGY FOR BUSINESS GROWTH

S.L. Gupta & Mukesh Sehgal***

The union government will reduce its stake in Industrial Development Bank of India (IDBI) from 72% to 58% by converting a portion of its equity into convertible preference issue. "The restructuring of IDBI's capital base is being done by converting Rs. 24.70 crore equity into 3 years redeemable preference shares at a dividend rate of 13% per annum" The Government has notified the preference share issue after getting the finance ministry's approval. With the rest, IDBI's capital base will shrink from Rs. 673.09 crore tc Rs. 432.39 crore.

Although the number of cross-border mergers and acquisitions was flat in 1999 compared to 1998, at 5100, the value of deals rose by 47% to a record high of $798 billion, according to a survey by KMPG corporate finance. Britain was the most happening country, accounting for $245 billion worth of deals, followed by America $155 billion, Germany $93 billion and France $92 billion.

Marriages are made in heaven, perhaps. But corporate mergers

* Chairman, Deptt. of Management, Kurukshetra University, Kurukshetra.
** Director-cum-Associate Prof., Shri Atmanand Jain Institute of Mgt. & Tech (AIMT), Ambala City.

are definitely not. Mergers and acquisitions between corporates are driven by earthly concerns rather than by heavenly bodies.What can be of more concerns to an organisation than competition from its counterparts? Therefore, one dominant reason for external restructuring acquisitions within an industry is the elimination of competition. Especially so, when the demand is not picking fast enough and the excess supplies are a cause for concern. Add to these woes are squeeze on profit margins, it is a clear case for the reasons behind the acquisition that gulfed the Indian industry? Quite possible, If the way the corporates are bidding each other out to get some prized restructuring, If the acquisition drive continues at the present rate,it cannot be ruled out that at the end of it a few big players will monopolize in India. Some analysts are already predicting that in few years time, major players like ACC, Birla Cement and Gujarat Ambuja will dominate the cement industry in India.

At this millennium's beginning the world is being turned topsy turvy by a technological break through, i.e., IT & communications.The following are the latest happenings ...

Banks Mergers on the agenda in ITLY.

Banks need to disclose more - crisis report

Banks told to crack the whip on errant big borrowers

Asahi Banks gives up on three way mega merger.

Corporate restructuring is a broad term to denote significant reorientation, reorganization or realignment of the assests, investments and liability structure of any company through conscious management actions with a view to drastically alter the quality and quantity of its future cash flow streams. This includes mergers, acquisitions, diversifications, spin offs, and all other internal management upgradations to cover all possible types of redesigns for a company. Corporate restructuring has gained added importance due to intensifying competition, globalisation and technological changes.

The practical general interest lies in these three issues:-

* why firm choose restructuring?
* which firms are likely to be acquired which acquiring, which diversing and so on?
* why do we see more Mergers/Acquisition in some periods than in others?

Rationale behind Corporate Restructuring

1. **Diversification**: Inorganic growth, HLL takeover of TOMCO (TATA Group—an example of conglomerate diversification) Acquisitions (For empire building)

2. **Economies of scale:** Where growth is stagnated or is in recession. India cements acquired visaka cement Raasi cement and a plant of CCI. Nicholas has acquired ROCHE and sumitra Pharmaceuticals (Bid to cut costs)

3. **Early Entry and market penetration**: Coca Cola acquired Parle Soft Drinks, GE Capital Acquired SRF Finance, ICICI Acquired ITC Classic Finance and Anagram Finance (to penetrate market)

4. **Tax Advantages**: Acquiring sick companies (take over of ALLWYN by VOLTAS)

5. **Regulatory Considerations**: Whirlpool merged its India wing Whirlpool washing machines with EXPO Machines and Kelvinator India to form Whirlpool India. Daewoo increased its stake in DCM DAEWOO JV from 51% to 85%.

6. **Size**: Mergers of SCICI with ICICI.

The way we trim though Indian Banks even in the public sector have done well to reduce costs through restructuring, an equal effort needs to be put in to increase revenues.

DEALING ON THE BANK STREET
Trends in transaction costs

	Average Annual Growth During The Period 1995-96 to 1998-99								
						Operating Expenses As % Total Assets			
BANK Group	*Interest expenses*	*Non-Interest OPE expenses*	*Establishment Expences*	*Total Expences*	*Assets*	*95-96*	*96-97*	*97-98*	*98-99*
SBI	15	9	7	12	15	3.1	2.7	2.5	2.5
Associate Bank of SBI	12	11	11	9	14	3.0	2.7	2.7	2.7
Nationalized Bank	14	10	10	11	14	2.8	2.7	2.5	2.5
Public Sector Bank	14	10	10	11	14	2.9	2.7	2.5	2.5
Old Pvt. Sector Banks	22	15	13	19	19	2.4	2.2	2.1	2.1
New Pvt. Sector Banks	46	52	47	43	46	0.8	1.7	1.7	1.6
Private Sector Bank	29	24	16	26	27	2.2	2.1	1.9	1.9
Foreign Banks in India	15	22	15	16	19	2.9	2.7	2.8	3.1
Total of SCBs	16	12	10	13	16	2.9	2.6	2.5	2.5

This rationale lies behind the spate of merger and acquisition in the corporate world today because such moves enable the corporate to consolidate their positions nationally first and after the merger of national companies, they can go global. In the case of Europe, there have been large no. of national mergers before the companies become the global players. In France, arch rivals are merging to form giant companies like the recent merger of Total Fina and ELF Acquaintance.

Globally, just about every IT major-Micro soft, Intel are constantly acquiring stakes in other companies for better market access and are being viewed as enhancing the changes of an increase of returns, higher share prices and dividends. In Europe (in the last three years), the increase in share prices was seven per cent greater through mergers and than from the stock markets as a whole.

One of the notable consequences of the liberalization of the trade and industrial policies has been the large scale restructuring of corporate enterprises.

Corporate restructuring has been the dominant global business theme from the mid-seventies. It has been fueled by a variety of forces like global competition, technological breakthrough, managerial innovations, regulatory changes, transformation of formerly centrally planned socialistic and communistic economics and expansion of international trade.

Now the companies are redefining their strategies to cope with challenges and restoring to restructuring by doing the following:

* Improvement in corporate governance
* Stronger organizational commitment to performance
* An active role of institutional investors
* A vibrant market for corporate control
* A meaningful privatization program
* Flexible mechanism for taking industrial sickness.

By and large corporate restructuring has been a resounding success. It has led to dramatic improvement in corporate performance. Observers of corporate restructuring believe that the gains are attributable to synergetic benefits, sharper focus, better corporate governance, improvement in managerial incentives and motivation, greater discipline power of debt and elimination of cross subsidies.

While the stock markets have been racing ahead at full steam over the last twelve month on the basis of some industries like pharmaceuticals and consumer durable and on the sentiment of the huge growth in the IT industry, the real economy has been rather lackluster paling into the backdrop. True, prices of commodities like steel and aluminum began firming up some time midyear world wide leading companies like Essar and the like to reduce some of their inventories. But the rate of growth was skewed towards some industries and was hardly remarkable, especially when compared with the sky rocketing captial markets. But things are changing now and herein lies the good news.

The data released by the Center for Monitoring Indian Economy (CMIE) reveals growth across virtually every sector and industry. the review for the month of December 1999 starts on a happy note. With industry recording and increase of 6.4% in the first half of the year 1999-2000 over the previous year that had recorded a growth of only 4% within the year, trends showed variation that were laudable with the second half of the year exhibiting a growth of 6.9% against 6% in first half of 1999-2000. Individual industries too faired well; while commodities continued their upswing.

The largest mergers include: British pharmaceutical giants SmithKline Beecham and Glaxo welcome are merging to forge world's largest drug giant. The new company will be know as Glaxo SmithKline.

The merger will be structured as an offer by Glaxo for Smithkime. With 04552 new share swapped for each Smithkline share valuing the transaction at around $76.37 billion Glaxo shareholders will own 58.75 % and SmithKline investors 41.25 % of the new group. In India, the merger is expected to result in the creation of the largest pharmaceutical company.

The world's largest traditional media company, Time Warner Inc.will merge with the world's biggest internet services provider, America on-line Inc. (AOL). Time Warner shareholders will receive 1.5 shares of ADL Time Warner for each share of Time Warner Stock they own, while AOL shareholder will receive 1 share of AOL Time Warner stock for each share of Adl they own. AOL shareholders will hold 55% shares of the merged company, while Time Warner shareholder will hold 45% shares. This merger amounts to $ 190 Billion.

Whereas amid rumors of big restructuring plans, Ford Motor Company announces that it was to give all its 350000 employed personal computers, as part of its plan to exploit the internet to the full.

Indian Overseas Banks

(Value addition through restructuring)

PERFORMANCE HIGHLIGHTS: 1999 - 2000

(A) PROFITABILITY

* Operating profits: Rs. 188.23 crores and increase of 31.67%

(B) BUSINESS

* Deposits: Rs. 243.18 crores, grown by 10.97 %.
* Advances: Rs. 11573 crores, growth of 14.39%.

(C) TREASURY OPERATIONS

* Net investments increased by 23.25 % to Rs. Rs. 1.25 crores
* Significant gains in securities trading

(D) GOLD DEPOSITS & LOANS

* Launching of Gold Deposits; Gold Loans for Jewelery Manufacturers

(E) TECHNOLOGY

* Any Branch Banking Services in Delhi, Mumbai, Chennai and Calcutta with inter-city connectivity

(F) STAFF PRODUCTIVITY

* Business per employee : Rs. 116.87 lacs, improvement

Rs. 1.25. crores by Rs. 13.09 lacs

(G) BRANCH NETWORK

* Total Branches went up from 1396 to 1419

Present Status of Corporate Restructuring in India

In the liberalized but developing economies like India corporate restructuring is regarded as an important instrument whereby the free play of market forces lead to the removal of structural imbalances or economic inefficiencies and the current recession. Even among the developed economies there is a wide diversity in the scope and extent of legislation and regulation. The existence of such diversities in many developed western economies pose a threat of duplicating the western realities to determine the extent to which these should be adopted.

The success or failure of measures adopted to restructure any company or organisation depends upon how realistic an appraisal was carried out.

Of late, Indian companies have been constantly trying to gear up for competition like SBI, Reliance Industries and Nirma Washing Powder. They are willing to grow by leaps and bounds either by grabbing the market share or doubling the growth rate. Therefore , takeovers and acquisitions have become the need of the hour for them. Takeovers and acquisitions are perceived to the best routes to achieve corporate milestones and to cope with the present problem of recession.

Today in India industrialists feel merger is one of the best routes to achieve a size for their company which is comparable to the global companies so as to effectively compete with them. Because today in the era of LPG (liberalization, privatization and globalisation), BIG is considered beautiful as against the age old theory of small is beautiful. The whole purpose of restructuring today is to withstand growing competition with in and outside the country and to keep the country floating profitably· against all those risks and threats which the top management anticipates and prepares itself to face those problem challenges by restructuring suitably. The top management always finds the company growing and earning even in the fierce competition and if it can be done successfully the company gains more recognition and attracts more consumers and investors.

In developed free economies corporate mergers and amalgamations are a regular feature. In Japan USA and European nations hundred of mergers and amalgamations take place every year as a regular phenomena of combination and reconstruction of the business enterprises.

Witness the efforts of India's leading business houses to systematically revert to core businesses. For example, TISCO has divested its cement business to leverage of France: TELCO has spun off its construction equipment business into a separate company, and so on. In the two wheeler industry, after Piaggio LML not withstanding their differences raised their market share with four stroke engines. Rahul Bajaj has been forced to become more aggressive. Pharmaceuticals and the automobiles will also witnesses a new process of consolidation. Big concerns too are likely to sell their stakes to foreign partners like Siddarth Shriram to Honda and Anand Mahindra to Ford.

Inter - company cross holding in Rs.3000 crore Murugappa group are being restructured -unrelated invest-met in group flagship companies viz. EID Parry (India) Ltd and Tube Investment Ltd have been transferred to other group companies .the main phase of M&A starts in two years to come but for its peak tax laws have to amended accordingly. This is only the beginning of many more such activities.

Many Indian industries are likely to undergo changes in activity and ownership structured notably pharmaceutical, beverages, consumer non durable goods, white goods, auto ancillaries, paints, oil etc. to name a few.

The financial institutions are, for the first time willing to help the M&A game by selling their holding since financial institution have large exposures in term equity holding in the cement industries, a uniform policy would facilitate smooth takeovers and mergers IDBI has prepared a study on the cement industry covering almost every type of information like regional demand distribution of supply, performance, problem, and prospectus, if want the industry to adopt suitable restructuring strategies to improve technology, reduce cost and achieve economies of scale. So far FIs have played an important role in Six mergers over past two years including the Rs.450 crore acquisition of Rassi Cement Ltd.

The need to take advantage of the relaxation in government policy, which is allowing companies to take decisions that are based on economic realities. The government is chalking out a fresh agenda for corporate restructuring matters in order to expedite approvals and decision and improving the corporate efficiency. A separate entity to deal with the mergers and acquisitions is required because the laws related to these issues are very complicated and processing procedure is very time consuming.

A Careful Approach

As the model it has constructed contends, the key issue is to weave M&A into your corporate strategy instead of pursuing it opportunistically. Only then will your post-acquisition corporation go on to create more value than that of its parts.

Post M&A economic gain, or synergy, will be generated only if the two companies are worth more together than apart.

Since there is little scope for companies to learn from experience as M&A is a sporadic and time consuming process, how, then, can they tell the toads from the princes as they adopt M&A as their chosen means for restructuring? Importantly, how does a predator determine whether or not a planned acquisition will prove beneficial?

A word of caution

While restructuring via M&A route one must give consideration to certain issues. The object clause of the transferee must contain objects to cover the operations of the transferer company. The effective date of merger must be mentioned in the scheme of amalgamation. Valuation of shares of both the companies must be done by a qualified auditor. Since as per provisions of Company Act, voting at the amalgamation meeting is done only through poll. It is important that poll papers are properly made out.

While the resurgence in the market after a long haul is welcome sign there are some causes of concern. Does the scenario represent a bubble in making? "No". Selective stocks could be overpriced. This could happen in any kind of market. In a bullish phase all stocks tend to go up. Some deservedly so up to a point, some deservedly not so at all.

From the perspective of market cap, depth appears to be happening in terms of the wide spectrum of traded stocks. Yet a large part of the volume is not settled, 905 of the volume is getting squared of. The number of stocks in which the interests are going up, is a good sign. The rally is not narrow based. It is fairly broad based.

As far as growth in valuations is concerned there does not seem to be a balanced growth. First, it was the golden troika of IT, Pharma and FMCG stocks. The new trend appears to be in favour of IT, communication and media stocks. While the growth has been spectacular in these stocks, for the rest of them it has not been so high. This led a two tired segmentation of the market.

The rapid rise in the market barometer sensex appears to be skewed in favour of a few stocks. Stocks like Infosys whose market price grew sky high, got higher weightage in the Index thus pushing the index higher and higher. The index appears to be prone to this self fulfilling prophecy inherent to this design. That raises question over its representativeness of the market.

For capital markets to perform well both the secondary

and the primary markets have to move hand to hand. Presently, the secondary market is vibrant whereas the primary markets yet to revive in a reasonable way. An aggregate quarterly results for 500 companies which has gone for restructuring shows that it is infact a value added strategy for business growth as the % change in the sales (Sep. '99 in comparison to Sep. '98) is 10.9% whereas net profit has increased by 19.2% due to synergy effect.

Summary

Restructuring is a wider concept which includes mergers, acquisition, diversification, spin off etc. In the present era of liberalization, globalization and privatization—the competition is becoming stiff.

In the recessionary phases, as one going on presently, and to cope with the competition a corporate body needs strong financial muscles as well as complete specialization. Hence these days we witness a lot of merger and acquisitions. Whereby the main objective of the acquirer is to grow large so as to crush the smaller fishes in the pond. Spin-offs are generally resorted to concentrate on one particular area and specialize. Due to legal complications and lack of support from the financial institutions (in completing mergers), such type of practices were not popular in the past. However, with the change in the outlook of the Government and FIs the number of acquisition cases are increasing and in the next two years we can see more activity in this area.

REFERENCES

Globe, Devra L., and Lawrance J. White, "A Time - Series Analysis of Mergers and Acquisitions in the US Economy," Chapter 9 in Alan J. Auerbach, ed., *Corporate Take overs: Causes and Consequences,* Chicago Press, 1988, pp. 265-309.

Jensen, Michael C., "Takeovers: Folklore and Science," *Harvard Business Review,* 62, November - December 1984, pp. 109-120

Rohatyn, Flex G., "Needed: Restraints on the Take over Mania," *Challenge*, 29, May-June 1986, pp. 30.

J. Fred Weston, Kwany S. Chung & Susan E. Hoag Mergers, *Restructuring & Corporate Control,* pp. 2-6.

W.T. Grimm, *Mergerstat Review,* 1987, and previous years.

Financial Analyst, April 1999, Feb 2000 and various issues

Business Today, March and Dec. 7-21, 1998 & various issues

The Hindustan Times 12-6-99

The Economic Times 12-7-99 & 21-5-99

The Financial Express 5-6-99 & 27-4-99

The Tribune 23-5-99

The Economic Times (18 July, 1999)

Indian Management, Feb., 2000

The Economic Times, New Delhi, (8th June 2000)

The Economic Times, New Delhi (13th and 14th June 2000)

Indian Management, Feb. 2000

The Economic Times (8 June, 2000)

The Economic Times (13/6/2000 and 14/6/2000)

8

REENGINEERING MANAGEMENT

*A.S. Chawla**, *G.S. Batra*** & *D.S. Randhawa****

"Things refused to be mismanaged long."
— Ralph Waldo Emerson

Introduction

Future of business lies in innovations, new ideas, mental mobility, thinking ahead and better than feither competitors. To overcome competition, customer demands and pressures, cost cuttings initiatives in manufacturing. Reingeering is the order of the day. Reengineering about changing our management techniques, the way we think about, organise, inspire, deploy, enable, measure and reward the value adding operational work, it is about changing management itself. But who exactly, is the manager these days? There are self managers, enterprise managers. This paper deals with managers on all these levels.

Reengineering prescribes actions, not words and difficult long term actions at that and not just are expedients like down sizing or outsourcing. Reengineering basically deals four conceptual issues that is issues of purpose, issues of culture, issues of process and performance including performance of whole organisation or enterprise issues of people. We must look ourselves

---

* Professor of Management, Punjabi University Guru Kashi Campus, Talwandi Sabo.

** Associate Professor of Management, Punjabi University, Patiala

*** Research Scholar, Punjabi University Guru Kashi Campus, Talwandi Sabo

and to each other, to find the personal resources we find to do our jobs—the courage and trust. To face realities, managers today have to face the tensions, stress, odds of dynamic environments before passing them to others. We proceed to examine the challenges, realities and are keen for the battle and to win.

AIM

The aim of this paper is to discuss the process of reengineering in an organisation to improve upon business results while earning the hearts and minds of people who produce the products.

The paper proposes to discuss the process of reeingeenring in the following manner

(a) The ordeal of management.

(b) Customer and re-engineering.

(c) What reengineering thoughts are all about.

(d) When to reengineer?

(e) What people want to know?

(f) Purpose and vision.

(g) Culture and values.

(h) Weeds push out flowers.

(i) What we want?

(j) Teaching, living, enabling, defining, measuring and doing.

(k) Conclusion.

The Ordeal of Management

The core issue in the business is to improve business results by winning hearts and minds of people working around. Nothing is simple any more, nothing is stable, dramatically, perplexingly before your eyes. Now whatever do is not enough, everything is in question, everything must change. The old ways of management no longer work where we are used to in oriental way of management. The organisational charts, the compensation schemes, the hierarchies, the vertical organisation, the whole tool kit of commanmd and control management techniques no longer work. The changes not only touch the manages but go deeper to explore who they are, their sense of task,thier sense about themselves, not just what they know about how they think, not their vision of their world but their way of living the world. The question is not of bringing a change in an organisation, but bringing it fast and managing too. Whatever you do is not enough, nothing is simple. Everything is in question. Everything mut change. Peter Drucker puts it bluntly, "Every organisation has to prepare for the abdonment of every thing it does, the question is what is this everything and should be abandon it?

Customer and Reengineering

The era of smooth sailing is over where grand children enjoyed the wealth and fame of grand parents. Modern day customer as Fortune puts it, "The sharpest, most educated customer that marketers have ever faced. In today's market places, it is no caveat emptor, but caveat factor. Customers today are characterised by their relentless demand in quality, service and price, by their willingness to act on default of conduct, by their disloyalty. All this puts them away from the gentle grateful, legal customer of 1950's. Look at the range of choices being offered today. Sony turn outs four new products a day and a new walkman model every three weeks in 1992. Heinz introduced more than 500 hundred new products world wide. Rubbermaid turns out a new product at an average everyday.

In fact, the new power and freedom of the customer has destroyed, all the fond managerial assumption of smooth sailing era. No more inherited, unearned brand loyalties and no more protection by the government. Governments, with a few exceptions, realize that protecting business enterprises creates bloated companies. Unable to compete in global markets. The message is clear sure things are rough and tough out there. We can't help that. In fact for the customers sake, fight it out. But there is also lots of money to be made, get your share. You are at your own may the best man or woman win."

The first wave of managerial exodus came purely from the need to reduce costs in order for companies to remain in the competition and others in business. The second came with a challenge that some managers did not add business values. The third wave came with a little more forethought, a recognition that many managers especially middle managers, principally gathered and moved information through bureaucracy, and the information technology has obviated their need. And then came reengineering, with managerial accoutability being pushed down and out as work becomes more self managed, and the need of many manager is in an organisation is being challenged.

Customer being their new muscle are growing ever more exacting. They express their power by asking to speak to the person incharge as reengineering sees it. This question is the beginning of wisdom. Let us redesign our process so that costomer can talk to the person incharge to provide services, quality and solve their problems, to actually help them, to be real person incharge. The great corporate of Sloan sort were really cruise ships, huge facilities for enjoyment of passerngers, majestic powers of command and control for their top officers on boart, not much than a floating system of rewards, promotions and privileges---a self serving bureaucracy what counts for power, authority, responsibility—is what one can do, oneself with own skills and personal qualities. At the deepest level, then the ordeal of management is revealing something about a great change not only in the business organisations but in the larger society. The democracy of the customer voting with their money, is summoning a meritocracy of people and producers, corresponding with every thing they have got. Everyone not just the owners and the managers, now believes in great secular faith of growth. And the growth is just not economic, but personal, cultural and spiritual as well. Reeingineering will teach us for more to do with much less.

What Reengineering Thoughts are About?

Change down with the past! Revolutionize! Think radically! Lead experimentally! go on a limb, go over the cliff. Linear thinking, formulatic thinking, grand strategy thinking, conventional, produce only comforting illusions, bland rigidities, complacent passivity, all the slow working recipes for disaster. The fact is that one does not know what lies ahead, our times are all 'post' something post industrial, post modern, post cold war and no one knows what they are "pre" to.

American are good at moving on into changing, contigent, turbulenty, adverse and are largely in unpredictable univrse i.e good at meeting challengec, discovering(re) presenting is a word REENGINERING everything including themselves. Europeans and Japanese are welcoming to radical thought, the past is not crpse for them, but rather the basis for strong cultures and of beliefs. Yet managers in those countries are learning fast the virtues of new world thinking the question of reengineering is discussed in the following sequences:--

What is the business for?

What kind of culture do we want?

How do we do our work?

What kind of people do we want to work with?

What is this business for? Three good reasons for the question. First dramatic change is in the store, actually or potentially for all industries all over the world. Changes are dramatic, unending and remorseless. Technology is playing its role in communication and robatics. Economic politics within and amongst nations is baring up old rules of the game. The business industry is technologically empowered, world wide competitive, free for all, here the managers have ask a question what they are doing is worth doing or else they should be doing something else.The second reason is continuous change in the market place means continous change inside the corporation. Managers must ask what result we want in the market and then come up with how changes in core work and management process be defined. The third reason is the need and task of leadership everyone wants to know why they are in the business to make money (who is not?). If the task then it requires redefining in a vivid and a compelling way.

What kind of culture do we want? This question addreses the culture, values and behavioures, asking managers to develop a set of principle of desired behaviour so that a company's culture cannot be proclaimed or manipulated which consists of deeply shared values and beliefs of people who work in it. Managers have to draw out what is already there by leading and educating. It is laeders who have to change themselves who have to launch experimental voyage, they who have to embrace perfectionism and relentless betterment, who have faith in their fellows, who listen to the voice of people and learn improvement through "personal best." Managers who cannot get out of the old ways and pass into new ones, will not be able to manage for long.

How do we do our work? This aspect deals with managerial processes of day to day work, the process through which we manage value added work. This is dealt in detail. later in this paper.

What kind of people we want to work with? In new pluarist corporation where authority is not restricted in office but in the skills. Managers unilaterally deploy team members only at the risk of destroying team morale--that is at the risk doing harm to the business. It is the purpose and operational capabilities what will point a way to strength. It is our process and culture that how we want to design our systems. All this is based on hiring and developing people to meet challenges.

"At the end of every day of every year to things remain unshakeable, our constancy of purpose and our continuous discontent with immediate present." Is the viewpoint Roberto C.

Goizusta, Chairman and CEO of Coca Cola. There is a contradicition, in the consistency and discontent, which means thinking reeingineering. Intelligence of holding two contradictory ideas in one's head at the same time this requires character. This is the best sign of reengineering character may not only to hold contradictory ideas but to act on them. This is the main theme of this paper.

When to Reengineer?

Fortune once laid down the rule about re-engineering, there are two reasons why anyone undertake it, greed and fear. The asset of any leader is followers. The followers are not to be commanded and controlled but understood. To mobilize the company the leader must understand the needs of the people, articulate in deeper sense respond to them. This is pre-engineering challenge. If an organisation is not change ready, it is going to be very very painful and just won't be anywhere near as effective as it could be or it should be. That is where we need to focus our energies. People would like to know as where do they fit into change. To whom must the CEO speak, everyone around the corporation managers, non managers, vendors the surrounding community, investors and needless to say coustemers, labour and the workers. Mobilization has to up down and sideways meaning everybody should be in the know. No one is going to go through total mobilization for change without knowing why and what for? The successful managers is not those who is entrusted with secrects but the manager who wins trust by sharing what he or she knows. When we are trusted we win hearts and minds are wallets of customer. To gain this trust, we must be candid to forthright, open with everybody. This may seem like throwing away the guard but the knowledge in power. Micheal Walsh late chairman and CEO of TENNECO said it right and straight "To win trust you have to make yourself vunerable."

What people want to know? managers may not be able to

provide right answer to all the question of reengineering to people but definitely can give a reason and a picture.

A) *Big Picture Reasons:* All reengineering managers agree on one point that eventually what ever procedures are followed but people do like to know the history of background of own and other big concerns. The picture and reasons has to be convincing enough to mobilize people working under. To say 'Why we had to do it'-- reengineering. Capitalism is a system which works on fear. Some managers do use reasoning from the historical content like, "look I know reengineering is hard, but is not our fault, history is making us to do it". This is a copy to be used with great caution. History is at work here nudging, prodding, threatening. History does not tell us how to respond. People know about this but will not forgive for making wrong choices.

B) *Industry Specific Reasons:* Different industeries are going through change, industries are being compelled to change either by technology or socio-economic developments or combination of both. Media industry has technology and communication as driving force, Health care may be compelled to change by a political reason, deregulation is adding novel competion to industry there may be a fear of privatisation.

C) *Corporation Specific Reasons:* In the era of rough sea people want to know where the trouble is and it effects them. In the times of trouble get increasingly worried but distorted fears, fantasies need to address their concerns and little if any should facts and figures have a central place in the mobilization process.

D) *Purpose and Vision:* The essence of purpose and vision is that we start questioning who we wanted to become? This radical turning point where past and perilous present is considered- the corpse of memory and in Emerson's phrase-" and let in light of the new day." Examine the people how to do their job is a place of work. Changing the way of work done means giving up something people are comfortable. The kind of loss has to be taken seriously. People are not very familiar with words like vision, purpose or mission. What they need is the new vision of their future, letting them know what was expected of them. It is true that without a vision people perish, values come here too, something for the people to hang on to. Values are a part of company's culture, compelling images and practices of company to hold on. To site he example of Pepsi Co's Pizza Hut division, of vision and metaphor power. In mid 1980's when 90% growth in pizza chain was being gobbled up by Domino's. Untill then pizza hut managers thought that they were a chain of restaurants. But Domino's challenge prescribed them that they would better change metaphor from one that conjured up the picture of pepole sitting in a restaurant enjoying a meal to one that implied being served in a variety of location, malls, airports, museums etc. in short industries chain become a distributers system. Pizza Hut illustrate the requirement that the inspirational union of the company must be left to revision, revision and revision .

Usually in an enterprise, it is the manager who will see the need for change who must bring the proves of mobilising the entire company first. The process begins with clear eyed look to the future as well to the present and past and often starts with fears. It is not enough for a leader to have a vision, a leader needs to attract followers, associates, men and women, who can commit themselves focus. But if mobilisation process is to succeed these followers must become leaders too finding their own sense of purpose in the shared challenge and spreading the call and vision of change.

A) An organisation of leaders all showing the same vision and purpose can be powerful force. But for the new organisation to work everyone must be given real work to do, work that focusses on making the vision and purposes real in short that focusses on reengineering. What are we in business and for whom--the newly discovered customer.

B) The focus should be on customer and rest everything else should be stripped away. Mobilization should never stop. Change will continue to be constant, for reengineering to live the company needs to be reinforced with purpose and mission.

As a consequence, managers must continually walk in their market place asking the question that began the mobilization process. Mobisation begin at the top. The energy comes from pushing authority and accountability down to where action is.

C) Radical change is sometimes in some ways. The easiest to accomplish marketing a clear break with the past sends a jolt of energy through a compny but only when some people are given some sense of control over what happens next.Sink or swim is more a sound policy in management than it is in swimming pool, water wings are no good , either, just another form of control. The best policy is clean measureable guidelines --swimming lessons, guidelines are not enough. The reengineering manager think's of jolt as one part of it anyway as being constant conversation with people. New give us sense of security and tell us where do we stand.

You have to have a critical mass of people who believe in the future of the place of work and continually ask what they can do to make a difference. The challenge to get a large group of people energised and focussed and then keep them that way. These people have to build stronger relationship with customers based on value, high performance, culture, working together and supporting each other. The people who make difference requires to be suitably rewarded financially.

One reason that reenginering is a radical understanding that once you have begin , there is literally no containing it. One thing leads to another or better. Lest the whole endeavor collapse . one of the means of getting across implemeting self managed work team where groups of people are given more responsibility, give people more autonomy in terms of managing themselves, provide them technical skill, increased problem solving skills and increase interpersonal skills. All this means major investment in the training and development of people across the organisation. By these measures waste could be reduced and responsibility to intervene at the required time themselves if something goes wrong. The idea is to provide smaller groups with larger knowledge and skills to increase efficiency and problem solving.

Culture and Values

Obedience is still called for let it be any type of command and control structure. Not everyone can be an entrepreneur who can make something out of nothing. Most of us we want to climb in this world then we must have something to climb. Robert Hall author of the Soul of Enterprises: Creating a dynamic vision for American Manufacturing tells us "Future belongs to those who can frequently recognize the high moral teams around the needs of changing process. If that is true values becomes most important structural elements in enterprises. There is terific strains between high morals and frequent changes.That is where values are, at the cross roads between decency and sound profit and that is where culture must be built.

What Values?

Let us get down to it -- what kind of values do we want, what kind of culture? I wish there is a simple answer to it. Values take their shape and substance from many sources from the real business, from the realm of metaohors, from the political and social ideals of company's native land, from the individuals beliefs of people in the organizations. The source are so difficult that mix so differently in different organization that it is helpless to expect a single statement of values do emerge in successful organization are willing to:

a) Perform up to the highest measure of competence always

b) To take initiatives and risks

c) To adopt to change

d) To make decisions

e) To work comperatively as team

f) To be open, especially with information, knowledge, and news of forthcoming problems.

g) To trust or be trustworthy

h) To respect others and ones self

I) To answer for our actions, to accept responsibility

j) To judge and be judged, reward and be rewarded on basis of performance.

The first five represent work values, appropriate to the job and how it is performed the second five are human virtues, pure and simple, appropriate to living and working fruitfully in a larger orderly society and are based on social values. These social values are entered by most of the cultures in developed world and our encouraged by most of our parents, teachers, friends and fellow citizens. The first asks people to perform to highest measure and tenth asks for be judged judgements and rewards are invidous, especially with in a closed stressful environment look again the values of willingness and notice the inevitable tension. Inevitable comparisons will be made which will be painful to some, delightful to others thereafter arises degree of envy, discord, self regarding fear even malice. This is where the culture comes in or should, until it is strangely supportive of trust, respect and teamwork, these social values will become totally personal and private, disappearing underground.

A Case of Bad Value

On self audit we will note that in some organization mistrust and non performance prevails, the audit uncovers the following:

Only your friends are trust worthy.

Information shall be on need to know basis.

Employees are overhead not assets.

Disagreement is bad.

To get along, go along.

The boss always right.

Internal rivalries are healthy.

Me. Me-ism.

Excellent performance is not a core value.

For promotions qualifications don't matter.

The customer is incidental.

One will note that results of bad values is mistrust, lack of respect, conflict, lack of knowledge about organization goals and poor performance. It is a disturbing fact of our times that many of institutions where we used to find our source of personal significance in larger world-family, neighbourhood, clubhouse, religious institutions, philantropthy, government have lost much of their persuasive power. They donot connet us to teach other as they used to do nor do help us know ourselves as they did once. As a result many of us may fact more alone or in significant. It has come to many people in west that of all the support of ancient, traditional supports of humane selfhood only work remains strong. That is what at stake in value statement- our sense of ourselves in a larger human world. The choices are ours.

Beware: Weeds Push out Flowers

In a reengineering process to be successful managers have to cultivate their own culture. The new culture has to be very strong to overcome the old one and it has to remain strong to keep the old one out from the coming back. The reason is very simple. There is a law of corporate cultures, the best values tries to push out good social values first and then good work values. The fact is good culture requires hard work to establish while bad cultures do not Flourishing, fertilizing and weeding cultivating weedy garden's require low maintenance they go off themselves.

The greatest enemy of new reengineering culture of willingness is the old culture of cynicism, self-regarding fear and mistrust. It is always there like seeds of weeds waiting to infest the place again. Nevertheless there is an iron law that dictates. That rheotic expression and the statement of values do wear out. People get tired of hearing the same phrases with the same old tone of aggressive urgency, in the same old forums. Simply because they cannot hear them any more. Primarily by actually acting on the values and the expression they talk about so often but keep the meaning above.

What We Want?

Identifying the values that define a culture of reengineering-that is a culture that willingly embrace the need for constant change is only a necessary first step. To make those values and that culture thrive within your corporate community and remove all the weeds requires teaching, living, doing at all levels of the organizations values contemporary or actually attempting more radical cultural change.

Check the following:-

- Determine what values are deeply shared by people in the organization look at how people believe to see the real values they share.
- Assess what bad behaviours may have driven good behavior, where are the weeds?
- Articulate what values and behaviors you must move toward together with your aspirations as a community of people.
- Examine your management process do they support or contradict.
- Start teaching, doing and living the values you want to define culture.

Teaching

To share the behaviour of community of people, a common goal must be clearly expressed. Teaching must be both formal and informal there is a good power in using metephors to teach culture-a power that is compounded when teaching stresses the alignment process of personal and organization values. Teaching should happen regularly as part of person's work. It should be a chance for everyone, teachers and student alike to renew their commitment to the company's cultural values as well as a way of monitoring how well those values are working in practice. Sometimes the information teaching done on an adhoc basis can be the best way to keep the weeds from growing. The single most lesson which requires to be taught is the permanence of change.

Dealing with human potential, most people operate at 75% of their true potential. The organization requires to lap this potential by identifying. Ask poeple to give thier idea a beiginning to take roots. Basic teachings on dealing with angry employees, beyond unions, coaching for commitment and interpersonal dynamics which helps managers to see themselves as their employee may see them.

Doing

Behavioural change can be accelerated if you can formalize the doing beyond managers. A good culture is maintained by designing a way for people to monitor their own behaviour. Everyone must know how they are doing. We are to except them to assume acountability. Designing way to tell a customer that your company considers. Their business is important.

Living

Living a culture demands that everyone deals with potential, problems proactively, as everyone lives the culture, the change will become pervasive, energizing veterans and transforming new hires. Some times merely changing.your physical space can help reinforce a cultural change. It is not enough to tell people a new culture is good for the customer: to get employees its principle completely they have to see how new values are good for them too. Responsibility is not that is daunitng, responsibility means freedom too and people find that liberating. Given a responsibility to run their departments, individuals generally do not look over their shoulders. Once given anotonomy, the involvement and decision at their level becomes better.

The reason managers can actually manage in todays world markets running the race that begins at the top speed and then gradually pick up the pace is that they are running along. They are "We". We with our subordinates, we with our bosses and we with our pears. In some organizations the right word is associates which may be the best word of all. There are five core managerial processes, mobilizing, enabling, defining, measuring and communicating. To let do people do their job is to provide them with wherewithal to do the job and empower them with decision making.

Enabling

Enabling and learning go hand in hand. Viewing mistakes as part of the learning process is crucial, enabling means letting go of control. A symbolic action can be a potent means of signaling that you have indeed let go, it means that control must be more all the way to frontline. A road block in the middle of the road can stymie this movement and encourage old behaviours, tearing away the bureaucratic under growth that seperates the workers ability to help and the customer's desire to be helped. People must know that their idea will be listened to and if they have merit will be acted upon. If they do, it is possible to mobilize individual creativity on a very broad scale like all reengineered process enabling must be prepetually on going to be successful, and it must touch every one.

Defining

Organization to succeed have to define their standards and objectives from customer point of view. There will be impossibly ambitious as a result striving to meet them you may / will achieve the impossible. Customers are not interested in definition of job well done. They just don't want any mistake on their nickel, so set your objective of zero mistake. Be skeptical of the "May the best man win" mind set, in this context that means resisting the temptation to define work processes and responsibilities so as to set one unit in competition with others, over customers demand that we be one company. The goals and services have to define from the point of view of the customer and not what company can do.

Measuring

Ultimate measurement is the customer satisfaction. Measuring customer satisfaction can also be an effectivc way to keep managers in touch with the market place. In case of personal performances being measured then let the specialist who are knowledgeable they do the job. Performance measurement process should be designed on the assumption that people have potential to do the new work. These process should be supportive and not punitive. Measurement and records processes must reinforce the culture you want to create. Reengineering does not mean anarchy with increased control comes increased accountability. The self managed performance must be measured.

Communicating

Communicating the reengineering message begins with presenting the case for change letting people know the "why". Then they must be told how and what - the specific impact on their lives. The new communication flow may be threatening to many, we need to be shown how sharing knowledge can be in their best interest too. No communication process is too humble or too grand. So, use them all from the simplest to most sophisticated. Knowledge is power but does not come easily, you earn it by thinking and all we have to think about is information. So make sure that information "Gets around".

Conclusion

It seemed much simpler in the days of smooth sailing years of business reengineering was not thought of as the globalization of business and advancement communications and information technology reengineering became necessary to keep the business enterprises going. Thousands of companies small or large have undertaken the mission of reengineering yet as the reengineering revolution spreads. Throughout the world economy, a new familiar pattern seems to have emerged. Too, often reengineering stops at top echlons of corporations, and managerial levels remain unchanged or resistant to reengineering process. As a consequence the task of reengineering is stopped in its tracks and the anticipated benefits are never achieved.

In early 1990s, corporation changed from owner leadership to professional managers who began to run companies like controllable predictable machines. Now that corporations have taken pains to reengineering their operational processes, the management processes must change too. In this paper focus have been on mobilizing, enabling, defining, measuring, communicating in order to achieve business culture that enables a continous process of reengineering in order to achieve success.

Reengineering works up to a point. The obstacle is management. The only way we are going to be delivered on full promise of reengineering is to start reengineering management by reengineering ourselves.

REFERENCES

Dr. Nalini V Dave, *Vedanta and Management.*

S. Lomash, *Value Management.*

Gray Hamel, *The Concept of Core Competence.*

Nature and Value of Strategic Management.

Champy, *Reengineering Organization.*

James C Collius and Roy Chodhary, *Building your Company's Vision.*

B K Roy Chodhary, *Manegerlal Effectiveness.*

Fred Luthmans, *Organisational Behaviour.*

9

MARKET RESTRUCTURING: A KEY TO CORPORATE RESTRUCTURING

K. Eresi & S.V. Shridhara Murthy***

Introduction

Indian economy is going through a series of changes as a result of second-generation reforms resulting from the first round of reforms on account of Libralisation, Globalisation and Privatisation.

One of the main features noted as a result of these reforms is structural change in the marketing environment with the entry of global players in almost all spheres.

The entry of foreign business houses into the Indian market has led to paradigm shifts in the market. This development has led expanding of mental horizon of the Indian consumer resulting in a wave of consumerism pervading the market.

Indian consumer, as a result of exposure to newer products and services as also better terms of sale offered by foreign companies has become choosy. The main shift noted in the Indian market is the dominance of the buyer over seller.

Some business houses, which commanded virtual monopoly

* Professor, Department of Commerce, Bangalore University, Bangalore - 560 001

** Senior Grade Lecturer, Department of Commerce, NMKV College for Women, Bangalore - 560 011.

position till recently, have felt the heat of competition from foreign companies.

The paradigm shift in the attitude of buyers has put the traditional Indian companies on guard and the resulting exercise on the part of business houses has led to 'Market Restructuring' paving way for Corporate Restructuring.

We have attempted this paper on the basis of above mentioned developments. The main focus of the paper is to examine the role of 'Market Restructuring' in influencing the 'Corporate Restructuring' and various elements thereof.

Statement of the Problem

Corporate restructuring is being carried out in a big way by business houses in recent times obviously with the main objective of surviving in the market. It involves leveraging the corporate image and brand image. The resulting competitive edge will help the business to survive and flourish.

Development in the corporate world in the recent past has shown that mergers, acquisitions and joint ventures are being carried out leading to corporate restructuring.

An analysis of sequence of operations in a number of cases shows that corporate restructuring is an outcome of market restructuring affected either by the corporate intentionally or as a result of changes in the economic environment. It is worth noting that in either of the cases, corporate restructuring is an outcome of market restructuring. Hence, it calls for a study.

PART—I

CORPORATE RESTRUCTURING

Restructuring is an inclusive term that refers to the recombination of an enterprise by rearranging the enterprise building blocks in ways that would enhance the value of the enterprise. It deals with all the strategically significant changes that directly and indirectly affect the value of a firm as a going concern. The objective of restructuring is to realign resources and their use with the market needs in ways that enhance the value of the surviving enterprise. Matching the product and service delivery of the firm with those of the market requirements is one of the essences of restructuring. It is also intended to make the enterprise financially self-sufficient. There are certain other important issues like, the ownership, which gives direction to the enterprise, work force of the enterprise, which is responsible for taking the firm in that direction. All this ultimately lead towards meeting the customer's requirements, which is the core of restructuring.

Market Restructuring

One of the toughest challenges that the Indian companies are facing as a result of Liberalisation and Globalisation is matching market performance with the multinational companies and facing the competition from them. Many Indian companies are not in a position to match the infrastructure and financial resources of the foreign companies. These foreign companies are also sound in quality of managerial resources and strategic planning capability.

Corporate restructuring is one of the strategies that come handy in challenging the competition offered by the multinationals. Market restructuring in this context means restructuring of the market in qualitative and quantitative terms to the advantage of the enterprise. It involves mobilization of those resources that are the strongholds of the local enterprises and leveraging their effects by making suitable changes in the controllable marketing environmental factors. There are two possible alternatives in this strategy. One is to tie-up with one of the competitors to counter the challenges of the other competitors. Second possibility is to bring together the capabilities of the local operators by entering in to joint ventures. When the restructuring is aimed at reallocation, redesigning and refocusing of marketing capabilities, it may be termed as Market Restructuring. It may be either internal or external. Internal restructuring takes place when internal marketing factors are redesigned and re-oriented. External restructuring takes place when external factors are redesigned or restructured.

Market Restructuring essentially involves restructuring and reorienting of various components of the marketing functioning. Product, Price, Processes, Physical evidence, Market Segmentation, Sales force, Channels of Distribution, Types of intermediaries, Methods of Promotion, Techniques of positioning are the components in question in this context. Any one, all or a combination of these may be restructured and reoriented with the ultimate aim of capturing a market. Restructuring may be effected either unilaterally or as an outcome of mergers and amalgamations. It may also be an outcome of a temporary arrangement like joint venture.

Some Cases of Restructuring

Some cases of restructuring witnessed in the recent past in different spheres of the industry have been considered here for substantiating the statements made in the paper. The cases selected are relating to BPL Group in the Electronic Durable sector, The Silverline Group in software sphere and The Murugappa Group in the Financial Sector. Thrust is on the product line as mentioned above while discussing the restructuring exercise carried out by these organizations.

The BPL experience

In view of the challenges faced in the market as a result of the entry of foreign electronic giants, BPL, which had a substantial share in the consumer durables market, was forced to change its marketing strategy.

To start with, diversification of area of operation was resorted to. In 1995, BPL Mobil's Mumbai circle was set up and by 1999 it had a clientele of 2,20,000 subscribers and started making profits. Market restructuring was the challenge ahead. In the colour television market, looking at the threat from Japanese companies and their partners, BPL tied up with Sanyo looking at the emerging revelation that Product Life Cycle of the products is becoming shorter and shorter. State of the art technology is being applied in the field of manufacturing flat line television to counter the competition from Phillips and others. Brand leverage with the help of latest technology is the ultimate objective. Further a range of new products is being added. Domestic and international channels are being streamlined in order to make the presence of BPL in the market positive.

As a result of this a metamorphosis in systems, structures, orientation and marketing effectiveness has taken place across the organisation. In other words, large scale restructuring has taken place leading to restructuring in all spheres of functional management.

Being a multi- product company, constant absorption of talented staff at all levels has led to restructuring of the personnel department. High salaries, lesser number, better facilities, more freedom for decision making are the outcome of this restructuring. Though there were some hurdles in the beginning, the scheme has been implemented successfully and is settling down gradually.

As a result of this on going restructuring scheme, BPL has withstood the onslaught of the foreign competition and strength of its brand name is growing day by day.

The Silverline Story

The Silverline Company, which owns the SIL brand, was facing a problem of not having a better perception in planning. For overcoming this problem the group has gone in for a major scheme of restructuring. The Silverline group currently consists of Silverline Holdings Corporation (SHC) of the US, the parent company of the wholly- owned Silverline Technologies Inc. (STI) of the US and 51% owned Silverline Industries Ltd. (SIL).

Restructuring was planned on the following lines. First, STI·

was to be acquired by SIL at a cost of $46.25 million. There was a fresh issue of 4.5 million shares on preferential allotment basis to SHC at Rs. 445 per share in consideration of the acquisition. The main objective of this exercise was to remove doubts in the minds of analysts and investors about the business prospects of the Indian company. In fact, restructuring is a common practice in this group. The IPO of SIL in September, 1992 was used for purchasing a US based Staff Supplementation Company called Infocom, which had revenues of $5 Million at that time. This immediately catapulted Silverline as one of the top ten Indian software companies. India was still at early stage of liberalization and the image of 'snake charmers country' still dominated the average American mind, and overall engagement of Indian programmers in the US had not yet reached critical mass. The core-marketing problem was compounded by the inability of American subsidiary to get adequate working capital financing from US financial institutions.

Then the Indian management sought permission from Govt. of India to pump in finance from India to the US subsidiary. The Govt, said no after permitting supply of $5 million. So there was a need for a major spin off and it was carried out by creating a US holding company, SHC and by bringing in a venture capitalist to fund the exercise. The US subsidiary was divested in January 1997 and a reverse merger ("to re-integrate the companies") was concluded by the end of the year. Silverline USA was able to tap into a $15 million line of credit by an American Bank.

This encouraged the group to go in for market restructuring by adding a host of services in to the product range in the field of application management and product development. This led to ranking of Silverline as an important company in the American market with a size of $60 million.

The Murugappa Group Restructuring

The Rs.3, 100 crore Murugâppa group is presently working

on a scheme of restructuring to be ranked as one of the major financial institutions in the country with in three years. The present presence of the group in the financial market is not so appealing.

The Murugappa group has planned high growth strategies for Mutual Fund operations as a part of its renewed thrust to financial services. The first stage they have taken is to plan an elaborate restructuring of their marketing effort. They have set targets in the field of fund management quality, customer service, liquidity technology and distribution network. Though the group is already in the field of mutual funds, they have not succeeded in making a mark in the market place. They are revamping the product line by adding more lines of products in the form of a variety of schemes.

With the main objective of strengthening the survival strategy they are resorting to restructuring strategies in the fields of human resource management, infrastructure, information technology, R&D and Fund management capabilities.

In order to achieve this they have forged a joint venture by name Cholamandalam Cazenove AMC. They intend to increase the capital of the AMC from the present Rs. 12 crore with Cholamandalam Investments holding 51 % and Cazenove Fund Management 49%.

Strategic Building Blocks of Corporate Restructuring

As evident from the discussion of the cases so far the important areas of restructuring scheme are Capital, Infrastructure, Human Resource, overall management and strategic focus. Thus the strategic building blocks of the restructuring may include:

1) Assets

2) Liabilities

3) Work force

4) Management and

5) Strategic Focus.

PART-II
INFLUENCE OF MARKET RESTRUCTURING ON COMPONENTS OF CORPORATE RESTRUCTURING

A discussion on the corporate restructuring building blocks and the influence of market restructuring on them follows:

1. Assets Restructuring

Restructuring of assets begins with division and reassignment, rehabilitation, abandonment, and/or replacement of physical assets. Asset management may also include the technology status, the production process used, as well as certain non tangible assets like brand equity. This area is mainly related to production activity. Creation of production capacity and production schedule depends on demand for the product, which is an outcome of marketing effort. Thus modification of marketing plans may affect asset structure as well. In other words market restructuring may lead to asset restructuring.

2. Restructuring of Liabilities

Classification and formalisation of liabilities and reengineering of existing corporate debt to create a viable capital structure is an important aspect of liability restructuring. Sourcing of financial resources required for market restructuring may influence this field as well. Promotion budget, especially at the time of re-launching re-engineered products or new products may have a bearing on the liabilities and lead to their restructuring.

3. Work-force Restructuring

Restructuring of workforce is a very sensitive issue. It is an issue having socio-legal dimensions. It deals with the number of employees, the mix of skill that the enterprise requires and the conditions for early retirement schemes worked out. New marketing plans may or may not require more work forces. Recent trends show that large- scale mechanization is leading to depletion of work force and inducting of highly skilled highly paid workmen in place of large-scale unskilled workforce. In the Indian conditions, legal protection and trade unionism may become hurdles in the path of reconstruction. Golden handshakes and VR schemes may further burden the financial position of the company.

4. Management Restructuring

Management restructuring addresses the values, skills and capabilities of the management team. It also deals with the need for change of composition and quality of managers. Market Restructuring not only calls for new and dynamic management in the marketing function but also matching capabilities in other functional management areas. Managers that can meet the requirements of international standards are needed in all the spheres of management.

5. Restructuring of Strategic Focus

Restructuring the strategic focus relates to the mission and vision of the enterprise and any possible changes in this area. It has to redefine the objectives of the firm and envisage the ways for achieving them. It is an extension of restructuring of management. Decisions of globally accepted standards, statesmanship and public relations are the need of the hour to meet the market restructuring challenge.

On the basic of the above stated discussions we can draw the following:

1. Corporate restructuring results out of changes in the marketing environment, which in turn influences the demographic characteristics of the consumers and the demand-supply position for the products.
2. Market restructuring has a bearing on all other spheres

of corporate restructuring and hence becomes the most important sphere and starting point for corporate restructuring.

3. Adequate planning and decision-making skills go into effective market restructuring followed by sound and effective corporate restructuring.
4. Mergers, acquisitions and joint-ventures are a result of cut throat competition in the market generally.

Conclusion

Corporate restructuring largely depends on the availability of internal and external incentives arising out of the environmental and allied advantages that are forthcoming as a result of restructuring. Market conditions are vital parameters of position of the company and any shortcoming arising out of the winning edge of the competitors can be set right by resorting to market restructuring and the resulting corporate restructuring.

10

CORPORATE RESTRUCTURING: A VIABLE OPTION FOR PUBLIC SECTOR UNDERTAKINGS

Anil Sharma & Rajiv Kumar***

Introduction

Both in comparison with over all economic performance during the fifty years of planning as well as by certain absolute standards, the performance of the Indian economy since the mid-sixties has been very unsatisfactory.

India is a country with vast resources, large potential markets, low productivity, excessive population, scarcity of goods, high cost of production, less effective demand, mounting unemployment and a host of such attributes calling for effective efforts to implement policies and programs aimed at remedying the situation. It must be recognized that the recent weakening of the develop mental process is because of the somewhat continued structural rigidity of the economic system following the failure to effect any significant institutional and organizational reforms since Independence and partly because the performance ever prior to the mid-sixties was not so miraculous as in the case of Japan and China.

* Faculty Member, Dept. of Management , K.U.K.

** Research Scholar, Department of Management, K.U.K.

One of the most disappointing aspects of the performance of the Indian economy since the mid-sixties relates to the deceleration in the growth of output in organized industry, accompanied by sluggish investment, vast under-utilization of capacity and very meagre increase in employment in the organized industry. There had occurred a noticeable acceleration in the compound (annual) growth rate over the first three plan periods up to 1965 from 5.8 per cent in the first plan to 7.2 per cent in the second plan and further to 9.0 per cent in the third plan. During the next eleven years' period (1966 to 1976), the annual growth rate dwindled to about 4.3 per cent including a 10.6 per cent increase in 1976; excluding it, the ten year average work out to 3.7 per cent.

The growth rate during the recent period has been particularly depressing in the capital goods industries or input-based classification, in agro-based and mental-based industries.

Because of the misallocation of resources, the share of national product earmarked for domestic savings and investment declined for quite some years and made only marginal improvement in recent years. Following the disquieting performance of the public sector in this respect, the private sector failed to get the necessary impetus to investment and hence performed miserably. Savings and investments efforts particularly in the public sector curtailed, the public sector plan outlays were slashed initially and thereafter their growth arrested rather drastically, funds for the maintenance of past plan projects were not allocated adequately, resources mobilization efforts were both inadequate and inequitious, deficit financing was resorted to indiscriminately, and finally a significant proportion of the total public outlays was frittered away in non-deployment expenditure in the form of higher subsidies of various sorts from the national exchequer, transfers to the State Government on such pretexts as drought relief, and in many other forms. Simultaneously, the rigours of industrial controls-price and distribution controls, industrial licensing, capital issues controls etc. were diluted, giving rise to many distortion in the production and investment pattern in the private sector.

The important characteristics of Indian Economy in the preliberalization period may be summed as under:

- Poor domestic investment.
- Absense of any change in Investment Strategy.
- Goal of self reliance also not achieved.
- Poor performance of the public sector.
- Resource Divisions and Financial Indiscipline.
- Inadequate and Inequities Resource Mobilization.

Reverberating Effects on Private Sector Activities

The declining trend of investment in the public sector since the mid-sixties has had its reverberating effects on private sector output, employment and investment. Among these parameters, the worst to get affected has been the private sector employment and not investment. The funds so provided appear to have been disproportionate to the investment requirements of the private sector, they were certainly disproportionate to the niggardly growth in Private Industrial Employment. Mere pumping in of large financial resources without a sound policy direction regarding their appropriate end-use and deployment may turn out to be counter-productive. Mere additional funds for the private sector could not achieve higher investment and growth, the relaxation of industrial controls would also fail to do the trick. Any laxity in the scheme of Governmental discipline and regulations on Private Sector would further accentuate distortions in the economy. The process of industrial development since the mid-sixties could be summed up thus:

- The building up of illegal capacity and their subsequent regularization have become a regular feature of the industrial scene.
- The scope for diversification and expansion have created such vast possibilities for the creation of additional capacities

that the whole system of licensing has been reduced to a force.

Investment propositions are almost entirely left to be decided by private entrepreneurs without considering the appropriate priorities, which has accentuated distortions in capacities built in different industries. Output and investment structures have moved against mass consumption goods.

The unmitigated scope for diversification and expansion as well as the tendency to building unauthorized capacities have inflicted incalculable harm to the investment climate, particularly because of uncertainty arising from the lack of knowledge about the existing and prospective capacities in individual products for the new entrepreneurs. The concentration of industrial capacity as well as that of economic power has got increased rather sizeably.

How will the economy move from here and what is required to be done to recover the lost ground at least partially-are vital questions.

Objectives of the Study

In the present scenario where business world has become highly competitive, public sector undertakings are finding very difficult to cope up with this race. Time has come when the revival of these undertakings has become imperative and for making them competitive organizations. Government need to take some effective steps excepting the fact that the present time is the time of change towards betterment. More pragmatically, there is an insistence on the need to examine the relevance berth and effectiveness of all restructuring activities undertaken by government.

Finding (Options) for public undertakings to revive their performance

After having gone through the important indicators about the performance of public sector enterprises; question which arises now is, what to do with these undertakings? Where lies the true solution? In the competitive environment of today would it be advisable to restructure these public sector enterprises or adopt the any or more of other available options like, Disinvestment, divestment or privatization.

Given the challenges that India faces are the fronts of public sector finance and balance of payment. Keeping in mind the scarcity of resources and lack of competitive strength many public enterprises may have to be privatized. But we should not privatize in a hurry; not without doing our homework. Government must exercise considerable caution before rushing into privatizing the existing enterprises. The grass is certainly not as green in the private sector as it appears. We should not get illusions by the policies of those who want us to believe that all problems will be solved once this conversion takes place. Many PSUs were set in remote and backward areas and helped the local economy and population with job opportunities. Many public sector undertaking are models for efficient management and have performed very well in spite of constraints.

The pressures for change in public sector insist that we are witnessing a revolution in how the public sector is organized to make decisions and to deliver services. Reinventing governance, Re-engineering, paradigm shift, entrepreneurship and empowerment are some phases which can regenerate the public sector enterprises.

Corporate Restructuring—A CGL Experience

Restructuring of Public Sector Units may be undertaken by the following different options and methods. One good experience in this regard has been of India's largest private sector company namely Crompton Greaves Limited. This company has recently completed the restructuring process with an objective of improvement and betterment's in its operations. In case of PSU's restructuring some suggestions are extended on the basis of Crompton Greaves Limited experience. Crompton Greaves is a large Indian electrical engineering company. It began life as a British-owned company, Crompton Parkinson Works (India) Ltd. Producing ceiling fans and small electric motors in the Worli district of Bombay in 1937. Over the following 60 years, it diversified into a broad range of electrical products, adding transformers, electric motors and switch gears to its original consumer products range. By the mid 1990s it was the 21st largest Indian Private Company, and in 1995-96 it turn over reached US $416 million.

Corporate Vision of CGL (Objectives)

To achieve for Crompton Greaves a state of a world class company by March 1998 which will ensure.

- Customer satisfaction and preference
- Profitable growth
- Perpetuity
- Stockholder' satisfaction and pride
- Fulfillment of social obligations
- Total quality
- Resource productivity
- Cost effectiveness.

And by creating an environment which encourages team effort and where.

- Each individual's contribution is recognized and valued.
- Each individual enjoys his work and has an urge to excel.
- Each individual gives his best to achieve the shared vision.

The growing competition in the markets is forcing firms to engage in a process of industrial restructuring and assumed that final markets are increasingly competitive, fragmented and rapidly changing and firms gain competitive advantage from offering

CGL's Evolving Restructuring Agenda

Year of Introduction	*Area of Major Concern*	*Example of Improvement Activities*
1984/5	Focus on HRD	▸ Open house discussions in groups of 30-40 for 10 per cent of labour fource; then cascading these down to all employees. ▸ Commitment to training - development of 'training exposure measure'* and establishment of specific training targets.
1985/6	▸ Quality circles ▸ Value engineering groups to reduce costs by 3 per cent. ▸ Profit improvement plan to systematically improve productivity in eight areas.	Small group improvement activities (SGIAs) in various areas.
1986/7	▸ Value-added management programme introduced ▸ Total productive maintenance ▸ Process control	▸ JIT, cellular production, single-unit flow, zero-defect policies, single-minute exchange of dies, etc. ▸ TPM procedures ▸ Statistical Process Control.
1990/1	ISO accreditaton	Achieved at various plants
1991/2	▸ Continuous improvement programme ▸ Development of shared vision	SGIAs SGIAs among senior management and then discussions with all workforce.
1992/3	• Business process re-engineering initiatives	In plants particular
1992/3	QPCE programme	Renewed focus on quality, productivity, cost and employee SGIAs

1992/3	New TQW	▸ Customer focus ▸ Problem-solving methodologies
1994/5	Supplier development	▸ Reduction in number of supplies ▸ Emphasis on upgrading ▸ Partnership
1995/6	Focus on Technology	Corporate R&D centre and technology cells in each SBU
1996	Adoption of MRP2 programme for inventory control	Installation and use of computerised management information systems.

Source: Company documentation

Turnover in Current Rs. Million			*Profit/Sales %*	
Year	*Actual*	*Goals, Vision 1998 Planning Document*	*Actual*	*Goals, Vision 1998 Planning document*
1987/8	3,423		2.0	
1988/9	4,270		3.1	
1989/90	5,104		3.9	
1990/1	6,166		3.5	
1991/2	7,209		2.5	
1992/3	7,804		2.1	
1993/4	8,859		4.3	
1994/5	10,782	11,150	5.5	
1995/6	14,807	13,600	5.4	7.7
1996/7		16,600		9.0
1997/8		20,000		10.9

Source: Company documentation

variety, quality and improved time to market. It is observed that a change in business strategy must necessarily be complemented by a change in manufacturing strategy, the organization of the firm and its factories.

In order to understand the effectiveness and appropriateness of new organizational principles in India (and in other developing countries), the question of implementation has to be explicity addressed. Three important factors are involved in successful implementation are policy deployment, management restructuring and labour relations. The challenge of intra-firm restructuring can be seen in relation to the adoption of three groups of intra-firm organizational innovation. These involves:

a) just-in-time control of inventories and new procedures towards production flow.

b) the implementation of total quality control.

c) the introduction of mechanisms to ensure a process of continuous improvement.

The continuous improvement of any entity depends upon many factors, important ones are here as under:

1. The Institution of problem-solving cycles. This involves a systematic process of planning changes, implementing them, checking their results and them taking corrective action.

2. A focus on process issues, which means not only the mapping of the entire process under review, but also measurement so that the impact of change can be assessed.

3. Mechanism must be established for rewarding contributions for improvements.

4. The process of continuous change should be subsumed into a broader focus towards innovation, so that instead of adopting a scatter-gun approach at should be directed towards focused strategic goals.

The CGL in its restructuring plan has mainly focused on

three major areas namely, managerial restructuring, policy deployment and changes in labour-management relations. These areas may also be helpful to identify the important aspects of restructuring of Indian PSUs. In management restructuring the company's concern is solely with the elements needed to support effective implementation of IT and TQM.

The introduction of IT and TQM is associated with the basic elements of the current orthodoxy on management arising out of the need to orient production to meet customer needs. They are

a) the extensive use of cross-functional teams.

b) empowerment of managers through the devolution of authority to those who have the responsibility for making things work.

c) the abolition or lowering of departmental and divisional boundaries. These are the core of management restructuring packaged in a wide variety of approaches to the problems of the modern corporation. The aim is to create not only a more efficient organization, but also develop an organization capable of learning and changing. It is not uncommon for the number of layers of management in a plant to be reduced from eight or nine to four or five. This improves communication and speed of response and devolves authority down to those who are closest to the problems.

Policy Deployment

In large complex organization, strategic goals have to be translated into targets which are relevant to managers and worker at different levels,which are within their power to achieve. Given that restructuring involves changes in attitudes and process leading to change in outcomes, indicators and targets should focus on all three of these elements.

The development of indicators and targets presupposes the capacity of management to:

1. formulate targets in the areas of attitudes, processes and outcomes which are specific to the responsibilities of particular mangers or workers (or teams of managers and workers) but oriented towards the achievement of company goals.
2. Develop indicators which reflect the progress made in meeting these targets.
3. Monitor the success or failure in reaching these targets and
4. Take correctives action as required.

The approach adopted is to set organizational change in a wider context, as follows:-

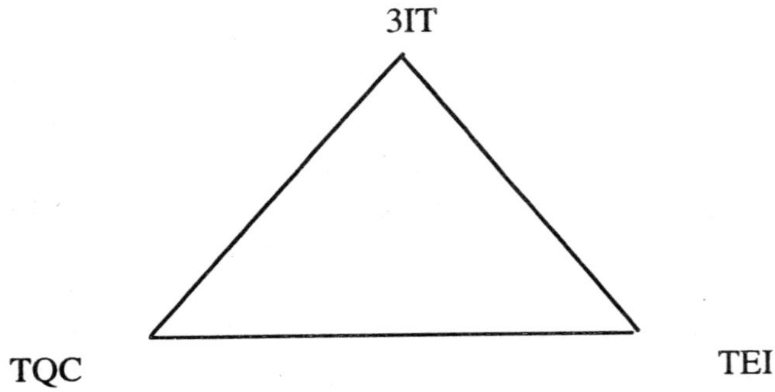

Source: Corporate Restructuring, John Humphrey, Raphael Kaplinsky, Prasad, V.Saraph.

The 'business challenge' - the firms strategic response—the introduction of new practices - their impact on performance.

A management review in mid-1993 identified opportunities for growth in both sales and profits which were to be achieved through -

1. A program of Total Employee Involvement (TEI) designs to enhance participation by all employees.
2. Adopting in principle of Total Quality Control (TQC).
3. A focus on the principles of production flow, summed-up in the phrase Just-in-Time (IT).

Progress could not be made without rapidly addressing the problem of supplier development.

- removal of suppliers who do not meet quality standards.
- putting an end to multi-sourcing of parts, although dual-sourcing may remain.
- shifting away from buying components to buying sub-assemblies or systems.
- tiring suppliers so that the first-tier supplier coordinates the work of second and third-tier suppliers.

The major changes in CGL are summarized.

1. In each case the decision was made to target greater product variety, enhanced responsiveness to customer and improved market share and profitable growth.
2. This was to be achieved essentially by a process of internal reorganization rather than the acquisition of new equipment; cells were introduced but usually within functional divisions, in both blue and white-collar activities, new quality practices and vendor development program were set in place.
3. Time taken to meet customer orders to be reduced.
4. On time deliveries to reach 95 per cent.
5. Inventory to be reduced.
6. Space utilization improved.
7. Adoption of new equipment, diversification, materials substitution and improved industrial relations.
8. An upgrading of manufacturing process.
9. A more practical approach to supplier development.
10. An increase in labour productivity, especially in white-collar occupations.
11. An increase in product variety.

Conclusion

The restructuring experience of CGL may prove to be useful while drawing the plans for restructuring of PSU's.

Managerial restructuring, policy deployment and change in labour management relations may be equally effective areas for review and reconsideration, where the restructuring team/group should pay desired attention. Changing managerial characteristics, redesigning labour management relation and shift in the policy of PSU's will help to improve the performance of these undertakings and the real objective of economic growth may be achieved.

REFERENCES

1. Pai Panadiker VA and Varde SD, "The Indian Economy under the First Three Prime Ministers", *Prajnan,* April-June 1977 (Vol VI No. 2), p. 133-148.
2. Bhaskar Chatterjee, The Privatization Debate, *MIG,* January/ March, 1994.
3. "Public Sector Enterprises: The case for restructuring," *Young India* 9 (23), 9 Jan 1999, pp. 7-8.
4. *Indian Journal of Public Administration* 42 (1) Jan-March 1996, pp. 105-107. Public Sector Enterprises in India.
5. Public Sector - The challenge ahead, *Monthly Common Indian Economic Conditions* 38 (1) Aug'96, p.55.
6. Sharat Kumar, "Adminisstrative reform in the context of political and economic restructuring," *Indian J. Public Administration* 41 (4) Oct. 95, 79398.
7. Arun Ghosh, "Privatization of Public Enterprises" *Economic and Political Weekly,* 29 (30) 23 JI'94 1929 31.
8. Rajni Kothari, Restructuring the Indian Enterprises, *Seminar* 401, Jan'93, p. 24-27.
9. Corporate Restructuring—Crompton Greaves and the Challenge of Globalisation, John Humphrey, Raphael Kaplinsky, Prasad V. Saraph.

11

APPLICATION OF MILITARY STRATEGIES IN CORPORATE RESTRUCTURING IN INDIA IN THE NEW MILLENNIUM

Dr Sunil Kant & Dr. Shakti Gupta***

Introduction

We have ushered in the new millennium along with multi-faceted and multidimensioned ongoing processes in the corporate sector. *Globalisation, liberalisation, privatisation and Information Technology are some of the vibrant processes which have not only affected but have got incorporated in the business world.* The consequent changes have had their direct impact on the corporate sector. No longer is the business cycle confined to the continuum of 'produce - sell – profit'. Businesses have to adopt multitude of tactics and strategies not only to thrive but to survive in the competitive era of today.

Does our corporate units need a restructuring? If yes then what are the strategies that will be effective in placing our business units at a strategic advantage in the global corporate world.

* Medical Officer (Hospital Services), Military Hospital Dehradun

* * Additional Prof. Hospital Administration, AIIMS, New Delhi.

Do we need a Restructuring of our Corporate Structure?

In a recent statement Shree K R Narayanan (1) commented "... if anything, liberalisation and globalisation are inevitable. Our three way fast lane of liberalisation, privatisation and globalisation must provide a safe pedestrian crossing for the unempowered in India also so that we can move towards equality of status and opportunity". There is no doubt that corporate restructuring is required both at macro & micro levels to adapt and obtain success in the global corporate activities. At the micro level disinvestment of PSUs, privatisation, global outlook are some of the parameters, where as at the micro level the essentials are enhanced productivity, profitability, quality assurance etc. We must realise that liberalisation is a process aimed at long term progress and development. In the initial stages the benefits may be too obvious at all levels. One has to swim and the choice is between a small river and a mightly occur. The former is easy, the latter far challenging.

War and Business—A Compatible Analogy?

"The business world is like a battlefield" is a popular Chinese saying. It is true that the business world is not unlike the battle field. In fact business have collapsed through poor planning, resulting in the loss of capital and employment. Businesses is a kind of war and the implications for the metaphor vary according to the seriousness with which the analogy is taken.

War is not merely a blind struggle between mobs of individuals, without guidance or coherance, but a conflict of well organised masses, moving with intelligent cooperation, acting under the impulse of a single will and directed towards a definite objective (2).

Militarization of Japanese Business Practices

Japanese military thought and strategies have tremendous

influence on Japanese management practice. Books such as "Book of Five Rings", "Annals of the Three Kingdoms" and "Journey to the West" are some the famous military treatise on strategies and are a must read for Japanese executives. The Japanese practices extend beyond the reading of books on the subject. Regular management camps for their employees and managers are conducted in the most militaristic manner and include such rituals as meditation, team work and survival techniques. The Japanese conquest of world markets is very much like a well orchestered military campaign.

The area of an analogy between the world of business and that of the battlefield is not a novel one. The metaphor is accepted, in regular use of such phrases as the US- Japan trade war. Indeed various studies relating the application of military strategies to business practices have been undertaken. A publication by Rics and Trout, Marketing Warfare (1986), chose to rely on the works of the German general Karl Nor Clause Witz which was written in 1832. (3) There are, however, some differences in the style and magnitude of application to the situation i.e. war and business. The following are some of the areas of application of military strategies to the corporate enterprises.

Planning

Detailed planning to assess the strengths and weakness of self and enemy is an essential requisite in war. As Sun Tzu comments. (4)

"He who has thorough knowledge of himself and the enemy is bound to win in all battles. He who knows himself but not the enemy has only an even chance of winning. He who knows not himself and the enemy is bound to perish in all battles".

The principle of detailed planning in war applies very much in business. Analysis such as SWOT are regularly done by business companies to identity possible areas in which the company is likely to be threatened as well as areas in which the organization has distinct advantages. In the Indian scenario, planning must be done scientifically e.g. disinvestment of the existing 240 PSUs should be done on a realistic time frame and implemented accordingly and not like the present proposed plan of collecting Rs. 10,000 crores by disinvestment of PSUs in the current financial year which has resulted in collection of about 25 % of the planned amount only.

Doctrine or Law

This factor refers to the organisation, control, procedures, rank structure, allocation of responsibilities. The way the army is structured affects the combat readiness capabilities and morale of the army.

Just like the army, a business firm's doctrine is reflected by the way it is structured and organised. This includes effective policies, operating procedures, communication, lines of authority and responsibility. These elements partially reflect the corporate culture or philosophy.

The organisation and structure must be considered in strategic planning, both in war and business. In an army structure, review is regularly done to assess the strength of the army units eg after the automation process strength of troops has been reallocated. The same procedure should be introduced in the corporate sector. Though presently the private owned enterprises do have realistic manpower strength, the government owned organisations have, in majority of cases, excess manpower. Retrenchment has not been possible due to pressures from political parties and unions. A militaristic approach to link numbers with productivity and achievement of goals will have to be followed sooner or later in all Indian organisations.

Formulation of Goals

In war, the ultimate goal or objective must be to win. In business one of the objectives is to make money. The aim in war is to win and win profitaby. In business the aim is to achieve maximum gains with minimum effort. In order to win in war or business, goals must be prioritised and achievable.

Consistency with Corporate Practice and Culture (Doctrine & Law Factor)

The strategy to be implemented must be in line with the way the company is organized and structured. The strategy must be consistent with the corporate mission, philosophy or values. It must not be in conflict with existing values of the company.

It should be noted that a winning strategy in the past may turn out to be non – effective as the competitors may have already learnt how to react to it. Sun Tzu's advise is applicable to both war and business. (5)

"Do not repeat the tactics that won you a victory, but vary them according to the circumstances"

Strategic Advantage

Sun Tzu has commented (6)

"The General in war should aim to be in a position of non - defeat while never missing the opportunity to defeat the enemy".

As part of successful and effective battle strategy, a general must be able to create strategic advantages in order to secure victory.

It is important to note that to ensure non-defeat one must have a strong defense. One's vulnerability should never be exposed. For example in the early years of the Japanese industrialization program, Japan never allowed foreign goods a free entry to domestic markets. This was because it was very vulnerable to foreign competition at that time. It was only in the last five years that the Japanese market gradually opened up, and protected its local markets vigorously in order to ensure a non – defeat situation. Yet it has never hesitated to strike its economic "enemies" when the opportunity arose.

Thus, to ensure victory and achieve a non – defeat situation both in war and business requires the use of both offensive and defensive strategies. Indian corporate organisations will have to ensure quality assurance to obtain a strategic advantage in the global corporate competition.

Strategic Timing and Implementation

Timing is one of the most important aspects of conducting war. Air radio, artillery bombardment, infantry assault need precision timing. In business too timing is equally important. Singapore Airlines- one of the few highly profit making airline company replaced its fleet of airplanes in 1986 when the aircraft industry was in recession and rates of airplanes were low.

Implementation consists of two parts: the human element and the operational element. The former involves clear understanding of the various roles and responsibilities of the various parties involved in the combat mission. The latter relates to certain principles that are required to ensure successful accomplishment of the mission. Sun Tzu commented.

"He whose Generals are able and not interfered with by the ruler will win. This clearly means that if the ruler has capable Generals to fight the war for him, then he should not interfere with the military operations."

It explicitly recognizes that there is a division of roles between the political sovereign and the military commander. In addition, it assumes, rightly, that the ruler in most instances will not have sufficient expertise to deal with the military aspects, which is a very specialized discipline. Such matter are best left to the General, who is the expert in war.

Applying Sun Tzu's concept of non – intervention to business would imply that the government should as far as possible, not be involved in business operations that compact directly with the private sector. Rather, it should confine its role to the construction of infrastructures like building roads, railways, and other transport systems, the setting up of communication networks like telephones, and the provision of utilities like water and electricity. In addition, it must ensure the existence of favovrable conditions for the achievement of economic prosperity and progress. In essence, the role of government should be to facilitate and assist the growth of business (so as to achieve national economic growth) In fact, privatization is fast becoming a buzzword in several countries and has taken so much prominence that some quarters in the United States are also considering privatizing their prisons! This mood of involving the private sector is motivated very much by the fact that these governments have begun to realize that private firms are much more responsive to market forces and would not hesitate to make quick and swift changes that will benefit profit making. Besides non – intervention in business, the government should also avoid appointing political figures as heads of business firms.

Another very interesting concept related to the principle of adeptability, as advocated by Sun, Tzu, is that of innovativeness. This can be illustrated by the following remarks: (7)

"Therefore, do not repeat the tactics that won you a victory, but vary them according to the circumstances. The General must be able to change his methods and schemes so that no one can know his intentions. He must be able to alter his camp – site and marching routes so that no one can predict his movements."

Innovativeness is also very much desired in business. This is especially so in the present environment where technology is becoming more and more important as a competitive edge. The following example is worthy of quotation

When carbon fiber, a medium that has an exceptionally high tensile strength first appeared, European and American companies immediately considered it for potential application in the aircraft industry (a difficult area). In Japan, the companies used this new material to manufacture golf clubs and fishing oars (an easy application). In doing so, mass – production technology was established and quality was achieved before using the material for large and more difficult products. This bottom – up approach resulted in Japan claiming 70 % of the world production of new carbon fiber. (8)

Creativity has increasingly become a feature of Japanese strategy. Indeed, without creativity entrepreneurship is difficult, if not impossible. Strategic initiatives, competitive advantages and distinctive competencies must be created. Moreover, as market competitive and environmental conditions change, these initiatives, advantages and competencies must be challenged and reshaped.

Element of Surprise

To mystify, mislead and surprise the enemy in a known strategy is war. The power of striking like a 'bolt from the blue' is of the very greatest value in war. Surprise has been the foundation of almost all the war strategical combinations of the past as it will be of those to come. In corporate restructuring the element of surprise will yield a competitive advantage to an organisation vis – a – vis the competitors eg the introduction of Nirma detergent powder with its pricing policy surprised even market leaders, Hindustan lever.

The Principle of Intelligence

The foreknowledge or military intelligence is necessary for the development of superior war strategies. At the macro level, when a country wants to export or penetrate a foreign market, it can conduct intensive studies on the needs and preferences of that market by interviewing and surveying their potential consumers and / or customers.

Military Espionage and Business Intelligence

The use of spies in military and political operations has never been questioned. In market intelligence, a company seeks information from the marketplace using "above – board" methods to improve its ways of doing business. Thus, there is nothing unethical about market intelligence. In fact, owing to the massive amount of information that must be processed on today's competitive business world, many top corporations in the United States have someone performing the functions of a Chief Information Officer (CIO). Specially, the CIO oversees the company's MIS (Management Information System) department, links Information Technology (IT) to the company's business strategies, and ensures that all parts of the organization can absorb and use IT effectively.

On a macro level, the success of the Japanese can be attributed to some extent to their market intelligence system. Over the years, Japan has created a massive institutional infrastructure that is geared to collecting information on various world markets. For example, the Japanese general trading companies (GTC), the Ministry of International Trade and Industry (MITI), and the Japan External Trade Organization (JETRO) have each established worldwide networks of intelligence systems. These organizations conduct all kinds of market – related research and information gathering and then compile, collate and compose them for use by Japanese companies. Indian organisations will have to restructure their setups and include business intelligence as an essential ingredient in the organisation. (9)

Information Technology

The last decade has been one of rapid change and discontinuities. The tectonic changes in technology have changed the landscape of our existence. The changes have been overwhelming but what we have seen so far may well just be the beginning .We seem to be at an inflection point in the history of human civilization. In the days ahead information technology will swamp our daily lives and play increasingly important role. We are now in an era of intelligent devices and ubiquitous computing . Information has become all encompassing to the convergence of media, telecom and computing technologies and the spread of Internet has interwoven business with information technology so closely that it is now impossible talk of either of them in isolation. Businesses worldwide saved over 17 billion dollars last year by adopting e-commerce .This is expected to increase to 25 trillion dollars in 2002. (10) Cost is just one of the reasons driving people to Internet. Thus e- business will soon form a large portion of industries in future We can foresee the emergence of a new era where IT occupies the center stage. The transition to this order is an opportunity for new countries and regions of innovation to reap rich dividends and India with its rich human resource base is ideally placed to take advantage of the revolution that is happening.

Knowledge Management: Ticket to Survival

Knowledge Management is a discipline which promotes a collaborative approach to creation, capture, organization, access and use of an enterprise's information assets. It is a systematic leveraging of information and expertise to improve organizational innovation, responsiveness, productivity and competency. Studies reveal that on an average in an organisation only 20 % of knowledge is used productively. The Indian corporate sector must adopt knowledge Management as a tool to optimise the available knowledge.

Bribery and stealing Secrets

While bribery is an accepted practice in war, there is no doubt that it is an unethical practice in business and should be eradicated. Though gaining insight through business intelligence is acceptable, Stealing of trade secrets is unethical. Though unethical, stealing of trade secretes is being carried out by developed countries. In a recent development Europeon nations led by France and Germany have sued, U.S and Britain after it was revealed that they operated a global electronic eaves dropping operation and passed on lucrative commercial secrets to U.S business houses. The operation was being conducted through Echelon Surveillance System., a network of the cold war intelligence effort against the communist block. This system is capable of monitoring telephone, fax and e – mail communication relayed by satellite anywhere in the world.(11)

Conclusion

Some of the essential areas of analogy in implementation of war strategies to business practices have been discussed. **War is assuredly no mechanical art**. In war intelligent cooperation is of infinitely more value than mechanical obedience. One of the ubiquitous requirements of a successful restructuring is the social restructuring. Personnel have to be explained the importance of restructuring, its objectives and advantages. Effective communication must be operational for a successful restructuring. **Napoleon's remarks are relevant to the corporate world. "The secret of war lies in the communication."**

We are constrained by large unemployment, consequent poverty, inequality, inadequacy of capital and technological gaps. To tackle these, we need harmonious coexistence of the public sector, a healthy and corruption – free cooperative sector for accumulation of capital. Import of technology and foreign investment should be confined to sectors where there are large technological gaps. Only such a balanced approach to economy will be able to benefit the poor. Application of war strategies, operations alongwith professionalisation of management will definitely aid in the corporate restructuring in India in the new millennium.

REFERENCES

Narayanan K R, *The Sunday Times of India,* Jan 30 2000 Pg 6, Col : 1

Henderson, CFR, *The Science of War,* Longman, Green and Company, London, 1920

Wee CH, Lee KS, Hidajat B. W *Sun Tzu : War and Management,* Addison to esley Publishing Company, Singapore 1997. Pg 2 – 110 Passim.

Shankar A, Knowledge Management : Ticket To Survival, *Dataquest,* Vol xvii No 5, Mar 1999, Pg 74.

Sen Gupta, J S, Threats to Globalisation, *The Hindustan Times,* Feb 3, 2000. Pg 11, Col . 1

Section III

FINANCIAL RESTRUCTURING

12

INDIAN CAPITAL MARKET: RETROSPECTION AND AGENDA FOR FUTURE

S.L. Gupta & Pardeep Gupta***

Introduction

The Capital Market in any country is one of the core economic indicators and is, at any point of time, a reflection of the state of the economy. The capital market functions as institutional mechanism to channel long term funds those who save to those who need them for productive purposes. It serves as a medium to bring together entrepreneurs, initiating activity involving huge financial resources and savers; individuals or institutions, seeking outlets for investment.

The capital market consists of the primary markets and the secondary markets and there is a close link between them. The primary market creates long-term instruments through which corporate entities borrow from the capital market and secondary market provides liquidity and marketability to these instruments. The depth of the secondary market depends upon the activities of the primary market because it is only when more corporate entities enter in to the market and raise funds through the market that more instruments are available in the secondary market for

* Chairman, Dept. of Management, Kurukshetra University, Kurukshetra.

** Lecturer, Dept. of Business Management, Guru Jambheshwar University, Hisar.

the purpose of improved activities in this market.

The capital market in India has witnessed as impressive growth and structural changes during the last decade of the 20th century. The volume of business, number of listed companies, number of investor and other participants, the type of financial intermediaries and services have increased considerably.

Theme of the Paper

The article primarily takes a retrospect view of the Indian capital market by discussing some of the features and trends in the last decade of the twentieth century. It also addresses the issue of resuscitation of primary issue market and secondary stock market and how, in turn, the small investors can be brought back into the Indian capital market to strengthen it.

Retrospection

The Indian stock market has undergone remarkable change in the last decade of the twentieth century. Certain steps taken by the government to place the market on a strong footing and develop it to meet the growing capital requirements of fast industrialization and development of the economy have significantly contributed to the development that took place in the Indian capital market during the last decade. The following tables depict some of the significant trends in the Indian capital market during the last decade.

It can be observed from the Table 1 number of companies which raised capital through public issues increased from 141 in the year 1990-91 to 2438 in 1995-96. However, the same decreased to only 32 in the year 1998-99. The number of companies which raised through Right Issues showed increasing trend from the 1990-91 to 1992-93. During this period, the number of companies increased from 209 to 488. But from the year 1993-94 to 1998-99, downward trend has been observed and the number of companies decreased from 384 to 26 only. For both types of issues, the number of companies increased substantially from 350 in 1990-91 to 1791 in the year 1995-96. However, the same decreased only to 58 in the year 1998-99.

Table-1
Capital Raised during 1990-91 to 1998-99

(Rs. Crore)

Year	Public Issues		Right Issues		Total Issues	
	Number	Amount	Number	Amount	Number	Amount
1990-91	141	1704	209	2251	350	3955
1991-92	196	1711	316	3851	512	5562
1992-93	528	6061	488	12630	1016	18691
1993-94	770	12544	384	9306	1154	21850
1994-95	1343	13312	351	6793	1694	20105
1995-96	2428	11822	291	6520	1719	18342
1996-97	753	11648	131	2724	884	14373
1997-98	62	3061	51	1743	131	4804
1998-99	32	7911	26	568	58	8479

Source: The Primary Directory, 1999, p. 0-3.

Table-2
Sector-wise Capital Mobilization

(Rs. Crore)

Year	Public Sector		Private Sector		Total
	Amount	%	Amount	%	Amount
1993-94	4763	35	8680	65	13443
1994-95	1251	9	12060	91	13312
1995-96	5059	43	6763	57	11822
1996-97	7539	65	4109	35	11648
1997-98	2644	86	418	14	3061
1998-99	7623	96	288	4	7911

Source: The Primary Directory, 1999, pp. 0-58

Table-3

Capital Mobilization Throughout Debt and Equity

(Rs. Crore)

	Debt		*Equity*		*Total*
Year	*Amount*	*%*	*Amount*	*%*	*Amount*
1993-94	2619	19	10824	81	13443
1994-95	0	0	13312	100	13312
1995-96	2940	25	8882	75	11822
1996-97	6977	60	4671	40	11648
1997-98	1929	63	1132	37	3061
1998-99	7407	94	504	6	7911

Source: The Primary Directory, 1999, pp. 0-59.

Almost similar trends have been shown with respect to capital raised through these issues. In the year 1990-91, Rs. 1704 crores were raised through public issues and the same increased to Rs. 13,312 crores during the year 1994-95. It showed downward trend afterwards and reached Rs. 3061 crores only in the year 1997-98. However, Rs. 7911 crores were raised during the year 1998-99. For capital raised through Right Issues, the amount increased from Rs. 2251 crores in the year 1990-91 to Rs. 12,630 crores in the year 1992-93. However, afterwards it showed downward trend and reached to Rs. 568 crores in the year 1998-99. For both types of issues, the amount increased from Rs. 3955 Crores. In 1990-91 to Rs. 21,850 crores in 1993-94 and fell down to Rs. 8479 crores in the year 1998-99, through it was higher than the amount raised in the year 1997-98.

It can be concluded from Table 2, that out of total capital mobilized by the public sector units and private sector units, the percentage share of the public sector showed significant upward trend was the private sector percentage share decreased among the years 1993-94 to 1998-99 except the year 1994-95 where it was vice-versa. The later part of nineties have been marked by an economic slow down, thus eroding investor confidence. This is what is being reflected in the investor preferences in the sense that they seem to repose more faith in the public sector as compared to private sector.

The Table 3 shows that for the years 1993-94 to 1995-96, equity was more popular among the investors as compared to debt instruments. The trend became reverse thereafter making debt instruments more popular because of assured returns on the investments. Though equity is an effective hedge against inflation, it is highly uncertain mode of investment. And when the economy and industry are going through a lean patch a rational investor would usually sacrifice some return in favor of a safer investment. Such a sensational seems to be justified by looking at the changing investor preferences as revealed by the data shown in the table.

The number of stock exchange has increased gradually and the capital market has expanded substantially. At present, there are 25 stock exchanges recognized under the Securities Contracts (Regulation) Act, 1956. The stock exchanges operate under the rules, bylaws and regulations duly approved by the Government and constitute an organized market for securities.

The establishment of National Stock Exchange of India Ltd. (NSE) Marked an Important Step in Institutional Reforms in India. Nse was incorporated in 1992 and started operations in 1994. NSE today covers 186 cities and towns, providing fair and equal access to investors spread across the length and breadth of the country, through its captive satellite communication system.

NSE operates two segments viz., the Wholesale Debt Market (WDM) segment and the capital market segment. Debt market operations presently average more than Rs. 5 billion a day. There are 99 members on the WDM segment where 504 securities are listed and 384 securities are permitted to trade as an April 30, 1998.

Capital market operations average more than Rs. 16 billion a day. There are about 1000 SEBI registered trading members on this segment of the exchange which include 20 foreign brokerage firms. There are 1358 securities available for trading accounting for a market capitalization of Rs. 5168 billion as on April 30, 1998. During 1997, NSE accounting for close to 50% of the equities trading in the country. In terms of the number of trades per day, NSE is among the seven largest stock exchange in the world.

The Over the Counter Exchange of India (0TC) was set up in 1992 expressly to provide investors with a convenient, efficient and transparent platform for dealing in shares and to help enterprising promoters to set up new projects or expand their activities by providing them with an opportunity to raise capital in a cost effective manner. The OTC Exchange is the ideal avenue for small and medium seized companies (with an issued capital ranging from Rs. 30 lakhs to Rs. 25 crores) to raise resources from the market through listing on it.

The shares debentures of the companies listed on the OTC Exchange can be bought or sold at any OTC counter all over India. The securities listed on the OTC Exchange cannot be traded on other stock exchanges. Certain shares debentures listed on other stock exchanges and units of UTI and other mutual funds are allowed to be traded on the OTC Exchange as 'Permitted Securities.'

However, the functioning of the stock exchange has shown many shortcomings with long delays, lack of transparency in procedures and vulnerability to price rigging and insider trading. The most glaring case in this regard is the notorious Bank Scam of 1992.

To counter these deficiencies government established the Security Exchange Board of India (SEBI) and was given statutory power by an ordinance promulgated on 30th January 1992. SEBI has wide ranging powers of control over the capital market.

A number of steps have been taken in recent years by the Government and SEBI to introduce improved practices and greater transparency in the stock markets in the interest of healthy stock market development. SEBI has been authorized to conduct inspections of various mutual funds to bring out various deficiencies of individual mutual funds, if any. Merchant banking has been statutorily brought under the regulatory framework of SEBI. They will have to adhere to stipulated capital adequacy norms. Merchant bankers have to abide by a code of conduct which specifies a high degree of responsibility towards investors in respect of the pricing and premium fixation of issues and disclosures in the prospectus or offer letter for issues. SEBI has advised the stock exchanges to collect from companies making public issues, a deposit of one per cent of the issue amount which could be forfeited in case of noncompliance with the provisions of the listing agreement and, non-dispatch of refund orders and share certificates by registered post with in the prescribed time. Regulations on insider trading under the provision of the SEBI Act have been notified. Such regulations will help in the protecting and preserving the markets integrity and in the long run help inspire investor confidence in the market. Stock Exchanges are advised to amend the listing agreement to ensure that a listed company furnishes annual statement to the stock exchanges showing variations between financial projections and projected utilization of funds made in the offer documents and actual. This will enable shareholders make comparisons between performance and premises.

The SEBI (Substantial Acquisition of Shares and Takeovers) Regulations, 1994 were formulated with a view to making the takeover process transparent and protecting the interests of minority shareholders. The Government has allowed foreign institutional investors, pension funds, mutual funds, investment trusts, portfolio management companies etc. To invest in the Indian stock market provided they register with SEBI. The Capital Issues (Control) Act, 1947 was repealed in May 1992, and office of the Controller of Capital Issues (CCS), was subsequently abolished.

In the year 1997, India ranked number one in the world for having listed the largest number of domestic companies in the stock market for the record year in succession in 1996. In total value traded, India ranked 17, behind the U.S. ($ 7.121 Trillion), Japan ($ 1.252 Trillion), Germany, UK, Taiwan, Switzerland, Netherlands, France, Canada, China, Spain, Korea, Malaysia, Hongkong, Australia, Sweden and Brazil.

Table-4
Number of Listed Companies in Different Countries

Country's Name	*Number of Listed Companies*
India	8800
U.S.A.	8479
UK	2433
Japan	2334

Source: Emerging Stock Market Fact Book 1997, released by International Finance Corporation.

Euro Issues: The globalisation of capital markets has encouraged issuers the world over to increasingly look beyond the borders of their home markets to expand their investor base and raise funds by way of equity and debt. While Indian companies have been tapping the foreign currency loan market since long, they were allowed to access the international equity market only after 1991, consequent upon the introduction of economic reforms and New Economic Policy (NEP). There have been issuances by Indian companies in the international capital markets by way of Global Depository Receipts (GDRs) and Foreign Currency Convertible Bonds (FCCB) commonly referred to as EURO Issues.

Global Depository Receipts: In India, the issue of GDRs is governed by the guidelines issued by the Ministry of finance,

Government of India. The Department of Economic Affairs, Ministry of Finance, gives permission to companies to float GDRs if they have a consistent track record of good performance for three years. This criteria, however, has been relaxed for infrastructure projects like power generations, telecommunications, petroleum exploration, ports, roads etc. Recently the govt. has allowed unlisted companies to issue GDRs. Companies raising capital through GDRs are allowed full flexibility in deploying issue proceeds with the restriction that investments in stock markets and real estate will not be permitted.

Indian companies have raised over US$6 billion in the form of GDRs. The first GDR issue by an Indian company was launched in 1992 by Reliance Industries. The year, wise breakup of the issuances are as under:

Table 5
Amount Raised through GDRs

Year	*No.*	*Amount* (US$m)
FY1993	2	240
FY 1994	17	1586
FY1995	30	2113
FY 1996	7	616
FY 1997	8	1438

Source: The Prime Directory, 1998, p. 0-22

Foreign Currency Convertible Bonds (FCCBs) : FCCBs were quite popular in the second half of 1993 and the first half of 1994 when a total of about US$ 1.1 billion was raised. Since then, the Indian Government had adopted a restrictive policy towards FCCBs since the bonds formed part of the country external debt till their conversion into equity. Since interest as well as redemption of the non-converted part would be in foreign currency, Indian issuers also not been very because of the exposure to the foreign exchange risk.

The *other instruments* which have been issued by Indian companies in the international capital market include American Depository Receipts, EURO Bands, EURO Convertible Bonds, European Depository Receipts, Floating Rate Note, Global Depository Receipts with warrants, Swiss Convertible, Yankee Bonds, Credit Enhanced Debt Indexed To Stock etc.

Table 6
Amount Raised through Euro Issue

	GDRs/EDRs		*ECBs*		*Others*		*Total*	
Year	*No.*	*Amount (US$M)*	*No.*	*Amount (US$M)*	*No.*	*Amount (US$M)*	*No.*	*Amount (US$M)*
1992	2	240.00	-	-	-	-	2	240.00
1993-94	17	1586.75	9	1020.00	-	-	26	2606.75
1994-95	30	2113.54	2	65.00	1	77.50	33	2256.04
1995-96	7	616.20	-	-	6	870.00	13	1486.20
1996-97	8	1438.15	-	-	15	1512.25	23	2950.40
1997-98	2	418.53	-	-	15	2005.00	17	2423.53
1998-99	1	185.00	-	-	1	70.38	2	255.38

Source: The Prime Directory, 1999, p. 0-38.

Financial Advertising Agencies: The corporate has now come to trust the advertising agencies in order to provide more marketability to their issues. SEBI has introduced a code of advertising for public issues for insuring fair and truthful disclosures. There are total 558 Financial Advertising Agencies in the country. Sobhagya has remained the number one financial agency in 1996-99 in terms of number of assignments whereas Adductors has remained number one financial advertising agency from 1995-98 in terms of issue amount. In 1998-99, Sobhagya remained number one in term of issue amount.

Foreign Investment: Till 1990, the strong belief in the complete state control and extreme distrust towards foreign companies resulted in almost negligible technology transfer and a limited foreign investment in India. But after the external payment crisis of 1990, there has been a shift in the policy priorities in favour of non-debt creating inflows of external finance. Consequently, India went for major changes in its industrial and foreign investment policy in 1991 in order to open up the doors of foreign direct investment. Some such important changes include the abolition of industrial licensing, virtual removal of import licensing on raw materials, components, intermediate and capital goods, approval of foreign direct investment up to 51% of share capital in high priority industries, setting up of Foreign Investment Promotion Board (FIPB), facilities for portfolio investments by Foreign Institutional Investors (FIIs) etc.[2]

Table 7 shows the Category- wise foreign investment inflows in the country. The table reveals that the amount of direct investment increased to US$3197 million in 1997-98 from a meagre figure of US$97 million in 1990-91. The portfolio investment increased to US$ 3312 million in 1996-97 from a meagre figure of US$6 million in 1990-91.

There are 556 foreign investment institutions registered with SEBI as on 13 May, 1999.

Table 7
Issues Offered to NRIs

Year	*Number of Issues*	*Amount (Rs. Crores)*
1992-93	125	322.70
1993-94	405	867.72
1994-95	410	900.00
1996-97	701	1085.37
1997-98	21	89.69
1998-99	8	41.36

Source: The Prime Directory, 1998, p. 0-63.

NRI Investment: Investment by Non-Resident Indians (NRIs) has gained notable encouragement from the Indian government in recent years. The major incentives offered to NRIs for attracting NRI investment in Indian industry include both repatriable as well as non-repatriable schemes. The NRIs have been allowed a 100% repatriation investment in Free Trade Zones. They have been granted special tax concession for investing in India. In 1998, NRI bonds were introduced in order to atract foreign currency. Table 8 shows the year-wise detail of the number of issues offered and amount raised thereform, from the NRIs.

Credit Rating Agencies: Credit rating has assumed great importance for individual investors, brokers and financial advisors with the expansion of money and capital market. There are now four credit rating agencies in India, viz., Credit Rating Information Services of India Ltd. (CRISIL), Investment Information and Credit Rating Agency of India Ltd. (ICRA), Credit Analysis and Research Ltd. (CARE) and Duff & Phelps Credit Rating India Pvt. Ltd. They rate the debt instruments of companies namely , commercial papers, debentures, bonds and fixed deposits.

Merchant Banking: Merchant banking has been statutory brought under the regulatory framework of SEBI and merchant bankers are required to abide by the stipulated code of conduct. Till 30th June, 1999 there were 1206 SEBI approved merchant bankers, of which 226 belongs to category I, 15 in category II 1,12 in category III and 953 in category 1V. Both in terms of number of assignments by issue amount, SBICAP has ranked no. 1 in the year 1998-99.

Custodial Services: Custodial services in relation to securities means safe keeping of securities of a client and providing services such as maintaining accounts of securities of a client; collecting the benefits or rights accruing to the client in respect of securities; keeping the client informed of the actions taken or to be taken by the issuer of securities , having a bearing on the benefits or rights accruing to the client, maintaining and reconciling records of the services etc.

To act as custodian, the capital requirement shall be a networth of a minimum of rupees fifty crores. At present, 27 member of Indian organizations are providing custodial services.

Mutual Funds Companies: A mutual fund renders the benefit of diversification of portfolios and adept financial advice and management to many small investors who may not be proficient in this regard. The increasing preference of investors in mutual funds have led to a arise in the number of mutual funds in India to 40 which were registered with SEBI till 30th June, 1999. This has been so due to the safety, liquidity and adequate return promised by them.

However, there have been certain shortcomings in the operations of mutual funds which have slightly obscured their lucrativeness. There is no specific law to supervise the mutual funds in India. There are multiple regulations e.g. UTI is governed by its own regulations, the banks are supervised by Reserve Bank of India and the Insurance Company mutual funds are regulated by central government regulations. Since mutual funds are not allowed to invest in smaller companies they become deprived of any benefits in the event of good performance by smaller companies.

Dematerialized Era: Dematerialized trading implies that transactions in securities are carried out by means of an entry in the participant's account and the securities are not kept in the physical form. The setting up of the National Securities Depository Limited (NSDL) in November 1996 signified the beginning of the move towards scripless and faster (rolling) settlement. NSDL is promoted by IDBI, UTI & NSE. Subsequently the State Bank of India, took a stake of 4.76 % in NSDL. NSDL is regulated by SEBI.

The depository system has gained acceptance among different segments in the market. 436 companies (issuers) have signed up with NSDL for providing depository services to their shareholders. These companies represent 83% of the market capitalization of the Indian market. They include all the companies in the S& P CNX nifty index and BSE sensitive index.

The number of Depository Participants (DP) through whom investors hold accounts in the depository stands at 97. All custodians providing services to local and foreign investors have joined the NSDL. The DPs are serving inveestors from 925 centres across India.

Mutual funds, financial institutions, and foreign institutional investors have dematerialized a significant portion of their holdings. 857.98 crore shares valued at about Rs. 1,52,900 crores have been dematerialized so far. In about 150 companies, dematerialization as a percentage of market capitalization (of the company) has crossed the 25% mark.

The retail investor base is growing rapidly. More than 7.75 lac retail investors from 1553 cities/towns in India and 40 cities abroad have joined the NSDL.

Buyback of Shares by Companies: Buy-back of shares has recently been permitted, though these may not emerge to be as popular in a growing economy like India as it is in the developed countries, as returning capital to the shareholders might not be an attractive option for most Indian corporates, who have capital expenditure plans on the anvil.

Agenda for Future

An important problem facing the Indian government remaining unsolved is how to revive the country's stockout market. The market continues to be in depression which started mainly due to withdrawal of retail investors. A staggering 84% out of total 3911 equity issue floated between April 1992 and March 1996 raising over Rs. 25,000 crores from retail investors are not quoted, listed or quoted far below the offer price. Until promoters of such companies are taken to task and made answerable for their misdeeds, no amount of pre-announcement are going to deter future offenders or assure potential investors. The Mumbai Stock Exchange has recently introduced the concept of `Z' category scrips. All companies not complying with the listing norms or not responding to investor grievances have been put in the `Z' category so that the investers are cautioned against investing in such companies.

It is found that the Indian market performs its monitoring role over corporate management very inefficiently and erratically, giving wrong price signals to investors because of the two factors, viz. (a) rampant price manipulation and (b) high volatility.[3] In India it is quite common for unscrupulous market intermediaries to work hand-in-glove with fraudulent corporate managements in floating unsound or even bogus enterprises at inflated issue prices and in rigging/manipulating share prices. This was exposed recently by upheavals of the so-called `Harshad Mehta scrips'.[4]

For healthy long-term development of the primary and secondary market and to ensure continuing participation by the small investor the under-mentioned issues[5] should be taken care of.

The compulsion to list on multiple stock exchanges under the Companies Act should be removed. Competition among the exchanges and all-India reach of exchanges would ensure the most efficient and cost-effective listing.

At least 10% of Public Sector Units shares should be divested in favour of retail investors to infuse interest in the capital market. This will not only help in widening the capital market but would also help proper price discovery for shares of such PSUs. This will also bring better corporate governance in PSUs as investor's demands would result in greater transparency and better performance.

In many cases, foreign companies listed in their own countries are allowed to hold 100% equity. stake in their Indian ventures established by them in India. In the concern is to have absolute control on management, a maximum of 76% of holding could be allowed. The balance 24% may be sold to public so that retail investors could participate in the growth and wealth creation by these foreign companies.

Protection of small investors could be ensured by permitting IPOs in the form of a secured debt issue such as debentures to be floated, listed and serviced successfully for at least three years without default or delay. Only then would an equity issue be permitted.

Auctions and book building need to be seriously looked at as means of determining pricing of new issues. These would not only result in market-oriented and realistic prices but would also help bring down the cost of raising funds.

In future, special attention should be given to the utilization of issue funds. The company's lead bank or financial institution could probably do the monitoring. Every company should be required to submit a quarterly status report on fund utilization to the stock exchange where they are listed and SEBI, while the annual reports should carry a detailed disclosure for the investor's benefit, duly certified by statutory authority.

It must be mandatory for a company coming out with a public issue for the first time to provide market making in its shares at least until such times they are regularly traded and quoted on the stock exchange. Care should be taken that spreads are controlled.

General Insurance Company and its subsidiaries presently have a corpus of about Rs. 20,000 crores, of which only about 15% is invested in equities. World-wide equity investments by GICs are anywhere between 30% to 50%. There is a need, therefore, for reconsideration to the proportion of investment by GIC and its subsidiaries in the equity market.

The investable funds of LIC are around Rs. 1,30,000 crores, of which currently only around 5% is invested in equities. Worldwide, life insturance companies invest between 10% to 50% in equities. LIC should earmark at least 15% of its investable fund for equity market.

Investments by banks in equity market should be accorded a priority status in the same manner as accorded to agriculture, exports and small scale industries. Banks can unleash a fresh wave of growth by earmarking at least 1% deposits for investment in equity.

At present, provident funds are not allowed to be invested in equities whereas in other countries a substantial portion of these funds is invested in the equity market. Employees should be given the option of investing at least 20% of their provident fund in the equity market through approved mutual funds aided with appropriate tax incentives. At least 5% of the retirement funds should be routed to the equity market through mutual funds.

Independent directors represent the interest of those shareholders who are not directly represented on the Board. At least one-third of the directors of any company above a certain size should be non-executive, independent directors. One way of ensuring their independence would be for credit rating agencies, industry organizations and chambers to make and circulate list of prominent personalities—lawyers, chartered accountants, financiers, bankers and economists who have the competence and the integrity to be independent directors.

Foreign Direct Investments (FDI) needs to be encouraged both in the primary (green field projects) and secondary (take-over) segments, with clear and easy guidelines. In the case of take-overs, whether friendly or hostile, the ultimate yardstick should be the beneficial impact on the economy, its employees, its shareholders and its future prospects. FDI in BIFR cases should be especially encouraged as it may often mean their only hope of revival.

Conclusion

The process of reforms in the capital market has only just begun. It needs to be deepened to bring about speedier conclusion of transactions, greater transparency in operations, improve services to investors, and greater investor protecton while at the same time encouraging the corporate sector to raise resources directly from the market on an unceasing scale. Companies should provide better governance, SEBI should contribute sensible regulation, and the stock exchanges should provide greater professionalism. This will give the investor resurgent buoyant capital market where he can put his hard-earned money with confidence and trust.

REFERENCES

1. *Manorma Year Book,* 1998, p. 544.
2. Kajipet, O. and Cary, P.K., "Foreign Direct Investment in India", From the proceedings of the National Seminar on *Global Trends in Indian Financial Markets: Thrust and Challenges,* Department of Management, Kurukshetra University, Kurukshetra, March 10-11-1994.
3. Gupta, L.G., P.K. Jain, C.P. Gupta, *Indian Stock Market P/E Ratios,* Society for Capital Market Research and Development, New Delhi, 1998, Chapter 3 and 8 which analyses Indian Market's volatility.
4. *The Times of India,* New Delhi, June 15, 1998, p. 17.
5. Adapted from Anand Rathi, "Strengthening the Capital Market? *"Prime Directory,* 1999, p. 0-9-12.

13

EQUITY CARVE OUT: REARRANGING THE FINANCIAL JIGSAW

Chandra Shekhar & Pardeep Gupta***

Introduction

. . .Once upon a time, in 1981, Condec coroporation of USA, filed a prospectus to the effect of selling 20% of the equity in its wholly owned subsidiary, Unimation Incorporation, to the public. The purpose of this "equity carve out" (partial public offering) was to the repay all outstanding long term debt and to keep the remainder for the working capital requirements. The market responded by bestowing a 19% per cent stock price rise. Why did Condec Corporation select this way of raising capital rather than the conventional way of issuing common equity shares? Moreover, what made the market respond so favourably to the announcement of the offering, especially when issue of common stock is considered bad news by the investors?[1]

This article intends to look into the working of an equity carve-out as an equity carve in as a modus-operandi for the financial restructuring of an organisation. An attempt has also been made to look into the "psychology" of the market, which,

* Reader, Department of Business Management, Guru Jabheshwar University, Hisar.

** Lecturer, Department of Business Management, Guru Jabheshwar University, Hisar.

surprisingly, tends to reward an equity carve out. To probe into the intentions of the partial public offering and to take a look at corporate India in its attempts at "carving" the equity, are other issues which have prompted this article.

Equity carve out: The Mechanism

An equity carve out resembles a usual public offering of stock in that cash is accumulated from the investing public. In an equity carve out, the parent company sells the equity of its subsidiary, thus making the subsidiary an independent identity. There are many features which distinguish between a 'partial public offering' from a 'regular public offering' in case of a voluntary spin off. In a spin off, well defined equity claims of a wholly owned subsidiary are distributed as dividend to the parent company's shareholders and they begin to trade in the public equity markets. In a spin-off as well as in an equity carve out, the equity claims of a subsidiary begin to trade independently from equity claims of the parent company. However, an equity offering of a subsidiary differs from a corporate spin-off in two major ways; First, in the case of spin-off, the stock of subsidiary company is distrubuted to the existing shareholders of the parent company, whereas an equity carve out is a sale of subsidiary's stock which raises new capital. Second, in a spin-off, the parent company relinquishes control over the subsidiary. An equity carve out, on the other hand creates a minority public interest in the subsidiary, instead of giving away the control.

The Urge to Carve Out

The carved out subsidiaries often undergo some kind of ownership reshuffling. One common reason for carve-out is the complete separation of the subsidiary from the parent by any means; spin-off, purchase by the subsidiary of its stock held by the parent, leveraged but-out, sale to another firm or if things don't go right-liquidation. Infact, the management may go for a carve-out with an intention to advertise the subsidiary. In such a case, the carve-out may serve as an intermediary stage of a process, which is aimed ultimately at divestiture. The parent may expect that the disclosure associated with a public market, for subsidiary's shares would eventually lead to a greater understanding and thus willingness to pay a higher price, on the part of potential acquirers.

Re-acquiring the carved out subsidiaries is also a possibility, though the chances are less. One possible explantion of why a parent may want to reacquire the carved out subsidiary is that the original carve-out might have been a mistake. However, another reason for reacquisition can be that it may become attractive to reacquire if the objectives of the carve-out can by accomplished with only a temporary publilc market for subsidiary shares. For instance, the need for external equity financing will decline if the subsidiary's investment projects mature to the point where they generate sufficient profits for internal equity financing. Put differently, the objective of informing individual investors and potential acquirers about a subsidiary' growth potential through audited subsidiary financial statements and other reports, as well as increased incentives for private information collection, may be achieved by a temporary public markekt for subsidiary stock.

Apart from ownership changes, a parent might want to retain a majority voting interest in the subsidiary because of two more benefits: First, effective control will allow any existing operating and/or financial synergies to be maintained. Second, a substantial voting control of the subsidiary may be needed if the subsidiary is to be consolidated for tax purposes. Tax consolidation is beneficial if operating losses or taxation sops which would otherwise go unused by either the parent or the subsidiary, can be used to offset taxable income of the more profitable firm, thereby reducing the tax liability to the consollidated firm. This kind of arrangement can be described as "having the cake and eating it too".

The Market Reaction

There are many ways of thinking as to why a positive market reaction is attributed to an equity carve-out. Some of them are examined in the ensuing paragraphs.

Most of what has been thought and said about the different market response to equity carve outs can be arranged under three categories, viz;(i)stand-alone financing for subsidiary investments, (ii) Public trading of subsidiary stock and (iii) restructuring of asset management and incentive contracts.

a) *Stand-Alone Financing for Subsidiaries*: An offering of seasoned parent equity simply increases the number of outstanding equity claims on the consolidated assets. In contrast, an initial subsidiary equity offering carves out the assets of the subsidiary from the assets of the original entity. Thus, an equity carve-out allows a subsidiary to obtain separate funding for subsidiary growth opportunities. The equity securities publicly offered represent claims on the cash flows of the subsidiary projects only.

Assuming that one purpose of a carve-out is to finance investment projects, a measure of the relative size of those projects is the proceeds of the carve-out offering as a percentage of the market value of parent equity. This size measure, it turns out, is positivsely correlated with share price reactions of parent firms; that is, the larger the carve-out as a percentage of the total equity of the consolidated company, the larger in general was the positive market reaction.

b) *Public Trading of Subsidiary Stock:* An equity carve-out initiates public trading of the common stock of the previously wholly-owned subsidiary. The subsidiary is thus subject to all financial and other reporting requirements of public companies. These requirements can impose considerable cost on the parent company's stockholders. These costs consist of the direct costs of preparing audited financial statements and other required reports for the subsidiary as well as any indirect costs of disclosing proprietary information to subsidiaty competitors.

Such costs, however, may be more than offset by the benefits to parent stockholders of the increased supply of a demand for information about the subsidiary's growth opportunities. The carve-out of subsidiary stock commits the subsidiary to supply audited periodic financial reports prepared in accordance with prescribed measurement and disclosure rules as well as other non-financial information about firm activities (such as the information in proxy statements). By making possible an equity investment in the subsidiary alone, the carve-out also increases the incentives of both individual investors and potential acquiring firms to gather and analyse information about subsidiary activities. The increase in both the supply of a demand for information about the subsidiary may increase the perceived value of subsidiary stock to individual and corporate investors.

c) *Restructuring of Asset Management and Incentive Contracts:* Many carve-outs are associated with a major restructuring of managerial responsibilities and incentives. Divisions are often re-grouped into a new subsidiary for the public offering with a consequent realilgnment in the responsibilities of various managers. Furthermore, the incentive contracts of subsidiary managers are usually revised to incorporate subsidiary share prices and profits as measures of performance. Such internal structural shifts are seldom associated with seasoned equity offerings.

A change in corporate focus through a restructuring program or a reduction by the parent of investment in the line with businesss of the carved-out subsidiary can also be one of the motives. The formation of the new subsidiaries typically involves combining the operation of existing units, divisions or subsidiaries under a single management. Finally, management responsibilities can also change to the extent that one or more persons resign the top management position with the parent to become president or CEO of the subsidiary.

Restructuring of managerial responsibilities and incentives

are frequently associated with equity carve-outs. To the extent the market expects such restructuring to lead to improvements in managements efficiency in using corporate assets, we would expect a favourable share price reaction.

Glimpses from Corporate India

In India, financial restructuring has been done with the help of "equity Carve outs" as well as "equity carve ins."* Equity carve-Ins are popular in India because companies fear that their subsidiaries will be taken over due to their low equity participation in them. Some recent examples of both"equity carve out" as well as "equity carve ins" are presenstesd in this sesction.

Equity Carve outs: The case of Nicholes Piramal is a case in point. Though it has usually resorted to acquisition as a means of expansion (In 1984, it took over Gujarat Glass, Nicholas Lab, Roche, Smitra Pharmaceuticals and Bochringes Manheim), it has shifted gears since 1997, when it decided to carve in by consolidating all these firms. Then, in 1998, it spun off and came up with Gujarat Glass and sumitra Pharmaceuticals again. To generate cash flow in order to use it for further expansion, it resorted to a carve out, when it sold around 40 % of its stake in Gujarat Glass to three foreign investors. Most of its Stake in the Sumitra Pharma has also been sold to a European investor. As such, the changed equity structure of Nicholas Pirimal (India) Limited now looks like this:

Promoters	=	46%
EM Warburg Pincus	=	9.99%
Roche	=	4.0%
Public	=	39.01%

Source: Wadhwani, C. "Of Mergers and Spin-offs", *Business Standard*, 2nd, March 1998, p. 3.

* An "equity carve in" mesans increasing the equity stake in group companies instead of generating cash through "equity carve out".

Financial restructuring has caught up with other business groups also. In order to increase focus of their operation, the Thapar group spun off their chemicals division as BILT chemicals. Then in 1997, the group was split up into three-BILT paper, BILT chemicals and BILT investment. BILT wanted to redeem some of its high cost debt. Since funds are required for that, it decided to issue up to 4.5 million nine, years deemable preference shares of Rs. 100 each for cash at par to Al, Mujran, which is owned by Bin Mahfonz and family, who are the owners of saudi Arabia's largest bank, the National Commercial Bank. Also BILT thought of issuing equity worth Rs. One crore on a preferential allotment basis which was expected to raise Rs. 500-600 million. As a result of all this, Thapars' share in the equity will come down from 28.9% to 24.06%, which is below the minimum of 26% needed to block the special resolutions under the companies Act[3].

Equity Carve-ins: As mentioned before, the Indian companies, in order to ward off the threat of acquisition, are trying to consolidate by either trying to improve their management (DCM Shriram Consolidated) or by getting hold of a WHITE KNIGHT* to come for rescuse (Sona Steering System issued preference shares to its partner so as to increase its shareholding from 12 to 20 per cent.[4]

Bhandari (1998)[5] was suggested some more methods for consolidation, viz; delisting of a company, preferentilal issue in one's own favour, creeping acquisition ** and share buy-back.

The Tata-group is also attempting to carve-in in order to

---

* In order to repel the moves of a raider, the target company can make an appeal to a friendly company to buy all, or a part of the company with an understanding that the friendly company will not dislodge the management of the target company. The friendly company is the white knight.

** Creeping acquisition means buying up to 2 percent of the company's stock every year.

counter the threats of a hostile takeover. Narayan (1997)[6] shares the story. Tata sons, the holding has a meagre share in these group companies. Moreover, the Parsi Charitable Trusts control around 65% of Tata Sons. The Tata family, Ironically, has only 3% stake whereas Pallonji Mistry has 18%. From over more than 80 companies, the Tatas intend to reduce to 30 companies and consolidate into 10-12 core businessess. They are frying to up their stake to at least 26% so that hostsile takeover bids are kept at bay. Shivaramu (1999)[7] has brought out the details. The modus operandi is as follows:

"The Tatas require Rs. 15.9 billion to increase their shares to 26 per cent in Telco (Tata Engineering & Locomotive Co.) and Tata Steel. The Tatas have started the centripetal pattern. The Tatas will increase Tata Sons' stakes in the operating companies. The operating companies will increase their stakes in the holding company. This will prevent predators from taking over any individual operating units. During the 1995-98 period, Tata Sons increased its stake in Telco from 1.78 percent to 2.82 per cent and in Tata Steel from 2.35 per cent to 8.44 percent. Similarly, the operating companies (Telco, Tata Power, Tata Chemicals and Indian Hotels) increased their stake to 11 per cent in the holding company. This was done through Rs. 2.99 billion rights issue by Tata Sons in 1995-96. Cach share (face value: Rs. 1,000) had a premium of Rs. 99,000 and the Tata Trusts renounced their shares in favour of the group's operating companies with an additional premium of Rs. 25,000. This cash was used to increase the stakes in the operating companies.

The Tata holding company has adopted the equity carve-out method to increase its equity base. A 20 percent equity stake in Tata Industries was given to Jardine Matheson. Tata Indusstries is becoming a holding company for many joint ventures within the Tata group.

In February 1998, the Tata group signed a joint venture agreement with Jardine International Motor Mauritius (JIMM), a subsidiary of Jardine International Motors, a Hong Kong listed company, which is in the automobile retailing business. This company belongs to the Jardine Matheson group. It has retail business in 11 countries. The joint venture is called Concord Motors Pvt. Ltd., with an initial equity of $24 million with equal stakes between Jardine International Motor Mauritius and the Tata group. The Tata group companies which got involved are Telco and Tata Industsries. The objective is to establish a passenger car dealership network in India"

Concluding Remarks

As a mechanism of corporate restructuring, financial restructuring has been resorted to for churning up more cash for new invsetment. Developed countries have done this by issuing subsidsiary stock to the public. This "Carving-out" of the equity has also been done due to many othesr perceived benefits like creating the public image of the subsidiary in order to divesst from or reacquire it later, taking tax benefits or to maintain financial synergies. Moreover, the markets seem to respond favourably to an equity Carve out decision. However, the Indian business houses have a different set of problems. Presented with a fear of hostile take-overs, they have been resorting to consolidation attempts through an equity Carve in, thereby increasing the shareholding in the subsidiary. Whatever may be the modes, restructuring has become imperative for survival of any businesss as the failures of over-diversified conglomerates become glaring, leading to breaking up of the companies into smaller, more focused operating units . . . as they echo, "small is beautiful".

REFERENCES

1. Stern, Joel M., and Donald H. Crew, Jr, *The Revolution in Corporate Finance*, Blackwell Publishers USA 1995.
2. *Ibid,* p. 1.
3. Srinivas, Alam, "Is there a crisis of control in India Inc.?", *Business Today,* 7 December, 1997.
4. Shiva Ramu, S., *Restructuring and Break-ups,* Response Books,

New Delhli, 1999, p.175.

5. Bhandari, Bhupesh, "Keeping Prowling Predators at bay", *Business World,* 1 February, 1997, pp. 58-59.

6. Narayan, Sanjoy, "Rebuilding Bombay House", *Business World,* 22 September, 1997, pp. 34-40.

7. Shiva Ramu, S. *op.cit.* pp.176-177.

14

SYNERGY OF COMBINATIONS: SOME SELECTED CASES

Mrs. Sudesh & Anil Mittal***

Introduction

Indian industry is ending the decade of the nineties with a lower growth trend, failing to avail of the sweeping liberalisation policies such as delicensing, freer imports, greater access to domestic and external financing and reduction in the levels of taxation unveiled since 1991.

Let alone the demands of competition in a globalising economy, and an inevitable structural transformation to be undergone, the record of industry in terms of productivity, exports or technological upgradation has been depressing. The annual average growth rate of industrial production declined in the 1990s from the eighties in all sectors-manufacturing, electricity and mining and quarrying. This is rue of the use-based categories, based goods, capital goods and consumer goods.

There has emerged in recent years a rising demand for consumer durables, which is reflected in the automobiles sector and a range of other "white goods" to meet the needs of affluent

* Senior Lecturer, Department of Management, Kurukshetra University, Kurukshetra.

** Lecturer, Department of Management, Kurukshetra University, Kurukshetra.

classes. The relative contribution of basic goods and capital goods to industrial production has fallen over the decade.

Against the around 8 percent average growth in the 1980s, industry grew by only 5.8 percent in the 1990s (till 1998-99). The share of basic goods declined from 43.6 to 35.8 percent in this period while that of capital goods from 25 to 7.1 per cent. An increase in intermediate and consumer goods offset the decline in the contribution of basic and capital goods sectors.

The decade has also seen a steady fall in corporate investments as reflected in new capital issues in the latter half (from 1996-97 onwards). The primary capital market had been in depressed conditions and resource mobilisation by non-government during 1995-96 to 1997-98 at an annual average rate of 48.1 percent, according to the RBI data. The rise in resource mobilisation in 1998-99 was on a low base of 1997-98.

Whatever the factors attributable to the stock market depression until recently, the slowdown in the economy, and industrial sector in particular, has affected the demand for funds from the primary capital market. For its part, the industry has been looking to the government to increase public investments which could trigger private investments and for lowering of both tax and interest rates. Several sections of industry has also been clamouring for protection against cheaper imports.

The relatively low contribution of basic and capital goods sectors to overall industrial output, according to RBI, reflect the impact of trade liberalisation, particularly imports, and of financial liberalisation that enabled the corporate sector to make financial gains through "other income."

Lack of competitiveness is writ large in many areas of manufacturing, but to become internationally competitive, industries would need to restructure themselves with modern technology. On the other hand, there are some leading industrial groups which are in the process of corporate.

Mergers, acquisitions and strategic alliances are the most frequently used words by the corporate managers today. And with the opening up of the global economy, corporations have to compete on a global scale, a scale not known before. Small corporations seek state of the art technology, capital, growth, etc. through such alliances where as big corporations look for strategic alliances to enhance their overall competitiveness.

Mergers, acquisitions and alliances are taking place not only between corporations in the similar fields but also between these from different cultures, different countries and sometimes different industries. Even their management styles are occasionally in sharp contrast to each other. This surely calls for special skills to structure the deals which put all the parties involved in a win position. The deals must enhance the total value rather than reduce it. They must make two plus two more than four.

If the combination is able to increase the wealth of equity shareholders only then, there will be economic justification. This paper is an attempt to study selected merger of companies by comparing merger of related (with more or less same product) companies and non-related (with different products) companies.

Methodology

For the purpose of the study, three companies have been selected, two of which have merged (in the same product line) and one has merged differently. Hypothesis to be tested is whether combinations in the same product line are more successful than combinations of companies dealing in different product line. The performance of companies has been observed over a period of three years before merger and five years after merger.

The study is based mainly on secondary data. Annual reports of the companies have been used. The data from these reports have been analyzed using appropriate financial and statistical tools with a view to evaluate the performance of companies.

Ratio is used for studying profitability and return on capital employed.

The efficiency of a firm and its ability to ensure adequate return to its shareholders depends ultimately on the profits earned by it. The crucial importance of profits earned by it. The crucial importance of profits for a firm cannot be over stressed. Profitability is measure of efficiency and the search for it provides an incentive to achieve efficiency. Besides, profits provide money for repaying the debt incurred to finance the project and the resources for internal financing of expansion. In order to observe the performance of merged companies profitability ratios based on sales and based on investment with some more ratios have been calculated.

The following companies (merger) have been studied.

(i) Merger of Gujarat Leasing and Finance Ltd. with Torrent Pharmaceuticals Ltd.

(ii) Merger of Tata Oil Co. with Hindustan Lever Limited

(iii) Merger of Ashoka Mills with Arvind Mills.

Analysis of Mergers (Companies with Different Product Line)

Here take the case of the Merger of *Gujarat Leasing and Finance with Torrent Pharmaceuticals:*

Ratios, highlighting the performance of Torrent Pharmaceuticals Ltd. before and after merger are given in Table 1 to 3. Gross as well as Net profit ratios have increased from 19.46 to 21.74 and 8.73 to 11.35 in 1995. Post merger average gross profit ratio is high in comparison to the pre merger ratio. Average Net Profit ratio has shown good increase over pre merger average. The average ROCE increased from 17.10% in pre merger to 27.5% in post merger period . Overall average Earning Per Share (EPS) of post merger period was Rs. 15.86 but for pre-merger period average was Rs. 51.31.

Analysis of Mergers (Companies in the same Products)

Merger of Tata Oil Co. Ltd. with Hindustan Lever Limited

The performance of Hindustan Lever Limited before and after merger is given in Tables 4 to 6.

As would be seen from Table 4 after merger, the net profit ratio of Hindustan Lever Limited increased from 6.42% in 1993 to 6.51% in 1994. The average value of this ratio increased from 6.07% in pre merger period to 7.15% in post merger period. There is a good increase in average value of return on capital employed from 28.86% increase in average value of return on capital employed from 28.86% in pre merger to 47.44% in post merger period. There is very significant increase in earnings per share (EPS) from pre merger to post merger period. It has gone up from an average of Rs. 7.74 in pre-merger to Rs. 22.94 in post merger period.

Merger of Ashoka Mills with Arvind Mills: (Same product line)

Different ratios, highlighting the performance of Arvind Mills before and after merger are given in Table 1 to 3. As would be seen from the table the net profit ratio increased from 12.81% in 1994 to 15.52% in 1995. Average gross profit showed a little increase from 27.81 in pre-merger period to 27.97% in post merger period. But average net profit has showed a decline in the post merger period. Average return on capital employed and average return on equity fund has declined sharply. Average EPS has declined in post merger period from pre-merger period. There is also decline after merger in average dividend payout ratio.

Conclusions

After the dilution of Foreign Exchange Regulation Act (FERA) and Monopolies and Restrictive Trade Practices Act (MRTP), and abolition of prior government approval for mergers and take over in 1991, there is an upswing in Merger and Acquisition activity in India. There have been more than 400 combination proposals in the last three-four years. Some companies are going for Merger and Acquisition for diversification of their risks like ICICI and ITC Classic Finance, Merger of Gujarat Leasing and Finance with Torrent Pharmaceuticals and Global Sugar to merge with Kitply Industries. Some are looking for growth in the same area like merger of Tata Oil Co. with Hindustan Lever Limited, Merger of Ashoka Mills with Arvind Mills; Times Bank to sign a MOU with Canara Bank to forge a correspondent bank in relationships; R.P. Goenka Group Cable Companies - Asian Cables, RPG Telecom and Upcom Cable Companies - Asian Cables, RPG Telecom and Upcom Cables - to merger into one company for synergetic reasons, merger of Tata Tea Ltd. with Teatly Ltd.

The cases analysed in this paper reveals that the selected companies which have merged in different product line i.e. Torrent Pharmaceuticals Ltd. with Gujrat Finance and Leasing Ltd. has shown growth after the merger. Its average net profits ratio, ROCE, ROEF, DPS, Divident payout ratio have improved in a significant manner. Similarly, the companies which have merged in the same product line i.e. Hindustan Lever Limited and TOMCO too have grown after merger. However, the performance of Arvind Mills after the merger has declined. Thus we can conclude that the merers/combinations of the companies whether in the same product line or different product line are equallyable to increase the wealth of equity share holders. However, we should keep in our mind that some other factors (not only the merger) affects the performance of the companies.

The ratios which will be used are defined below:
(for table 1, 4 and 7)

$$\textbf{Gross Profit Ratio} = \frac{\text{Earnings before depreciation, interest and taxes}}{\text{Net sales}}$$

$$\textbf{Net Profit Ration} = \frac{\text{Earnings after taxes}}{\text{Net sales}}$$

For (Table 2,5,8)

$$\textbf{Return on Capital employed (Pre tax)} = \frac{\text{Earnings (pre tax)}}{\text{Capital employed}}$$

$$\textbf{Return of equity fund} = \frac{\text{Earnings after tax}}{\text{Share holder's equity}}$$

(For table 3,6,9)

$$\textbf{Earning per share} = \frac{\text{Earnings after taxes}}{\text{No. of ordinary share outstanding}}$$

$$\textbf{Divident per share} = \frac{\text{Dividends paid to ordinary shareholders}}{\text{No. of ordinary share outstanding}}$$

$$\textbf{Dividend payout ratio} = \frac{\text{Dividend per share}}{\text{Earnings per share}}$$

Table - 1

Profitability Ratio of Torrent Pharmaceuticals Ltd. related to Sales before and after Merger of Gujarat Leasing and Finance Ltd.

	Pre-Merger Period			*Post-Merger Period*						
Year	*1992*	*1993*	*1994*	*1995*	*1996*	*1997*	*1998*	*1999*	*Pre Merger Average*	*Post Merger Average*
G.P.R (%)	19.61	19.73	19.46	21.74	25.28	29.95	18.61	18.60	19.60	22.77
N.P.R. (%)	5.08	9.85	8.73	11.35	12.4	13.1	12.2	12.7	7.89	12.35

Table - 2

Profitability Ratio of Torrent Pharmaceuticals Ltd. related to Sales before and after Merger of Gujarat Leasing and Finance Ltd.

	Pre-Merger Period			*Post-Merger Period*						
Year	*1992*	*1993*	*1994*	*1995*	*1996*	*1997*	*1998*	*1999*	*Pre Merger Average*	*Post Merger Average*
ROCE (Pre-Tax) (%)	14.86	18.1	18.1	20.2	47.0	50.4	11.6	8.3	17.10	27.5
ROEF (%)	5.08	9.85	8.73	11.35	24.4	23.4	19.7	16.1	7.89	18.99

Table - 3

Earnings and Dividends of Torrent Pharmaceuticals Ltd. before and after merger of Gujrat Leasing and Finance Ltd.

	Pre-Merger Period			*Post-Merger Period*						
Year	*1992*	*1993*	*1994*	*1995*	*1996*	*1997*	*1998*	*1999*	*Pre Merger Average*	*Post Merger Average*
EPS	33.1	109.3	11.52	11.32	15.84	15.55	19.3	17.3	51.31	15.86
DPS	1.8	2.02	1.39	3.5	3.53	6.09	5.5	6.7	1.74	5.06
DPR	5.0	2.0	12.0	31.0	22.0	39.0	28.6	38.8	6.0	31.88

Table - 4

Profitability Ratio of HLL related to Sales before and after Merger of Tata Oil Co.

	Pre-Merger Period			*Post-Merger Period*						
Year	*1992*	*1993*	*1994*	*1995*	*1996*	*1997*	*1998*	*1999*	*Pre Merger Average*	*Post Merger Average*
GPRin %	12.41	12.76	13.53	12.43	12.96	10.78	12.00	13.3	12.90	12.29
NPR %	5.95	5.83	6.42	6.51	7.4	6.14	7.2	8.5	6.07	7.15

Table - 5

Profitability Ratio of HLL related to investments before and Table after merger of Tata Oil Co.

	Pre-Merger Period			*Post-Merger Period*						
Year	*1991*	*1992*	*1993*	*1994*	*1995*	*1996*	*1997*	*1998*	*Pre-Merger Average*	*Post Merger Average*
RCE (Pre-Tax) (%)	24.16	24.84	31.57	30.92	40.2	46.3	61.1	58.7	28.86	47.44
REFin (%)	30.75	30.11	33.95	33.8	30.3	34.4	44.9	47.0	31.60	38.08

Table - 6

Earnings and Dividends of HLL before and after Merger of Tata Oil Co.

	Pre-Merger Period			*Post-Merger Period*						
Year	*1992 Dec.*	*1993*	*1994*	*1995*	*1996*	*1997*	*1998*	*1999*	*Pre-Merger Average*	*Post Merger Average*
EPS	6.39	7.17	9.35	12.38	16.93	20.2	28.5	36.7	7.64	22.94
DPS	3.85	4.2	5.6	7.86	10.0	13.2	18.7	22.0	4.55	14.35
DPR in %	60.0	590	60.0	63.0	59.1	65.1	65.7	60.0	59.67	62.58

Table - 7

Profitability Ratio of Arvind Mills Limited related to Sales before and after Merger of Ashoka Mills

Year	*Pre-Merger Period*			*Post-Merger Period*					*Pre-Merger Average*	*Post Merger Average*
	1991	*1992*	*1993*	*1994*	*1995*	*1996*	*1997*	*1998*		
GPR in (%)	23.10	30.92	29.42	32.11	33.42	33.63	27.73	12.95	27.81	27.97
NRP in (%)	8.42	14.44	12.81	15.52	15.65	14.60	11.3	1.6	11.89	11.73

Table - 8

Profitability Ratio of Arvind Mills Limited related to Investment before and after Merger of Ashoka Mills

Year	*Pre-Merger Period*			*Post-Merger Period*					*Pre-Merger Average*	*Post Merger Average*
	1991	*1992*	*1993*	*1994*	*1995*	*1996*	*1997*	*1998*		
RCE (%)	13.48	10.60	7.56	8.73	10.9	11.6	6.7	1.5	10.55	7.89
REFin (%)	22.71	18.91	7.26	8.83	10.4	11.81	8.5	1.2	16.29	8.15

Table - 9

Earning and Dividends of Arvind Mills LImited Before and after Merger of Ashoka Mills

	Pre-Merger Period			*Post-Merger Period*						
Year	*1991*	*1992*	*1993*	*1994*	*1995*	*1996*	*1997*	*1998*	*Pre-Merger Average*	*Post Merger Average*
EPS	14.71	10.26	7.57	9.08	11.40	12.67	10.00	1.40	10.85	8.91
DPS	2.08	3.17	3.45	3.99	4.49	4.92	2.80	00	2.9	3.24
DPR in (%)	21.0	31.0	46.0	44.0	49.0	39.0	27.8	00	32.67	29.96

15

INTELLECTUAL CAPITAL AS A KEY TO FINANCIAL RESTRUCTURE —A New Concept

*Gopa Kambagiri Swamy**

There is a growing realisation the world over that the edge enjoyed by companies over their competitors comes more from insights, experience and superior solutions than from sophisticated machines and gross block. This is the big lesson of the modern industrial era. The first phase of industrialisation some 200 years ago was marked by entrepreneurial capitalism. As an increasing numbers of companies prospered and the first generation of nation-builders gave way to their successors, it became more critical to run these companies successfully. Thus evolved managerial capitalism. With managers becoming increasingly skilled over time, businesses becoming more complex than before and industries turning more competitive, it became necessary to evolve better systems and processes to stay afloat. This has given rises to the third phase in the sequences: intellectual capitalism.

Corporate managers are unanimous that companies that prosper in future will be those which can successfully leverages the knowledge at their disposal, or can unleash their brand equity or can deliver solutions that are better than the rest at a price which

* Research Scholar, Department of Commerce, Bharathiar University, Coimbatore-641046, Tamilnadu.

is lower, in a form which is more attractive, and at time that the customer wants it. But this is only a one dimensional focus. Intellectual capital goes beyond. It deals with the expertise-creating system within an organization that makes it competitive. It identifies the building blocks of a corporation's edge. It increases awareness.

Why intellectual capital is the candle to a confusing future is simple. No company can sustain growth if its keeps driving only the hard numbers. Nor if it keeps writing out stiff targets in its annual budgeting exercise in the hope that as the months go on, the numbers will fall into place by magic. Because, as analysts have discovered, it is the soft numbers that hold the key. Some day in the future not too distant-companies drawing out their budget exercise at the start of a financial year will write out growth targets for 'mandays of training' and 'customer response time' with as much of conviction as they draw out 'Sales' and 'Margins' today. The cause will gradually take precedence over effect.

Traditional accounting practitioners may differ on the different ways of calculating Intellectual Capital- right down to insisting that it cannot be done- done- but those tracking the stock market have already figured out a way of arriving at the figure. Simplistically, Intellectual capital is the difference between the market capitalization of a company and its book value on that date.

The reason why this appears to be a reasonable practice is clear: when one buys a stock at Rs. 250 while its book value is Rs. 100, it is clear that the incremental amount is paid for competitive skills not reflected in the balance sheet which are expected to drive corporate profits in the coming years. An averaged calculation over a period of time enables a more stable and corrected reading of a Company's Intellectual Capital.

Perhaps that biggest modern-day driver of shareholders value is intellectual capital. Modern thinkers have developed tools that enable us to ascertain whether shareholders value has been created or destroyed over time. The three principal tools in this direction are Market Value Added, Total Shareholder return and Economic Value added.

Economic Value Added and Market Value Added

Maximizing shareholder value ought to be fundamental goal of all business emperical evidence indicates that increasing shareholder.Winning companies create relatively greater value for of all stakeholders, customers, labour, goverment (through tax paid) and suppliers of capital yet there are additional reasons to adopt a system that emphasizes shareholder value.They are first value is the best metric of performance. Second, shareholders are this only stakeholders of a corporation who simultaneously maximize their own. And finally companies that do not perform well will find that capital flows towards their competitors.

The value of the company's equity is the value of its operations,less the value of its debt and adjusted for any non-operating assets or liabilities value of business equals the present value of its expected cash flows discounted at an appropriate discount rate.Company value is determined by its discounted future cash flows and value is created when companies invest capital at returns that exceed the cost of capital.

Free cash flows are gross cash flow(Net operating profit less adjusted taxes plus depreciation) minus gross investment (increase in working capital expenditure). Since value is based on discounted free cash flow the underlying value drivers of free cash flows there are two key drivers of free cash flow and ultimately value, they are return on invested capital and growth.

Hence to increase a company's value one or more of the following should be done:

- Increase the level of profits earned on the existiing capital
- Increase the return on new capital investment

- Increase growth rate but only as long as the return on new capital exceeds weighted average cost of capital.
- Reduce cost of capital.

Economic value added is a measure of financial performance that combines the familiar concept of residual income with principles of modern corporate finance specifically, that all capital has a cost and that earnings more than cost of capital creates value for shareholders.Thus EVA is the financial performance measure that comes closer than any other in capturing the true economic profit of an enterprise and is directly to the creation of shareholder wealth over time.The most revealing of EVA is that it takes into account a factor no conventional measure includes (i.e) the the cost of capital. One of EVA's most powerful properties is its strong link with share prices. EVA measures may be applied at two different situations firstly, to calculate the quantum of value the concerned organisation have added from the current operations for its shareholders and vice versa. Secondly, to deploy the technique in the strategic planning process where it provides for the basic information for additional value creation true. If a company's return on capital exceeds its cost of capital, it is creating true value for the shareholders. Companies consistently high EVA are top performers that are valued highly by shareholders.

Market value added is a measure of the real wealth a company has created for its investors. In effect, the MVA shows all the cash floes from and to the shareholders. MVA is a cumulative measure of corporate performance that looks at how much a company's stock has added to (or taken out of) investors pocket over its life and compares it with the capital those it investors put in to the firm. If MVA is a positive number the company has made its shareholders richer. A negative MVA indicates how much shareholders wealth has been destroyed.

Calculating Eva and MVA

The cost of capital is the minimum of rate of return on capital required to compensate debt and equity investors for bearing risk. e.g. a cut-off rate to create value. It can be expressed as:

EVA	=	(rate of return-cost of capital)—capital
then EVA	=	(rate of return-cost of capital)—capital (cost of capital—capital)
EVA	=	Net operating profit- cost of capital—capital
And EVA	=	operating profits-a capital change

The calculation of EVA is based on the premium factor called beta. Beta refers to the sensitivity of the security returns (dependent variable) to changes in market returns (independent variable). Once the security and market returns of a sufficient negatively long period have been computed to get large number of returns, the simple linear regression technique can be used to estimate beta.

EVA shows the business profit left after adjusting for the cost of servicing the capital employed in the business. If the EVA, is positive the business has generated wealth in excess of what is expected by the shareholders and vice versa. If the figure for a particular year drops below zero, it indicates that the expectations of the shareholders are not being met. /The usefulness of EVA is that it can be applied to various divisions within a company to improve its efficiency.

Research has shown that there is a fundamental correlation between economic value added and shareholder value.

An increase in EVA reflects

- Greater Efficiency in utilization of existing capital
- Investment of additional capital in projects that return more than the cost of obtaining the new capital i.e. profitable growth

Liquidation of unproductive investment that do not cover the cost of capital

MVA enables one to conclude whether the company has been valued by the market in excess of its total funds. In instances where this is so, the assumption is that the market is willing to place a premium on the company's value in recognition of its future earnings potential. To calculate MVA, the capital of the company over its span of existence is taken and adjusted to capitalize certain past expenditure like R&D. This adjusted capital is compound to a firm's total market value, which is the current value of the company's stock. In formula form

MVA • [(shares outstanding * Stock Price) + Market Value of Preferred Stock + market value of debt]-total capital

The Economic value added's fundamental strengths, namely that it:

Measurers true, economic returns on total invested capital

Explicitly acknowledges a cost of equity capital and

It positively correlated to share holders value.

In every case, Economic value added directs professional manager's attention to actions that will improve returns to shareholders. It attempts to reduce agency problems by motivation manages to feel like business owners. An Economic value added compensation system provides a frame work for focusing attention on investment efficiency and profitable growth that aligns professional manager's objectives with those of the shareholders.

The Economic Value added has powerful appeal. However, systems such as Economic Value added are based on the concept that maximizing shareholders value is the company's primary directive, a theory proposed by financial economists.

Unfortunately, the link between management investment actions and long term shareholders value is only loosely defined. Others have proposed that shareholders are only one constituency and that the long term success of the company depends on benefits received by a broader set of constituencies including customers, employees and suppliers-labor, technology and capital. The long-term shareholders value is maximized only when all of these constituencies prosper.

Shareholder Return

Dividends and expansion in market valuation are the two principal ways in which shareholders can be enriched. Total shareholders return takes into account the sum of these two features. The increase in market capitalization is added to the dividend paid out by the company during a financial year. This sum is then expressed a s a percentage of the market capitalization of the company at the start of the financial year under review.

Estimation of future growth rates play a key role in valuation. Growth rates can be estimated in three ways. First by using past earnings, second by forecasts made by other analysts who follow the same firms and third relates growth rates to fundamentals.

Shareholder's wealth = Market Value added
= Total Value - Total Capital
= Net present value
= the present value of future Economics value added

by aubtracting the cost of capital, Economic value added automatically sets aside a return sufficient to recover the value of the capital that has already been or will be invested.

The model that companies has used over the years to create Intellectual Capital is five-pronged.

1. Human Capital
2. Technology Capital

3. Structural Capital
4. Customer Capital

'The customer is most important part of the production line'

—W. Edwards Deming, quality guru

5. Brand Capital
6. Efficiency Capital

Human Capital

The management of the companies strongly believes that organizational effectiveness is best achieved through the proper development and utilization of human resources. It also believes that organizational contribution to individual development and satisfaction is generally reciprocated manifold by the individual. In keeping with this core belief, the Companies are firmly committed to meeting the following objectives

- To plan and induct competent manpower in terms of knowledge, skill and attitude.
- To provide opportunities for growth of the employees in terms of skill and career upgradation.
- To practice equity and fairness in all its dealings with employees.
- To continously enhance knowledge and the skill-level of the employees for the performance of their present and future tasks through continuous education and training.
- To create an organizational climate conductive for optimal contribution by a highly motivated work force and
- To prepare employees for a smoother and quicker adaptation to change.

'A tool is but the extension of a man's hand and the machine is but a complex tool, and he that invents a machine augments the power of man and the well being of mankind'

Structural Capital

Structural capital represents those assets of an organization, which the employees leave behind at their place of work when they leave for their homes in the evening. Structural capital includes a number of efficiency drivers which effect productivity and in turn, profitability.

Even though the use of Information Technoiogy is no guarantee of a Company's success, there is little doubt that companies which have successfully leveraged IT have emerged increasingly successful in a competitive world. The use of IT has unleashed latent corporate potential : it has increased the flow of information between various divisions; it has improved corporate morale, the use of sophisticated technologies like ERP, data warehousing, internet/ intranet etc., have made it possible for companies to become information-rich at the press of a button, importantly, IT has helped in aligning the shop floor to shelf place and has led to more productive use of capital.

'In the business world, everyone is paid in two coins: cash and experience. Take the experience first; the cash will come later.'

--H. Geneen, Ex- Chairman of ITT

Brand Value

Since the earliest times producers of goods have used their brands or marls to distinguish their products. Pride in their products has no doubt played a part in this. More particularly, by identifying their products they have provided purchasers with a means of recognizing and specifying them should they wish to repurchase oı recommend the products to others.

The use of brands has developed considerably, especially in the last century. Indeed, the words 'brands' and branding are now such common currency that their original meaning is in danger of being weakened. However, the function of a brand as distinguishing the foods of one producer from those of another and thus allowing consumers a freedom of choice has remained unaltered..... As a result of this development, it has been acknowledged by financial and marketing communities like that brands do not merely have 'consumer' value, and that this value can be measured. Various techniques for measuring financial brand value have now been developed.

Power brands are those brands which are particularly well adapted to the environment and which thus survive and flourish. They are the ultimate examples of an organization's marketing skills - their finest and most valuable productions. Power brands can be either goods or services, can act as corporate names ass well product brand names and can be very specific products or ranges of related products. What they have in common is that they all embrace products which are well priced and offer good and consistent quality to consumers. Hence the brand, in a sense, acts as a credible guarantee for the product or service, allowing the consumer to clearly identify an specify products which genuinely offer added value. *The Brand Valuation exercise attempts to put a value to the brand.*

Section IV

RESTRUCTURING: ORGANISATION & HRD

16

REDUNDANCY : A FALLOUT OF RESTRUCTURING

*P.K. Gupta**

Introduction

Only thing constant in a changing world is change itself. In normal course of events, i.e., without divine/evolutionary/managerial intervention, we observe a certain commonality in the pattern of changes in the medium/long term in the biological, technological and business processes. The pattern of change is that represented by the very familiar 'life-cycle curve' consisting of four segments, viz., introduction, growth, stablisation and decline. In the case of biological process, it can be said that a steady state is maintained through divine/ evolutionary intervention such that by the time a process or species in this case is declining, another process takes its place. In the case of technology and business such renewal/replacement requires timely human intervention. It is the specific job of the manager to bring in such renewal and, therefore, a common saying in "Manager is the agent of change'.

However, such smooth transition/renewal is not a universal phenomenon. Sometimes the change is kept in abeyance over a period of time till it reaches the stage of inevitability and unavoidability. Finally, when it occurs, the effect is drastic and

* Birla Institute of Technology and Science, Pilani -333032

usually accompanied by upheavals which affect specially the people in the immediate environment, such as, the employees of the business.

In this paper, we take a critical look at this phenomenon including some of its causes and a fallout in the Indian context.

Indian Context

In pre Independence India, most of the businesses and industries were owned by the Britishers and for obvious reasons many of them were more interested in repatriating the profits to their home country rather than spend part of it in the renewal process. This tendency because more pronounced in the 1930s and 1940s when it become apparent that India is going to achieve independence very shortly and it was only a question of time.

When India became independent, many of these enterprises were saddled with outdated technology, ramshackle equipment and obsolete processes. After independence, many of the foreign owners of industries, wanted to leave India and the industries were taken over by the Indian businessmen. With notable exceptions (for example, Tatas) the Indian businessmen were mostly traders and not industrialists. They were interested in quick profits, sometimes employing unscrupulous means and rarely thinking of modernization as an essential part of business.

After Independence, many new industries came up both in public and private sector usually using the then modern technology. For reasons that we are not going into here, Indian industry both public and private sector, from the beginning also enjoyed protection from competition.

The economic policies under which Indian industry operated were those of 'mixed economy'. It is a combination of two approaches: (a) free market approach which permits the private sector to use their resources and skills in business and (b) socialistic approach which propounds involvement of government in all facets of planning and implementation of economic activities.

In the mixed economy as practised in India, private initiative and ownership were permitted but these were controlled and regulated less by factors of free market economy and more by government regulation. At the same time, the Indian industry enjoyed a protectionist regime which made the concepts of productivity and quality largely unimportant for the time being, since in the captive market it was easy to make profit through cost-plus pricing. More so, in the public sector where lack of accountability and red- tapism compounded the inefficiency. "Of the 244 PSUs of the central government and about 800 PSUs of the state governments, 45 per cent are estimated to be sick, encurring heavy losses."[1]

In addition, by our interpretation of socialism and social responsibility, further government actions aggravated the problems in two ways –

(a) Nationalisation of some viable private sector industries, such as coal, which under government administration, started making losses.

(b) Government taking over sick and non-viable private sector units.

Soon enough, many of these industries needed government subsidy to survive which can be termed as the ultimate in protectionism.

In this dismal scenario, the problem of unemployment and underemployment and the resulting hardship were major issues. Only about 10% of the employable population were employed in the organised industry and 90% were somehow surviving (either working in the unorganised sector or unemployed). However, this 10% benefited the most from the protection conferred by the labour laws and trade union movement which virtually guaranteed life time employment. The political and social compulsions to generate more jobs led to overmanning in the public sector undertakings,. almost without exception. "It has been affirmed time and again that while social security is a fundamental right for citizens, handing out doles and subsistence support in the absence of productive jobs deprives people of pride, self confidence and hope.[2]"

Into the Eighties

In this dismal scenario, there were honourable exceptions and during the decade of eighties there was significant increase in the rate of the industrial output as well as development of the service sector. However, some of the industries which were set up after independence (say, for example Hindusthan Motors producing Landmaster and then Ambassador cars) were using, by now, outdated technology and still surviving because of the protected market and at the expense of the consumer. The white paper prepared by the Economic Advisory Council under the chairmanship of Late Prof. Sukhamoy chakrovarty highlighted certain disturbing aspects of economic growth, such as, mounting budgetery deficits, large foreign debt and overall paucity of resources. Low productivity, population growth and unemployment also continued to remain significant problems.

Productivity in the Organised Industry

Most worrisome issues in our organised sectors were erosion of productivity, lack of innovativeness and high cost of infrastructure all adding up to the high cost of end products. Some of the comparative data regarding productivity are given below:

Table 1
Labour Productivity in the manufacturing sector (1960-80)

Country	*Growth % p.a.*
South Korea	10.0
Japan	8.2
West Germany	5.0
USA	2.6
India	2.5

Table 2
Total factor productivity growth (1960-80)

Country	*Growth % p.a.*
South Korea	5.7
Japan	3.1
India	-0.6

The Decade of 90s

Realising the situation of our own economy, and seeing the example of several other countries, India embarked on a policy of liberalisation, through which we can augment our resources by utilising the resources available globally. This can lead India into a sustainable high enough growth rate which can help reach the country to the take off stage.

In the liberalised economy, Indian industries are facing the competition from world class global industries. Indian market with its immense potential and growing purchasing power is attracting businesses from all over the world. Indian industry would have to improve product quality, process efficiency and cost of production in order to survive in this environment. When this is accomplished, the Indian consumers and ultimately the whole country will be the gainers.

The inevitability of this change becomes more accentuated at the turn of the millenium when the world is moving from industrial age to information age and then to knowledge age. Multinational and transnational conglomerates have already taken note of the situation and started restructuring themselves. (For example, ABB world wide are going away from their businesses based on manufacturing).

Restructuring and Redundancy

Considering the above scenario, Indian industry and business has no option other than modernisation and restructuring. While modernisation and restructuring has many facets, in this paper we are focussing our attention on one of them, viz. redundancy of manpower.

- The reasons for redundancy of manpower are well known. We enumerate some of them below –
- Recruitment of more manpower than required to satisfy the urge to make quick profit (cost was not so important) in the short run
- Reduction of manpower requirement due to shrinkage of market demand of product.
- Manpower in the payroll of sick and closed industries.
- Recruitment of more manpower than required in the part, considering provision of employment as a part of social responsibility of business, especially in the public sector.
- The above are the historical reasons for surplus manpower in industry. Added to this, further redundancy is arising and will arise in the post liberalisation period as a fallout of restructuring and modernisation.

The redeeming feature of this scenario is the expectation that the very process of industrial growth and modernisation will add to both direct and associated opportunities for generating employment. The jobs so created will have to be kept delinked from redundancies and loss of jobs in sick industries in so far as the two phenomena are qualitatively different. However, in the balance one will have to first compensate for the other and then overtake it significantly so as to make a sizable difference in the employment scenario.

As mentioned earlier, the focus in this paper is the redundancy and how to deal with it. Before proceeding further, let in reiterate two points:

One, a large portion of this redundancy was already a fact of life in the preliberalisation period. It has only been exposed and brought into focus the restructuring process,

And two, "loss of jobs is an inherent cost of restructuring a high-cost and uncompetitive domestic industry into a modern, vibrant and low-cost one"[3].

Dimensions of Redundancy

The following information emerge through a study covering the period 1990-91 to 1994-95. In the industrial units having a capital size of more than Rs. 100 crores and a 62% share of the total capital of the industrial sector, the average employment size per unit has fallen by around 36%. A similar trend has also been observed in the industrial units with capital size ranging from Rs. 50 crores to Rs. 100 crores[4].

Extrapolating this trend on the estimated total employment in the organised sector, the total dimension of redundancy appears to be of the order of 10 million jobs. In 246 central public sector units in 1992 number of surplus employees were of the order of 0.2 million[5]. It is certainly an area which require urgent attention along with the realisation that " life after liberalisation can be built only through hardwork, economic growth, human ingenuity and endeavour and not be pretending that there is some easy route[6]". As regards the people rendered surplus, a solution must be implemented in a humane manner and this has to be considered a social obligation. In the sections that follow, some experiences, perceptions and insights will be shared. Most of these relate to worker level redundancy in traditional industries some of which claim to be professionally managed.

HANDLING REDUNDANCY - POST FACTO

Preparing the Ground - 1

The most important and also the most difficult process is to gain understanding and acceptance of the situation by the people who are directly affected.

- A typical worker profile is as given below:
- Age around 50 years, good health
- Primary to middle level education.
- Number of years on the job : 20+ years.
- Only skill learnt on the job : one or more speical purpose machine operation (not a trade such as, turner, welder, etc).
- Reasonable earning and benefits.
- Respect and faith on the company[7].

For such people, it is difficult to believe that redundancy can happen to them. The company has been the "Annadata"[8]. (more than "Karmadata") for many years. To explain the situation to them is as painful as it is difficult and the requirements are absolute transparency and infinite patience. Dialogues have to be continued formally at the union level and among the opinion makers. The political mentors of the Union and concerned Government agencies have to be taken into confidence and convinced.

Preparing The Ground – 2

Detailed homework has to be done to explore all avenues of gainful redeployment of the surplus work force preceded by retraining. The following options among others may be explored

- Redeployment in another unit of the company.
- Employment in ancillary unit setup by entrepreneurs assisted by the company.
- The above options made available to the sons of the employees.
- Helping the employee to startup on his own (for people with some general skill, such as the electrician).

It is obvious that there options cannot come with existing wages and benefits continuing to be protected at the same level.

Legal Option

The Industrial Disputes Act, 1947 (IDA) has explicit provision of retrenchment of surplus employees with payment of statutory benefits only in the event of partial discontinuation of operations of the company. In practice, the provisions were found to be obstructive and ineffective. It is found that the concerned government lacks the political will to accord approval for retrenchment.

In this background, the idea of voluntary retrenchment scheme (VRS) has been evolved envisaging the reality of industrial compulsion and at the same time ensuring protection of human needs as far as possible. While this route was already being taken by some private sector companies with proactive thinking, publication of model VRS by the Department of Public Enterprises in October, 1988 effectively made the IDA route totally impractical and unusable.

Last Option – VRS

VRS, a practical, humane and 'best compromise option' will be considered in some detail in the following sections. The focus is on the industrial workers (a typical profile presented earlier) who form a significant proportion of potential VRS candidates.

Designing the scheme

Experience shows that a tailor- made scheme has a better chance of success than an omnibus scheme. The following points are to be taken into account.

Objective of the scheme – number of employees to be separated and the targeted segment of employees, if any

Gathering of data

- Distribution of the employee population in terms of age,

length of service, years remaining to normal retirement, emoluments, etc.

- High probability VRS candidate data, such as chronically ill, debtor, having alternate plan of livelihood, etc.
- Forecasting of VRS population – This depends on the expected VRS amount and other factors; various forecasting methods of nonquantitative type including intelligence gethering can be used.
- This being a business decision, optimisation of cost and benefit is to be attempted.
- Design of the scheme will synthesize the above areas and attempt to match the forecast with the objective while optimising the cost to the company and the benefit to the employee.

From the foregoing discussion, it is obvious that a tailor-made scheme should give better results than an omnibus scheme.

While appreciating the Government's intention to contribute to VRS effort through income tax relief for the VRS amount (provided the scheme follows the DPE model), it may be suggested that a joint committee of industry and government look into provision of I.T. relief even in case of tailor-made scheme.

Helping the employee decide

It is recognized that the decision is probably the most difficult one that the employee has to take throughout his working life. A survey among the potential VRS candidates (profile given earlier) shows that very few employees can logically prefer VRS over continuing employment. A typical worker has a feeling of incapability of doing anything else, has not learnt any universally useful skill and faced with the situation, has a strong sentiment of insecurity and anxiety[11].

Taking note of such reality, management has to take a multipronged humane approach.

- Counselling both individual and group with patience, transparency and sympathy.
- Provide all help to the employee to acquire new skills including possible business skills
- Identify opportunities and customize them for individuals.
- Organise investment of post retirement funds with full safety and adequate return.
- Help in tax planning and payment.

Helping the union to help the employees

This presupposes absence of mistrust and hostility between the management and union. Both union and its political mentors have to be taken into confidence and explained the compulsions. While its unrealistic to expect active support for VRS by any union, achieving understanding and acceptance is a must. Most notably, VRS has to be realised as the insurance for continuity of the balance work force.

Negotiating VRS

In extremely rare cases, union may be negotiating a VRS as part of overall settlement resulting in what is known as 'Agreement VRS'. However, through collective bargaining it is possible and necessary to fix the number of surplus employees preferably departmentwise. In the bargaining process, some amount of 'give and take' will be there. As regards the scheme itself, it will be helpful if the unions expectation can be assessed through formal and informal interaction.

Redundancy Avoidance

This problem can be minimised/avoided by following some well known time tested methods.

- Plant capacity and technology to be used are carefully decided with due regard to the forecasted external environment.

- Manpower requirement is determined in a rigorous manner following well established methods of job design, work measurement and fixing of standards.
- Concepts of productivity and capacity utilisation are given primacy right from inception on an ongoing basis and corrective action, if required, are taken promptly.
- Training and development of employees are made integral part of business plan and executed.
- Technology, processes and product development are updated appropriately to keep the operations viable and self sustainable.
- The above suggestions hold good both for individual units and for the country as a whole.

Conclusion

If appears that the country as a whole has to go through the process of restructuring in order to achieve reasonable results from the reforms agenda. There will be some painful chapters on the way. An attempt has been made to look at one of them in this paper. We expect that the story will have a happy ending.

REFERENCES

1. Arun Monappa & Mahrukh Engineer, *Liberalisation and Human Resource Management*, P.62, Response Books, New Delhi, 1999.
2. Ashok S. Ganguly, *Industry and Liberalisation*, p. 116, Allied Publishers, New Delhi, 1994.
3. Ashok S. Ganguly, *Industry and Liberalisation*, P. 142, Allied Publishers, New Delhi, 1994.
4. Taneja K.C., Impact of Liberalisation on employment in the Indian Industrial Sector, Summarised in *Times of India* (Business Times), New Delhi, October 22, 1998.
5. Sapru, R.K., Workforce Restructuring under Liberalised Economy, *Indian Journal of Industrial Relations,* Vol. 34, No.3, January 1999, p

348-355.

6. Ashok S. Ganguly, *Industry and Liberalisation,* p. 227, Allied Publishers, New Delhi, 1994.

7. Study Report on VRS by A Specialised Agency at a member company, CII, Eastern Region, January 1990.

8. Study Report on VRS by A Specialised Agency at a member company, CII, Eastern Region, January 1990.

9. Omkar Goswami Committee Report on Restructuring Quoted by Sapru R.K., *I.J.I.R.,* January, 1999.

10. Aloke Mukherjee, Preface of Publication on VRS, CII, Eastern Region, January 1990.

11. Study report on VRS, CII, Eastern Region, January, 1990.

17

RESTRUCTURING NEED FOR EMOTIONALLY INTELLIGENT LEADERS

Etinder Pal Singh & Arshi Naim***

The ongoing wave of massive downsizing, multi billion rupee mergers, acquisitions and constant restructuring has left the people perplexed and disoriented. Restructuring is both an 'episodic exercise' as well as a 'continuous process.' Corporate entities have to constantly change on all operating and strategic parameters to prevent themselves from being drowned in the maelstrom of corporate aggression. The corporate sector views restructuring in terms of structural and technological change whereas employees regard it as physical resetting of work environment as also of interpersonal relationships. Both the viewpoints are valid and important, since changing structure involves making an alteration in both authority relations and coordination mechanisms, and job design or similar structural variables.

Hence the need for change in the people as well changing people refers to changs in employee attribudes, skills, expectation, perception & behaviour. It also illustrates the need for an effective

* Presently working as Faculty member in the Dept of Business Management, H.N.B.Garhwal University, Srinagar (Garhwal) and has been a business executive for four years.

** MBA student class 1997-99.

leadership. Leadership if not in size, then at least in quality. If not the biggest then the best, or the most unique or most specialized. In the present context, leadership means growth. Companies must grow to survive. And today, leadership in business is no longer an option but a necessity. But what type of leadership is required in the world of change which could possibly and positively contribute as a catalyst for future organizations?

With old motivational tool kit depleted, leaders need new ways to encourage high performance and build commitment. For these objectives, leaders find emotional constraints as a major hindrance. The leader's mission is to inspire others with the power and excitement of their vision and give people a sense of purpose and pride in their work. People want to be recognized and a leader should not just try to lead, but should give recognition. Thus, the leadership style which could serve the future corporate structure should have the feeling of empathy towards its fellow people for understanding their needs and to motivate them towards organizational goals. Accordingly, the leaders should have the ability to take necessary emotionally intelligent steps in their way to success. This new species of emotionally intelligent leaders will re-engineer the ways the organizations work and manage change.

What is Emotional Intelligence?

Emotional Intelligence (EI) refers to the ability to recognize our own feelings and those of others, to motivate ourselves and to manage emotions well in ourselves and in our relationships. Salovey and Mayer (1990) defined EI in terms of being able to monitor and regulate our own feelings, and to use feelings to guide thought and action. EI does not really mean 'being nice.' On the other hand, it some times mean bluntly confronting someone with an uncomfortable but consequential truth they have been avoiding. Further, EI does not mean giving free rein to feelings - " Letting it all hang out." Rather if expressed appropriately and effectively, feelings enable people to work smoothly towards their common goal. Unlike IQ, EI changes over time; our level of EI is not fixed genetically, nor does it develop only in early childhood, it seems to be largely developed and continues to develop through out life.

Need for Emotional Intelligence "why it matters now"

More and more companies are realizing that enhancing EI skills is a vital component of any organization management philosophy. You do not compete with products alone anymore, but how well you use your human assets in change.

As business changes, so do the traits needed to excel. Past data relating to the talents of star performers over several decades, reveals that two abilities that mattered relatively little for success in the 1970's have become actually important today: team building and adapting to change. Entirely new capabilities have begun to appear as traits of successful people like change catalyst and leveraging diversity. New challenges and changes demand new qualities, skills and talents.

There are two levels of job competence, first level deals with the "threshold competencies", which people need in order to get the job done. These are the minimum skills needed to carry out the tasks associated with a given position. Second level deals with "distinguishing competencies", the competencies that set the star performance apart from the average. A study of star performance by Spencer Jr. at Hay/Mcbre (1993) includes competence studies at 286 organizations, two third in the U.S. and one third in the 20 other countries. Of the 21 competencies Spencer identified, all but three were purely cognitive competencies, two were intellectual; analytical skills and conceptual thinking. The third was technical expertise. This means that more than 80% of general competencies that are instrumental in the performance of star performers depend on EI, not on purely cognitive ability.

It is not that I.Q. & technical skills are not important, they do matter, but they are not the only thing. On the basis of these of these it can be said that Emotional competence is something that makes the 'star' a star.

Emotional Intelligence is the sine qua non of leadership

Goleman (1998) strongly asserted that EI is the sine qua non of leadership. Without, it a person can have the best training in the world, an incisive, analytical mind, and an endless supply of smart ideas, but he still will not make a great leader. Emotional competence is the nucleus of leadership, a role the essence of which is to get others to do work more effectively. Goldman went into the extent of saying that, "for star performers in all jobs, in every field, emotional competence is twice as important as purely cognitive abilities." For success at the highest levels, in leadership positions, emotional competence accounts for virtually the entire advantage. The author stressed on five key components of EI:

Self awareness, Self regulation, Motivation, Empathy and Social skill. Out of the above five competencies Self awareness, Self regulation, Motivation comes under personal competence i.e. 'how we manage ourselves.' Empathy and Social skill can be put under social competence i.e. 'how we handle relationships'.

Self awareness

The first component of EI, means 'know thyself' or having a deep understanding of one's emotions, strengths, weaknesses, needs and drives. Self awareness gives rise to three emotional competencies that are-

Emotional awareness: The recognition of how our emotions affect our performance and the ability to use our values

to guide decision making, in other words, recognizing one's emotions and their effects.

Accurate self assessment: A candid sense of our personal strengths and limits, a clear vision of where we need to improve, and the ability to learn from experience, in other words, knowing one's inner resources, abilities and limits.

Self confidence: The courage that comes from certainty about our capabilities, values and goals, in other words, a strong sense of one's self worth and capabilities.

Self regulation

It is that component of EI that frees us from being prisoners of our feelings. We can not do away with our feelings and emotions. But we can do much to manage them. People engaged in such a conversation undergo bad moods and emotional impulses just as everyone else does, but they find ways to control them and even to channel them in useful ways

Self regulation contains two skills- handling impulses and dealing with upsets, which are at the core of 5 emotional competencies that are-

Self Control: Managing disruptive emotions and impulses effectively i.e. keeping the disruptive emotions and impulses in check. This helps the people in staying composed, positive even in trying moments and also help in thinking clearly and stay focussed under pressure

Trustworthiness: It is displaying honesty and integrity, makes people act ethically and above approach, help in building trust through their reliability and authenticity, admitting their own mistakes and confront unethical actions in others, help in taking unpopular but tough and principled stand.

Conscientiousness: This means dependability and responsibility in fulfilling obligations and taking responsibility for personal performance. Conscientious people meet commitments and keep promises, hold themselves responsible for meeting their objectives, are organized and careful in their work.

Adaptability: It refers to being flexible in handling change and challenges. One of the most important competence in the time when the only constant is change is adaptability. People with adaptability smoothly handle multiple demands, shifting priorities and rapid change. They adapt their responses and tactics to fit dynamic circumstances and are flexible in how they perceive events.

Innovation: It refers to being open to novel ideas, approaches and new information. Innovative people seek out fresh ideas from a wide variety of sources, entertain original solutions to problems, generate new ideas, take a fresh perspective and are flexible in their thinking

The Self regulated people who are reasonable are able to create an environment that is based on trust and fairness. In such a kind of environment politics and infighting is greatly reduced and productivity is high. Talented people will join the organization and are tempted not to leave. It has a trickle down effect, fewer bad moods at the top means fewer throughout the organization.

Motivation

If there is any trait that is present in all the effective leaders, it is motivation; the emotional tendencies that guide or facilitate reaching goals. The three motivational competencies that every outstanding leader has are as follows-

Achievement drive: Striving to improve or meet a standard of excellence. People with this competence are result oriented, with a high drive to meet their objectives and standards, set challenging goals and take calculated risks, pursue information to reduce uncertainty and find ways to do better, and learn how to improve their performance.

Organizational commitment: Embracing the organization's or group's goals and visions. The people with this competence have congruence in their personal and organizational goals. These people readily make sacrifices to meet a larger organizational goal, find a sense of purpose in the larger mission, use the group's core values in decision making and clarifying choices, actively seek out opportunities to fulfill the group's missions.

Initiative and Optimism: Twin competencies that mobilize people to seize opportunities and allow them to take set backs and obstacles in stride. The people with these competencies are proactive and persistent. The people with initiative are ready to capture opportunities, pursue goals beyond what is required or expected of them, cut through red tape and bend the rules necessary to get the job done and mobilize others through unusual enterprise efforts.

An optimist leader persists in seeking goals despite obstacles and setbacks, operates from high hopes of success rather than fear of failure, and sees setbacks as due to manageable circumstances rather than a personal flaw.

Motivation is one of those components which contributes maximum to the performance of effective leaders as it helps in keeping people optimistic even when in dire straits. If the leader will set the performance bar high for himself, he will do the same for the organization. Leader with a relentless drive to surpass goals and an interest in keeping a score can be contagious. Such type of leaders can often build a team of managers around them with the same traits.

Empathy

Of all the dimensions of EI, Empathy is the most easily recognized. It represents the foundation skills for all the competencies important for work. In a broader sense, it means awareness of other's feelings, need and concerns. This includes a cluster of social competencies.

Understanding others: Sensing other people's feelings and perspective and taking an active interest in their concerns, people who understand others, are attentive to emotional cues and are good listeners, sensitive and understand other's perspective help out based on understanding the needs and feelings of other people.

Developing others: Sensing other's development needs and bolstering their abilities. People with this competence acknowledge and reward people's strengths and accomplishments, offer useful feedback and identify people's need for further growth, also acting as a mentor- give timely coaching and offer assignment that challenge and foster a person's skills.

Leveraging Diversity: Cultivating opportunity through different kinds of people. People with this competence respect and relate well to people from varied background, understand diverse world views and are sensitive to group differences, see diversity as an opportunity, and creating an environment where diverse people can thrive, challenge bias and tolerance.

Political Awareness: Relating social and political currents, politically aware people accurately read key power relationships, detect crucial social networks, understand the forces that shape the views and actions of clients, customers and competitors, and accurately read organizational and external realities.

The above cluster of social competencies make the leader more empathetic. It does not mean adopting other people's emotions as ones own and trying to please everybody. Rather empathy means thoughtfully considering employees' feelings - along with other factors in the process of making intelligent decisions. Empathy is particularly important today as a component for leadership for at least three reasons, the increasing use of teams, the rapid pace of globalization, and the growing need to retain talent. But empathy does not get much respect in business, people wonder how leaders can make hard, harsh decisions if they have a " feeling" for all the people who will be affected. But leaders with empathy do more than sympathize with people around them. They use their knowledge to improve their companies in subtle but important ways.

Social skill

Empathy and Social Skill are those components of EI that deal with managing relationships with others. Social skill is not as simple as it sounds, it is the essential sense of handling another person's emotions artfully. It does not mean friendliness rather, it is friendliness with a purpose; moving people in the direction you desire, whether that is agreement on a new marketing strategy or enthusiasm about a new product. Social skill comprises of several competencies are as follows-

Influence: Wielding effective tactics for persuasion. People with this competence are skilled at winning people over, fine tune presentations to appeal to the listener, use complex strategies like indirect influence to build consensus and support, orchestrate dramatic events to effectively make a point.

Communications: Sending clear, convincing messages and listening openly. People with this competence are effective in give and take, registering emotional cues in attuning their message, deal with difficult issues straight away, listen well, seek mutual understanding , and welcome sharing of information fully, foster open communication and stay receptive to bad news as well as good.

Conflict Management: It means negotiating and resolving disagreements. People with this competence handle difficult people and tense situations with diplomacy and tact, spot potential conflict bring disagreements into the open and help de-escalate them, encourage debate and open discussions, orchestrate win - win solutions.

Change Catalyst: It would help in initiating or managing change. People with this competence recognize the need for change and remove barriers, challenge status quo to acknowledge the need for change, champion the change and enlist others in this pursuit, and model the change expected of others.

Building Bonds: It refers to nurturing instrumental relationships. People with this competence cultivate and maintain extensive in formal networks, seek out relationships that are mutually beneficial, build rapport and keep others in the loop, make and maintain personal friendship among work associates.

Collaboration and Cooperation: This refers to working with others toward common shared goal. People with this competence balance a focus on task with attention to relationships, collaborate sharing plans, information and resources, promote a friendly cooperative climate, spot and nurture opportunities for collaboration.

Team Capabilities: This denotes creating synergy in working towards group goals. People with this competence model team qualities like respect helpfulness and cooperation, draw all member into active and enthusiastic participation, build team identity, espirit de corps and commitment, protect the group and its reputation and share credit.

Social skill is one of the most important components when compared with the other components of emotional intelligence. The major task of the leader is to get work done through other people, leaders need to manage relationships, no leader is an island and it is the social skill which makes that possible. Social skill allows leaders to put their emotional intelligence at work.

Making of an Emotionally Intelligent Leader

Having discussed the Emotional Competencies that make a leader, the issue at hand is how to build an Emotionally Intelligent leader. Whether the Emotionally Intelligent Leaders are born or made. There is a good news that EI can be learned. All emotional competencies can be cultivated with the right practice, unlike IQ, EI can improve through out life. As recent study by Reuven Bar On (1997), on growth of EI found small but steady and significant increases as people go from age group to age group with a peak occurring in the forties. There is an old fashioned word for this growth in emotional intelligence: maturity.

Emotional Intelligence, the deciding factor for success in leadership

While stressing upon EI, it is not meant that IQ, Cognitive ability, Technical Expertise are not important. They are important but that which differentiates the star from the average leader, is the mastery of these 'soft skills'. And it becomes even more important when we are facing such a turbulent time where change is ubiquitous.

The only answer to uncertainty, change because of continuous restructuring is the creation of Emotional Intelligent Leaders. Not a Leader, but many leaders. The most favorable leadership style for future organization would be when many people will play leadership roles because the process of change is complex and too difficult for a single leader to handle.

Some Essentialities/ Characteristics of Emotionally Intelligent Leaders in Change

Eats Change for breakfast & serve it up for every meal

The leader of future has to be very adaptive who will acts as a change catalyst with high levels of influence, commitment, motivation, initiative and optimism.

Remember that real assets go home at night

As Alfred P. Sloan said, "Take my assets but leave my organization and in five years I will have it all back." Neither machines nor bank accounts nor corporate policies will determine the success or failure of an effort to adapt to change, successful change depends on individual people and their collective actions. By showing trust and respect for all employees, manager can empower people to do the jobs to the very best of their ability.

Guts to say NO

They can say no firmly and definitively. They know when to be assertive. Can be tough if needed.

Omnipresent

Tom Peter(1994) unraveled the concept, 'leaders Manage by walking around' (MBWA). They interact with people down the ladder asking about their families and their personal matters, they want to be informed, creating an environment of openness where it is easy for every one to communicate.

Organization builder

Leader, as Peter M. Senge (1990) cites is the creator of 'a learning organization.' Leader acts as a designer, steward and teacher. He will create the organization in such a way where people will love to work. He will act as what Butler and Waldrop (1999), called 'job sculpting' to retain key people.

John Wayne is dead

John Wayne model of leadership does not work any more. The arrival of groups, teams, communities, partners, stakeholders on the business scene, announced the death of John Wayne. Leader of tomorrow will work in a team. He will 'lead by getting led', or what Senge (1990), called 'Team learning'.

Abundance Manager

The successful leaders are those who possess what Covey (1992), called abundance mentality. "It is a bone deep belief that there are enough natural and human resources to realize my dream and that my success does not necessarily mean failure for other, just as their success does not preclude my own."

Focus

The leader of tomorrow does not focus on problems but on opportunities, does not focus on short term goals but on long term goals, does not focus on circumstances but on purpose, does not focus on doubts but on trust.

Last Word

John Kotter (1990) cites the difference between "management and leadership." He says that 'management' refers to the way complex enterprises are kept orderly, nonchaotic and productive, 'leadership' by contrast refers to effectively handling the changes that the competitiveness and volatility of the time have wrought. He further adds, " Motivation and inspiration energize people, not by pushing them in the right direction as control mechanisms but by satisfying basic human needs for achievement, a sense of belonging, a feeling of control over ones life, the ability to live up to one's ideals. Such feelings touch us deeply and elicit a powerful response. So leadership of this kind, then is an emotional craft.

Even Covey (1992), puts it similarly that one should manage from left and lead from right. He is emphasizing on the research of brain theory. That although both the hemispheres are involved in logical and creative processes, the left works more with logic, right work more with emotions. He means that left is rational so manage with left, as right deals with emotions so lead with right. He again was emphasizing on emotional intelligent leadership.

Last but not the least, it can be said that recipe of success in today's world is not complete without emotionally intelligent leaders who are the answers to change, who will bring change, who will create change, who will catalyze change and who will change 'change'. These EI components which were once considered "nice to have" are the ingredients that leaders "should have" to survive in the future.

REFERENCES

Butler Timothy and Waldrop James (1999), "Job Sculpting", *Harvard Business Review*, Sep-Oct.

Covey Stephen.R (1992), "Principle Centered Leadership", New York: Fireside.

Goleman Daniel (1998), "What Makes A leader", *Harvard Business Review*, Nov-Dec.

Goleman Daniel (1998), *Emotional Intelligence At Work*, New York: Bantam.

Kotter John (1990), "What Leaders Really Do"; *Harvard Business Review*, May-Jun.

Peters Tom (1994) , "Pursuit of Wow", New York.

Reuven Bar-On (1997), "Bar On Emotional Quotient Inventory: Technical Manual" (Toronto: Multi-Health System)

Salovey Peter and Mayer John.D (1990), "Emotinal Intelligence", Imagination, Cognition and Personality.

Senge Peter. M (1990), The Fifth Discipline: *The Art and Practice of The Learning Organization*, New York: Currency.

Spencer Lyle. M. and Spencer Signe M (1993), *"Competencies At Work: Models For Superior Performance,* New York: John Wiley and Sons.

18

HRD STRATEGIES FOR CORPORATE RESTRUCTURING FOR THE 21ST CENTURY

*S.A.Mufeed**

Introduction

Just a few months ago the world entered into the 21st century, in developing countries like India we have to think about doing things differently, creatively and in an innovative way, if we wish to catapult ourselves to the forefront of the world economy. Today, as we stand in the year 2000 AD that beacons us with a challenge to continue the need for and paramount importance of human resource development (HRD), to furthering the human heritage and to make this world of ours a better place to live in. The year 2000 AD does not merely signify the end of a decade or even a century, but the end of a millennium and the beginning of a new one. It gives us vantage point where from we can scan the twentieth century and foresee the 21st century very carefully. We can learn from the past and prepare ourselves for the present as well as future HRD challenges and strategies for business.

If one looks at a micro level, it will be witnessed that 20th century has seen the rise and fall of many large corporations.

* Senior Lecturer, Department of Management Studies, University of Kashmir, Srinagar - 190006, J & K.

GM and Ford are no longer leaders in automobile industry; Toyota and Honda have surpassed their excellence. Kodak and Xerox have humbled by Fuji and Cannon in photographic arena. GE and Philips which one time leaders in the medical electronics, had to make way for Hitachi and Toshiba. The question arise, that can a organisation either MNC or a Indian business house hope to get an edge over its rivals? The answer is quality, which is being determined by the customer's satisfaction. Innovation in the market and a originality of service. Only one factor could provide all the three abilities i.e., knowledge. And its only source is human resource with potentialities and capabilities.

The approach to managing human resources in recent years has undergone a drastic and a revolutionary change. By the 1970s a shift in professional values was discernible with a focus on developmental status. During the period 1980s- 1990s professionals began to talk about new technologies and HRD challenges and strategies and the emphasis was on human values and productivity through people. In the Acknowledgement of the decadel changes there is a growing realisation that global competitiveness can be achieved not through the machines, money, material, science, best technologies and plants but by effectively motivating employees to perform at global standards. Presently, there is practically no government or international agency that does not see the importance of HRD. The World Bank, the United Nations and its constituent bodies including UNDP, UNIDO, WHO and ILO etc., all recognize the need for and the importance of HRD. Research indicates the HRD systems, instruments and strategies which they practice as being of strategic importance at a given point of time, for or given country or a group of countries: may vary, but the focus and emphasis in uniform (Rao, 1996)

HRD Strategies for Business

Every organisation has a vision, a mission and a strategy to fulfill a need, a purpose in society to survive, develop and grow.

The prescription for improving the goodness of fit between an individual, the organizations and the environment includes focus on the strategy of the organisation. Organizational survival and growth in the given environment need balance between functional strategies and Human Resource Planning. The lack of integration between human resource management and strategies business planning is a major cause of implementation failures. Very less research work in the Human Resource development strategy area has revolved the nature of links between corporate and Human Resource development strategy. HRD as a strategy is of very recent origin, basically it emerged in well run organizations to prepare people to meet business challenges.

Past research studies indicate that HRD is important in strategic management in two distinct ways, such as, a strategy formulations and strategy implementation. The elements for formulation of strategy are vision, mission, comparative advantage, goals and objectives shared values and action orientation(Toft, 1989). And also the participation of the top and senior management groups in the choice of a long term vision for the enterprise. According to Mary *et al* (1981), a strategic decision making process should be put into place to involve key Human Resource staff at many levels of the strategic decision making process so they understand and are committed to the Human Resource strategy. Another research study indicates that to encourage employee loyalty and commitment, organizations must share with employees information about goals, missions and strategies. They can then expect employees to be more self-reliant and take greater responsibility for their performance and career (William and Hermine, 1990). While as, the strategy implementation refers to the basic objectives of the enterprise which are achieved through proper execution by the organisation, and refers to the participation of top management in executing divisional strategy decisions, such as, changes in product market mix, pricing channels in make or buy, changes in technology, communication and conflict resolution and changes in employee relations, employees feed back and participation , values, HRD climate (Octapace culture) and HRD systems- sub systems and mechanism for workers and managerial development.

The fundamental strategic management problem is to keep the strategy and Human Resource dimension of the organisation in direct alignment. "There is a linkage of some kind between HR policy and practices and overall organizational strategic aims and the organizational environment" (Kapoor,1998 and Truss, *et al,* 1994). Thus it is apparent that Human Resource planning is an integral part of business planning which facilitates the personal function to link itself with the long term organizational strategy.

Research indicates that there are number of Human Resource management strategies currently receiving attention from leading business houses(Michael, et al, 1993 and Purchell and Bruce, 1994). A variety of links have been identified and it is possible to classify those inters of a 'reactive- proactive continuum'. Once the corporate strategy is se (independent of Human Resource input) Human Resource policies are implemented to aid in the delivery of the strategy. Human Resource strategic management is therefore, a stream of decisions, issues an options that leads to the development of an effective strategy to help to achieve strategic business objectives. An example of Human Resource strategic issues analysis model can be found in Figure 1.

Human Resource Development strategies should therefore contribute to winning employee commitment, promising values, culture of trust and openness, give the need to build a self disciplined work force and responsive organisation. To achieve HRD strategic values and challenges for the 21st century, it creates a need to give much emphasis on the specific HRD mechanisms which are linked to each other and are currently receiving a great deal of attention for organizational maturity. Therefore, the importance of HRD strategic issues linked to each other and to company's business goals need to be focused seriously. These HRD strategic issues, covering five component shall be discussed as follows:

Selection

For improving and retaining a strong talent base strategy, management must continue to ensure that the promotions and selections process for all levels will be impartial, reliable and accurately predictive and certainly more so in the 21st century. Motivating, attracting, managing and nurturing talent will be one of the most critical HRD strategic issue. This strong talent acquiring strategy will be the key differentiating factor, that we will have to grapple within the present century. Doing this company's must look at two important interlinked components, such as, a) first companies will have to create an organizational ambiance where talent can bloom. A corporate culture that cares for people and gives them room to grow will be a company's strongest magnet for attracting good people. Secondly, they have to put in place systems that help unleash their potential.

Performance Management

To ensure that organizations have attracted the talent with high performance and high potential, can help organizations to achieve employee commitment, loyalty and organizational goals, missions and strategies. Employers need performance-management system that allow employees to become more autonomous. HR professionals may want to institute performace"contracting"' ensuring that employees know what is expected of them and what standards will be used to evaluate their performance. Employees also need performance feedback systems that allow them to monitor their own performance.

Training and Development

The most widely felt HRD strategy need is training and development (T and D).

An intensive efforts in it generates constructive pressures towards other HRD strategies and mechanisms. The focus of T an D programs should be on behavioral aspects both at office as well as at home levels, career planning, continuing education and retraining. T and D will also have to concentrate upon the values, emotions and sentiments of people in order to confront the problems of interpersonal relationships rather than evade or escape problems. Such a focus will reduce the chances of skills obsolescence and will increase self- directed leadership, self motivated team work, self generated creativity, self confidence and an employees sense of autonomy.

Reward System

As we have seen above that with the first three phases of company's integrated HRD strategy focusing an acquiring and developing employees with the potentialities and capabilities to fulfill corporate objectives, a system of good setting, evaluation compensation is being used to directly link organizational objectives to individual performance. Reward- mechanism options are key to motivating talented employees. Instantaneous performance rewards, quarterly bonus and quality of life enhances will also become ways to recognize performance. By ensuring that individual rewards are available only if corporate goals are met, the HR strategy for business should work in a way to prevent people from expanding their energies on activities that bear no relationship to organizational objectives. Attention should also be paid to non-momentary rewards such as recognition and opportunities for growth.

Organizational Kick

No longer can employee now(irrespective of their status) hope for and companies afford to provide life long employment irrespective of the company's fortunes. Instead, it is the market that is becoming the only guarantor of employment. In fact, there are no two opinions about the fact that in the present competitive

Figure 1
Human resource Strategic Issue Analysis

market, employees will have to exceedingly perform well so as to retain the organizations position in the 21st century. And employees with low performance and low potential should be asked to improve their performance levels, in case if they fail to improve, planned separation process should be initiated without any delay.

Conclusion

In the preceding paragraphs, an attempt has been made to outline some of the characteristics of HRD strategies for business. These business strategic implementation issues, which though may not be as new to the west as it is to India, will change the entire complex of our age old traditions of managing people in this 21st century. In any business strategy, people are more crucial than plans. HR strategy implementation, is therefore, possible only, when HR professionals shall be able to attract the best talent, motivate people to work, to implement satisfactory compensation reward packages, to introduce effective and result oriented career planning and be able to implement satisfactory managerial and worker exit practices. To sum up, on the strategic Human Resource side, the key issue is to determine the kind of people needed to run the business in the long term, choosing the specific policies and programs for the long term development of Human Resource for the 21st century. Moreover, HR professionals must become strategic business partners and employees must more actively manage themselves.

REFERENCES

Kapoor, B.M.(1998) "Globalisation of the Indian Corporate Sector-Requirements of Human Resource Development," *JIMS,* Jan-March.

Mary Anne, Charls F and Noel Tichy(1981), "Human Resource Management: A Strategic Perspective", *Organizational Dynamics*, Winter.

Michael, J.M. and Dean W. Engle(1993),*"Global Human Resource*

Development" Enlwod Cliffs, Prentice Hall.

Purchel J and Bruce (1994), *Human Resource Management in the Multi-divisional Company"*, Oxford University Press.

Rao, T.V.(1996), *Human Resource Development Experiences Interventions*" Sage Publication, New Delhi.

Toft, Graham, S. (1989) "Synoptic Approaches to Strategic Management", *Hand Book of Strategic Management,* Marcal Dekkar *INC,* New York.

Truss, Catherise and Gratton, Lynda(1994), "Strategic Human Resource Management-A Conceptual Approach", *The International Journal of Human Resource Management,* Vol. 5, No 3.

William H. Wagel and Hemine Z (1990), HR' 90: Challenges and Opportunities," *Personnel,* June, Vol.6.

19

ORGANIZATIONAL RESTRUCTURING: A CHALLENGE FOR HR PROFESSIONALS

Mukesh Dhunna & Ajay K. Rajan**

The triumvirate of liberalization, globalization and competition has changed the rules of the game for corporate India. In view of the unprecedented challenges posed by economic turbulence, emerging new world order, shifting in workplace paradigm and global competition, there is a continuous refixation of 'milestones' in the business organizations in respect of higher quality of products, new technology, productivity, innovation, cost digression and several such parameters. All this is happening at a much faster pace than before. "Teaching an elephant to tap dance" is what most Indian organizations are aspiring today. This requires shedding the unnecessary flab that has accumulated during the past years and concentrating on doing those things that it does best by changing the alignment of its critical parameters and functions (Ghosh *et al.,* 1995). In other words, business organizations, in a bid to survive and grow in the present turbulent environment, change their shell through corporate restructuring. Hardly a week goes by without one or two instances of one corporation purchasing another, two corporations joining forces, or companies undergoing massive reorganizations either by cutting

* Both the authors are Reader at the Institute of Management Studies & Research, M.D University, Rohtak (Haryana).

layers of hierarchy and restructuring the work forces or by gaining economies through combining efforts. Corporations across the world see in restructuring the cure for all ailment and it is being viewed as an unavoidable and inevitable part of doing business. Restructuring is a process of realignment and redeployment of company's resources which is akin to reawakening and rebirth of the organization. It means taking a realistic look at one's company and deciding to reshape it partly or completely to remain competitive.

Nature of Restructuring

Corporations restructure to gain strategic, financial and operational leverages (Monga,1997). Mainly three types of restructuring are usually undertaken:

Portfolio restructuring - It involves responding to market needs by concentrating on its core competencies, through effective configurations of task to achieve synergy, acquisition of synergical firms and divestiture of peripheral activities.

Financial restructuring - It aims at achieving better return on investment; reduce takeover threats, innovate financial instruments, explore global financial resources and absorb volatility in the capital markets.

Organizational Restructuring - It is designed to increase the efficiency and effectiveness of personnel through significant changes in the organizational structure. It involves delayering, downsizing, realignment of business units etc.

Though each type of restructuring has its own utility which complements each other, the business organizations in India have shown maximum lee-way to initiate organizational restructuring as compared to the other forms of restructuring. Corporations undertake organizational restructuring exercise more easily and frequently as the cost involved is lower and it can be carried out in incremental steps, unlike the other form of restructuring which call for a quantum and expensive leap.

Organizational restructuring in its true sense, needs to put the people into their new roles, which would impose new responsibilities and relationship on them, forcing new attitudes and behaviours to emerge as 'organization people' (Sarangdher,1995). It enables the firm to become strong enough to face competition and ensures the composition of an educated work force that is compatible with new environment. Organizational restructuring is not a new phenomenon, it has been a part of industrial climate for decades (Chandler,1962), it is the pace and volume that is expotenential today. Speed is the essence of restructuring now. Either the company be quick to restructure itself or cease to exist.

To weed out the in-built skilled incompetence in their systems, and to gain superior efficiency, effectiveness and structural fit, the corporations may resort to organizational restructuring in following manner:

1. Divisionalising the organization by creating strategic business units to better implement the corporate strategy.
2. DelayeringÄ It is aimed not at eliminating but reclassifying or regrouping jobs to reduce decision making levels to respond faster to customer.
3. Rationalizing pay structure considering increased job responsibilities and complexities.
4. Downsizing and right sizing of organization.
5. Better HR practices —Flexible control structure, Transparent and development oriented performance appraisal, Team building & shift towards younger work force.
6. Changing work profile—Relook at individual job responsibility
7. Training and redeployment—Unlearn old technology, learn new one, rearrangement of human resources.

HR Implications of Organisational Restructuring

Organizational restructuring generates favourable response among business leaders and HR professional as it helps in formation of result oriented team, extracting faster response, instill high degree of empowerment and catalyze the attainment of quality system in easier, economical and convenient manner, as attested by a recent survey (Personnel, 1994) in which HR professional ranked organizational restructuring as the second most important issue for the 1990s (behind health care only). However, the non-economical cost of such restructuring is the highest as it changes the essential fabric of the firm i.e. its culture, which have wide ranging repercussions.

The process of restructuring a corporation is likely to be perceived by many people to unfairly rattle the status quo. It can lead to change in individual's organization status and prospects leading to direct materialistic, social and psychological implications. It may also lead to retrenchment (at least in the short run), disruption in the organizational design which may create an environment of fear, mistrust and discontent and also create a feeling of sense of void among employees. Employees are left wondering what, if any, role they will play in the 'new organization' resulting into decrease of loyalty quotient to the organization. Employees are likely to face following threats as a result of organizational restructuring:

- Loss of job, pay and benefits
- Change in job—new roles and assignment
- Transfer to new job and/or geographical location
- Change in compensation and benefit package
- Change in career possibilities
- Change in employees organizational power, status and prestige
- Staff changes—new colleagues, bosses and subordinates
- Change in corporate culture and work climate

Executives and consultants responsible for restructuring the organization have shown creative expertise in conceptualizing, formulating and implementing the restructuring plan, but unfortunately they have not exhibited corresponding creativity and expertise in understanding and dealing with psychological trauma that the employees have to face in restructuring process. Continued failure to do so will likely to undermine the success of structural adjustment exercises. While working in the organization, employees attach themselves to their jobs, co-workers, work routines, work locales, the application of personal skills and career goals (Schweiger *et al.,* 1987). When they get affected by the organizational restructuring programme, many of them experience a powerful sense of loss as the strong attachments are destroyed or changed. This sense of loss may be manifested into shock, anger, depression, frustration, helplessness, which may result in to the problems of absenteeism, indiscipline, insubordination and turnover, if employees are not provided with psychological protection and suitable counseling. Are our HR professionals prepared to deal with these organizational behavioural problems the employees may experience in anticipation of, during and after the culmination of restructuring programme? Recent strikes in power sectors in UP, supported by employees associations all over the country, postal strike, strike in insurance sector attest the fact that there has been little preplanning for HR issues on the part of top management.

Tasks Ahead of HR Professionals

Restructuring is inevitable in the present era of uncertainty. To bar restructuring will mean making the organization stagnant, sick and putting it out of race. Corporations have two options before them - either to reorganize or restructure or perish. Hence, there is no use to swim against the current. But no restructuring programme is likely to serve its purpose, if appropriate measures are not taken to handle the human resource issues emphatically. Caught up in uncertainty and ambiguity about future, top management may be preoccupied with their own situations, hence, unable to pay enough attention and time to employee concerns. HR professionals can not only act as buffer between top management and employees but also can exercise greater influence on employees behaviour in such case. Therefore, the importance of HR professionals as enabling force to achieve excellence is increasingly being recognized in corporate circles. The challenge before the HR professionals, nowadays, is to help organization initiate and implement restructuring programme without tears in the eyes and fear and suspicion in the minds of employees and thus preparing them to take assignment as a part of restructuring programme.

Following tasks may be undertaken by HR professionals to achieve the desired results:

1. Emphatic listening to employees concerns

Most often, all that the HR managers need to do is just provide opportunity to subordinates to let vent some of their anger and frustration. This will serve as an excellent catharsis. We open our heart to a person whom we trust and feel listen our problems sincerely. HR professional should instill such confidence among the employees. As a result, the employee-manager relationship will be strengthened; fears, anxiety, anger and misconception can be circumvented and employees emerge with an increased sense of self-esteem and worth, ready to take up any challenge with courage and conviction.

2. Handling Outplacement with dignity

Decision to downsize the organization should be taken with great care and caution. The strategy to downsize the organization i.e. reducing head count to make organization leaner to improve its competitiveness, can make sound sense but only in short run. Right sizing, rather than downsizing, would be an appropriate strategy, because downsizing can make organization thinner not necessarily fitter. Employees are scared of organizational restructuring mainly because of prospective downsizing, which they consider the basic outcome of restructuring. There is little doubt that the employee morale and commitment is greatly affected by the radical lay offs and retrenchment. Employees who are not privy to decisions that underlie the restructuring, may bear the burnt of radical cuts in work force.

HR professionals can do a yeoman service by easing out the pains of employees associated with retrenchment. Outplacement services can be provided to the outgoing employees and thus they can be helped to find another jobs. How people are let go have significant impact on those who stay in the organization.

3. Personal Counseling

Personal counseling may be the appropriate strategy in diffusing and eliminating the fear of unknown that may arise due to organizational restructuring. Employees must be helped to understand the acute necessity of organizational restructuring and share with them what consequences could have followed to the industry, organizations and subsequently to the employees, if it were not for organizational restructuring. They must be helped to understand the nature and shape of new business deal, its genesis, prognosis and implications. Personal counseling should also be aimed at gradually inculcating the new management philosophy, work ethos and practices after discussing its connotation from the angle of employees, business and customer.

4. Proper Communication

To prevent rumour mongering and unavoidable apprehensions on several sensitive issues, a deliberate communications programme need to be developed. In view of organizational restructuring, there is a lot of anxiety among the employees and they have queries in the form of how are departments going to be absorbed or how is the manpower going to be developed etc. (Kaura, 1997). Employees want accurate and honest information so that they can plan for their future and make personal and career decisions. HR professional can be called upon to encourage and generate a healthy debate over vexed issues, initiated with the help of well thought out campaigns, meetings, specially designed workshops and open house meeting by involving all those key functionaries who have the responsibility of implementing the change. Enable people to find practical and pragmatic solutions.

It has been observed that, the employees often resist more out of unfounded fear, uncertainty and possible redundancy, which they visualize, the organizational restructuring may bring (Nandakumar, 1995). HR professionals, therefore, are required to increase interaction/communication with people down the line to instill in them a feeling of security amidst such changes. They must also ensure that all the line managers are in a position to serve as effective communicators who are capable of ascertaining the validity of information and, there after allowing the information to percolate downwards, unfiltered.

5. Career Planning

HR professionals can play an important role in providing the employees of integrated organization better growth and development prospects and thus help in employee retention and bring about a more motivated work environment. They must map the career paths emerging in the post-organizational restructuring scenario for different categories of employees and get them plotted on different new assignments that enhances their professional development.

Many times employees may not be in a position to prioritize career moves in the organization for want of information particularly during the phase when restructuring programme is going on, and employees are perceiving job insecurity consequently. HR professionals will then have to resort to a lot of convincing, personal cum career counseling so as to ensure employee retention. In post restructuring period, the essence of career planning, is prompt identification of available talent and creation for them of a new vision for their career (Mc Cann & Gilky , 1988).

6. Revamping Training and Development System

For sustaining and reaping the benefits of organizational restructuring, for removing the resistance to change, for removing the fears and myths and apprehensions of employees that arise due to organizational restructuring and for upgrading the skills of employees, the training and development system needs to be revamped. Malia et. al (1995) advocate for the creation of a 'Learning Organization', where employees themselves perceive the need for upgradation of their knowledge and skills resulting in increased training effectiveness.

A mental shift from job security to employment security and increasing the employability of employees should be cardinal purpose of training and development programme. Employees must be encouraged to undertake retraining and accept reallocation of job wholeheartedly. Adequate training and development activities can certainly help the organization in smooth transition from the old business practice toward new systems, policy and procedures emerged as a result of restructuring efforts.

7. Total Employee Involvement

To make organizational restructuring successful, it is important to make effort towards employee involvement. Employee involvement must be supported by training as regards skills as well as mind set. HR people must advise the Management to pursue inclusion strategy by including more and more people into organizational restructuring process. Organizational restructuring cannot deliver result themselves if people at large are not contributing to it. Hence, the needs and wants of employees have to be considered first for getting them involved in organizational restructuring process.

A total employee involvement system must be developed in order to tap the full potential of employees, because total employee involvement will help the company realize the following benefits:

A Complete coordination in the team functioning at departmental and inter-departmental levels.

B. A wider acceptability of decisions and faster implementation of the same.

C. Emergence of a participative work culture throughout the organization with increased sense of commitment of the employees.

Conclusion

Restructuring has become imminent for every organization in this era of economic uncertainty if it wants to become a business enterprise to reckon with. For real revitalization of an organization, it is critical that restructuring is driven by a sound, logical and well thought out strategy. No sensible restructuring strategy can afford to undermine the importance of human resources. People support gained through effective HRM policies and practices is the only answer to ensure organizational restructuring programme deliver results and meet the challenges of uncertain future successfully.

REFERENCES

1. Gokhale, Chetan., Kulkarni, V.D. and Agarwal, M.G., "Corporate Restructuring — Case Study of Siemens Ltd., Nasik," *Restructuring to Change*, Excel Books, New Delhi, 1995.

2. Kaura, Anupam. "Mergers and Acquisitions in India: Implications for Human Resource Management Strategy," *South Asian Journal of Management,* Jan-March, 1997.

3. Malia, B.S., Ranjan, Sunil and Pudi, S.K. "Corporate Restructuring - A case Study of JCT Electronics Ltd.", *Restructuring to Change,* Excel Books, New Delhi, 1995.

4. McCann, J.E. and Gilky R. *Joining Forces: Creating and Managing Successful Mergers and Acquisitions*, Prentice Hall, New Jersy, 1980.

5. Monga, M.L., "Corporate Restructuring: The Search for a fit by Indian Organizations", *South Asian Journal of Management*, Jan-Mar, 1997.

6. "Most Important HR Issues for the '90s", *Personnel Journal*, Match, 1994, p.12.

7. Nandakumar, D.V. "Human Resource Management in Organizational restructurings," *Indian Management*, Vol. 34 No.1, Feb. 1995.

8. Sarangdhar,V.V.; Pednekar, M; and Rajappan, Prasad, "Corporate Restructuring—A Case Study of Mahindra & Mahindra Ltd., Bombay," *Restructuring to Change*, Excel Books, New Delhi, 1995.

9. Schweigar, D.M., Ivancevich, John M, and Power, Frank. R., "Executive Actions for Managing Human Resources Before and After Acquisition," *Academy of Management Executive*, Vol. 1(2), 1987.

20

TOTAL-EMPLOYEE-INVOLVEMENT & TRANSFORMATIONAL-LEADERSHIP-DRIVEN-MANAGEMENT—TOOLS FOR CORPORATE RESTRUCTURING

*Urvashi Makkar**

For long in the past, corporates performed in a stable and predictable environment. However, few organisations today can treat change as an occasional disturbance. Every organisation today faces a world of constant change. Several factors, both external and internal act as triggers of change in organisation. Interestingly, organisations, which practically initiate changes in Technology, Marketing or any other dimensions of business faster than their competition are found to be successful.

The challenges facing India in this millennium are undoubtedly complex. Will the future of the global corporation belong to India? How many Indian corporates will feature in the FORTUNE 500 in this century? A tough question, but largely it will depend on the speed and efficiency with which Indian corporates adapt to the changing scenario. The future belongs to those who are able to crystal gaze into it.

This century will see the emergence of the major trend in which corporation will be an extended leadership team and be

* Faculty Member, M.A., Institute of Management of Technology, Jagadhri (Haryana).

"leadership-driven", because management is not enough any more.

Internal Restructuring

In the not-so-distant part, the business environment was relatively uncomplicated. Today, however, companies find themselves at the beginning of a period of radical change. Companies have already been forced to rethink their business models. Indian companies will be subject to intense competition this millennium.

Those companies that survive and succeed in this millennium will possess the capability to change whenever, necessary. In the words of K. V. Kamath, CEO ICICI, "In new millennium only people – management driven companies can survive. And millennial managers will have to be a leader who is responsive to the needs of the entire organisation". It calls for an attitudinal change in the organisation & internal restructuring is basically revaluation of the assets of our organisation & I want to strongly emphasise Human Resources in the present context.

"Expertise in the Human Resources area" has been ranked as second in importance, next only to "expertise in strategy formulation " Clearly the competitive advantages of an organisation in global economy depends primarily upon how well its Human Resources are managed. Undoubtedly the financial, technological and other material resources are also critical to the organisation success. But it is the people's industriousness, talents, creativity and above all commitment and involvement that generate and effectively deploy these resources.

Internal Restructuring, which is a form of change, does not only mean improved profits and turnover but mainly a transformation, which depends upon two major factors namely —

Total Employee - Involvement

Transformational–Leadership–Driven Management.

This trend will be the revolutionary overhaul of the old concept of Personal Management and a leap into much wider canvas of Human Resource Management, generating **Employee – Involvement** as an integral part of strategic planning.

Total - Employee - Involvement

There is an urgent need to broaden our perspective about Human Resources. In order to maintain the organisational setup which is seen as advantageous, a number of HR initiatives in the area of organisational restructuring have to be undertaken. One of the most important initiatives is to create Employee - Involvement & Commitment. The various issues which must be focused for creating **Total - Employee - Involvement** are:

- Recognition Of Employee Contribution.
- Wholesome Development
- Empowerment
- Participation

Recognition of Employee Contribution

Larsen & Toubro Ltd. is a Public Ltd. company with a turnover of around RS 5400 crores and assets of around RS 5090 crores in which recognition of the employee contribution is considered integral part of the HR - strategies.

Performance - Based - Reward - System is functional which gives boost to the Employees Morale and Motivation levels. Moreover, **Achievement – Motivation,** in which accomplishment is important for its own sake, not for the rewards that accompany it, must be provided to the employees.

Wholesome Development

Wholesome Development happens when the material and spiritual aspects of life are seen as one unitary process, all moving in the direction of evolving people towards total well - being.

The concepts like Total Quality Management, Customer

Orientation, Continuos Improvement etc are different facets of the same basic process of the Wholesome Development. But the question arises, who to generate Wholesome Development in our employees? The answer lies in the **OCTAPACE** value system provided by Prof. T.V Roa. The acronym, which stands for Openness, Collaboration & Teamwork, Trust, Authenticity, Proaction, Autonomy, Confrontation & Experimentation, has become more relevant than before.

An **OCTAPACE** culture needs to be developed in an organisation to achieve Holistic Development. Openness brings new ideas, approaches, skills & talents. Openness combined with proactivity encourages self-expression and the way for growth. Collaboration and Teamwork provide the strength to organisation to perform. The **"WE" feeling** created serves many purposes and ultimate resultant is **Total-Employee-Involvement** and Commitment.

Empowerment

In our Indian scenario, most work organisations have a number of employees who believe that they are dependent on others and their own efforts will have little impact on performance. This powerlessness contributes to frustrating experience of low self-efficacy. **Self-efficacy** is the conviction among people that they can successfully perform their jobs and make meaningful contributions. Now, practical examples have proved the fact that self-efficacy levels can be raised by empowerment of the employees. **Empowerment** is the process of identifying and removing the conditions that cause powerlessness and enhancing feelings of self-efficacy.

To generate maximum levels of employee involvement, empowerment is an important tool. The two - step process has to be followed to generate Empowerment -

- Removing conditions of powerlessness (by giving proper training, encouragement & verbal feedback designed to raise self-confidence)

- Enhancing Self-efficacy (by giving emotional support & positive reinforcement)

When, these two approaches are followed honestly, employees begin believing that they are competent and valuable. In effect, their efforts result in great performances.

Participation

Participation is the mental and emotional involvement of persons in group situations that encourage them to contribute to group goals and share responsibilities for them. Without participation of employees, no organisation can survive in this millenium. Hindustan Lever LTD's CEO K.K.Dadiseth, who is being called as PEOPLOCRAT, went to the extent saying-that a persons entire **"SELF"** is involved, not just one's skill. A person who participates is "ego-involved" instead of merely "task involved". Ultimately, participation results in providing opportunities for people to create organisational spaces for themselves and make an impact in their own ways in each of the job they perform.

Transformational-Leadership–Driven-Management

The second initiative, which needs to be taken by the organisations, is to realise the highlighting role of Transformational Leadership-Driven-Management.

Developing "Transformational Leadership" as an integral part for forming an 'Enlightened Team of highly motivated employees' is must for introducing any type of restructuring activity.

Transformational leaders are the managers who initiate bold strategic changes to position the organisation for its future. They articulate a vision and sell it vigorously. They attempt to create learning individuals and organisations that will be better prepared for the unknown challenges that lie ahead.

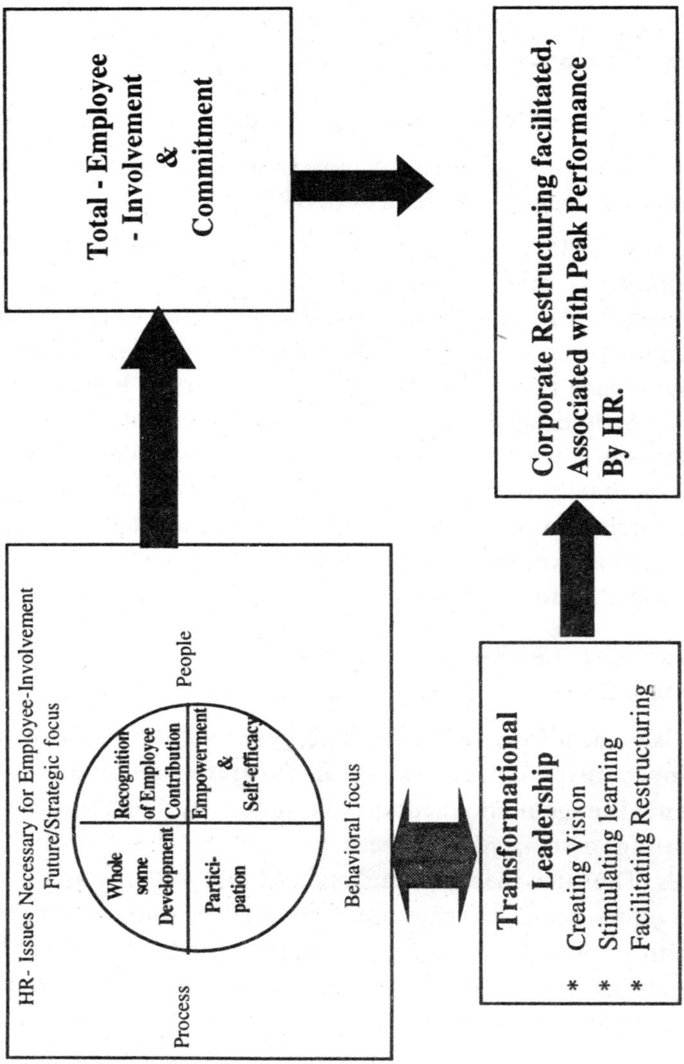

"MODEL FOR INTERNAL RESTRUCTURING"

Thus, Transformational- Leaders play key role in initiating & implementing change successfully. So for success implementation of corporate restructuring, **Transformational-Leadership-Driven Management** is an essential pre-requisite.

A Model For Internal Restructuring

How can we proceed for internal restructuring of an organisation keeping our focus on HR?

How can HRM practices can be tailored to generate **Total – Employee - Involvement** & commitment. on part of our employees.? How can **Transformational Leadership Driven Management** create marvels in an organisation? An attempt has been made to develop a **Model For Internal Restructuring**, in which leadership and employee involvement are the important tools. It would not be surprising if the managers find these questions to be perplexing. It is only in the last two decades that the researches in the Industrial and Organisational Psychology have begun to explore the influence of the employee involvement and leadership to generate quality and excellence.

(Please see Model for Internal Restructuring given on page 257.

It is evident from the model that these two factors i.e. **Total Employee Involvement** and **Transformational Leadership Driven Management**, facilitate the process of corporate restructuring, associated with peak performance by Human Resources. Thus this model if implemented true to the words , can create effervescent changes and Corporate restructuring in the competitive world will not be a distant dream. Moreover the corporations will be ready to face challenges with courage, conviction and innovativeness.

REFERENCES

Business-Led HR Strategies, AIMA, Excel Books

Organisational Behavior, Davis, Keith; Newstrom, John W.; Tata McGraw Hill .

Organisational Behaviour, Robbins, P. Stephen, PHI.

The Essence of Human Resource Management, Essence of Management Series, PHI.

The Essence of OB, Essence of Management Series, PHI.

HRD, In the New Economic Environment, Tata McGraw, Hill.

21

ORGANISATIONAL RESTRUCTURING IN INDIAN STEEL INDUSTRY

*R.P. Das**

There is a general consensus today that at the start of the new millennium, the management of business enterprises in India is on the threshold of major transformation. The liberalization and globalization of businesses, the emergence of common currencies, the integration of financial markets and information revolution together have put a lot of challenges to each and every sector of our economy. Rahul Bajaj (2000) points out that "globalization comes with responsibilities .it calls for better management of multi-cultural environment, faster response to change ,and subscription to globally accepted standards of quality and price." Infact Indian industries in general are seem to be working hard, and are undergoing transformation to be globally competitive .It has become a matter of their survival .To meet the challenges, Indian corporates have been restructuring post haste in the past one year in order to become globally competitive (Sengupta, 2000). According to Sunderajan (2000) , to thrive in the new millennium, organisation will need be designed to meet the challenges.

* Reader in Management, Pt. J.L.N. Institute of Business Management, Vikram Unviersity, Ujjain (M.P.).

Organisational Restructuring Defined

In deed ,organisational restructuring is one of the forms of the corporate restructuring. Usually it is understood as the mechanism to match organisation's structure with strategy .According to Sundreajan (2000), historically organisational design meant organisational structure and today it means the alignment of structure ,management processes, information system, reward system and people. Professor Dwivedi (1998) observed that in general , organisational structures are moving towards a delayering or flattend system. Bowman et al (1999) observed "recent organisational restructuring has included the redrawing of divisional boundaries ,flattening of hierarchic levels, spreading spa s of control ,reducing product diversification ,revising compensation, steamlining process and reforming governance. Downsizing of employee ranks is often a by product of such restructuring efforts, though in some instances it has been defined as an end itself ." According to Arun Maira (2000) the chairman of the Boston Consultancy Group (India) the organisation form that is now required must possess the flexibility to change easily as the environment changes in unexpected ways .It must operate even more effectively." Thus, from the above ideas, the objectives of organisational restructuring can be well imagined.

Objectives of Organisation AL Restructuring

As organisational restructuring strategy itself is quite broad ,therefore ,objectives of organisational restructuring are many. Companies go for organisational restructuring to make them flexible enough to keep pace with the changes in the environment. This strategy is adopted to design the companies that are sufficiently decentralised to encourage innovation in all their parts ,and sufficiently centralised or coordinated to adopt best practices quickly. Here it is intended to make a company innovative and efficient which necessitate to use a new and different approach for organising people and the work . Mr. S. Sundarajen (2000) the Chairman and Managing Director of Bharat Petroleum Corporation emphasized that while the hard aspects of organising people must be combined with the soft aspects: values .visioning, new ways of thinking ,and new means of influencing behaviour. Bowman et. al. (1999) pointed out that normally management of organisations go for organisational restructuring to provide greater satisfaction, reduce turnover increased efficiency and better communication. According to Bowman *et al.* among the leading nationals for organisational restructuring are preparations for expansion in to new market or product lines, actions to improve decision making or operational efficiencies, and steps to reduce operating costs. Likewise, Dwivedi (1998) observed that the objective is to speed up decision making and provide adequate freedom to work. In a recent article Sengupta (2000) pointed out that many companies in restructuring process are going for drastic downsizing to bring down labour costs as well as operating cost.

Inking performance with pay is helping them to cut down middle level management. Many are also offering VRS to trimdom the labour force and concentrate on core competencies. As the competition is everywhere in every industry the present article is written on Indian and Steel industry.

Indian Iron and Steel Industry—A Brief Profile

Steel to Pandit Jawaharlal Nehru was a symbol of the economy and a portent of the glory of India of the future. In India, there are some richest iron ore mines with the highest iron content. At one point of time, the cost of production of steel was the lowest in the world. The industry which is both in public and private sector employes 2.5 lakh workers. Now India is only 15th in the world ranking of steel producers. From 1.5 million tonnes of crude steel in 1950-51, in 1996-97, nearly 24 million tonnes of crude steel was produced in our country. During the same period , the production of finished steel rose from 1 million to nearly 23 million tonnes. An important feature of Indian iron and steel industry is its self reliance now in research, design and development. Even now we are in a position to set up new steel plants without depending on foreign countries. However in recent years she industry is facing stiff competition due to liberalisation of import-export of steel materials and abolition of price and distribution controls and successive reduction of import duties on iron and steel products. As a result, in addition to external factors, steel is one of the six crore sectors in the country facing problems like heavy expenditure on social over Heads, poor labour relations and underutilisation of capacity. Therefore, the organisations both in private and public sectors are carrying out various forms of corporate restructuring in order to overcome the current crisis and cope with the challenges of competition.

One the above backdrop, presents the pictures of restructuring in selected Indian steel industry.

Organisational Restructuring: Case of SAIL

One of the largest public sectors companies THE STEEL AUTHORITY OF INDIA (SAIL) was created in 1974. It is the third largest Steel maker in the world and Country's largest Steel producer. In the last decade, many things have happened for which this Rs. 16403 crore company is now not worth it's weight in steel. Mr. V. Krishnamurthy converted the sick giant into a profit -making undertaking.

Concerted efforts made by Mr. Krihnamurthy to accomplish goal clarity, teamwork and evolve product mix, marketing strategy and systems and followed a change-centered leadership approach.

Because of customer orientation of SAIL by Mr. M.R.R Nair during his tenure as chairman, quality emerged as a key factor. Mr. Nair made a most challenging form of restructuring; redesigned the collective mind set of it's 1.9 lakh employees. According to Mr. Nair "we are making fundamental changes in our ways of doing business.

And these changes are all about the culture of coping with change" *(Business Today,* 7-21, 1994, p.162).

- Earlier SAIL modernized it's manufacturing plant and was expected to be better placed than other PSUs to face competition.
- Efforts were made to change organizational culture by workers involvement programs, establishing work discipline.
- Rs.15000 crore modernization program with the message that machine alone cannot do the job, so people involvement is essential.
- Under a retraining program, the surplus manpower was proposed to be used for construction work and retrained for new process, which motivated workers to support organizational changes.
- 1987-88 captive power plants were commissioned at Rourkela and Durgapur.
- SAIL modernized in Durgapur plant and modernization programs of Bokaro and Rourkela steel plant is still on.
- During Krishnamurthy's tenure, a memorandum of understanding with Government was signed to secue autonomy and freedom from usual interference from administrative ministry.
- Marketing department change its philosophy to manage the change from seller's to buyer's market.

In order to promote human resource development programme, SAIL established a training institute at Ranchi to develop organizational cultural, full time faculty member increased from 6 to 16 and the staff was extended to its line manager.

SAIL has identified 650 key customer from among a total of 5000 and by moving from the concept of all customers equal. Out of these 650 customers, those that can order 1000 tonnes per months are high stake customer and medium stake customer are one who can order 500 tonnes per month. One senior executive of the marketing department is attached to high stake customer and three medium stake customer are to looked after by one middle level executive SAIL has invested Rs.700 crore over the last one decade in modernizing its stock yard, which is better than that of TISCO. Thus all these strategic efforts in the last one and a half decade have made SAIL a Rs. 1500 crore, exporting to 70 countries with its 500 special grade Steel. While it has plans to double its crude Steel production by 2005 and to export 3.5 million tones saleable steel, but the entry of private sector into steel business and more liberal policy of the government to import steel, the company has been facing hardship from last two year. By March 31st, 1994, SAIL'S titak borrowings stood Rs. 16403 crore and one time the company was to resort to barter system by asking its debtor to accept steel in likely of cash to discharges its obligation. The company registered a net loss of Rs. 1574 crore during last fiscal Year 1998-99 which may exceed Rs 2000 crore in the current Year. Very recently the Government of India has initiated some measures to over come the current crisis. Some of the organisation restructuring measures are:

- Government has permitted SAIL to take a minority stake in a joint venture with any strategic partner for the revival of the ailing IISCO *(Hindustan Times*, Feb 16th, 2000, P-13)

- Selling of various power plants at Rourkela, Bokaro, Durgapur, Bokaro, Durgapur, Bhilai of the company installed at different sites, as power generation is not a core activities of SAIL.

- The company also intends to hive off an oxygen steel of bhilai and a fertilizer unit into a joint venture.

There is also proposal to hive off VISL Alloy and Salem Steel *(Hindustan Times*, Feb. 25th, 2000. P-7) Through there is no encouraging response but SAIL intend to shed 10000 employee under VRS-99 with eligibility criteria in its corporate restructuring exercise. It needs to reduce its employee to 100000 over the next Five year in order to increase its competitiveness. (*Hindustan Times*, Feb. 16th, p-13)

Organisational Restructuring: Case of TISCO

Tisco one of the largest and oldest iron and steel company in the county in private sectors was founded by JRD tata is existing in Jamshedpur, Bihar. The company holds 15% market share in the steel industries. TISCO has established its credibility being the best in class in terms of quality and reliability. The cons of one tone of hot metal in TISCO Is Rs. 6000 against the global average of Rs. 7200 to Rs.8000 pe tonne. Every thihg is not rosy in this old outstanding company in the recent years. As a result, the company has adopted the following strategic moves:

The company hired Anderson consulting to execute project top gear, a comprehensive exercise aimed at reducing production cost, improving quality and building a seamless organisation.

- The modernisation programme carried out in TISCE to make its operating parameters comparable to the best in the world. The company has increased production of high value flat products, which are in great demand.
- In order to overcome the problem of transportation cost TISCO is setting up a mega plant in Gopalpur Orissa.
- TISCO is bench marking itself not against SAIL or other domestic producer but POSCO the 25 million tones South Korean giant.
- In its restructuring of efforts, TISCO solds its cement division to French construction giant lafarge, to use part of its proceed to buy sister company TATA SSL'S cold rolling division (*Business World*, Feb. 7,1999, p-31).

- In restructuring execuse, the complany want to chang from abureaucratic multilayed company to a ceat, fully empowered organisatin and make fast decision.
- Company has reduced its manpower from 77000 to 59000 in order to cut the wage bills.
- Company has moved up the value chain in terms of the product mix. The company will increase the production of float products. (*B.T.*, April 7,1999, P-31).

Arther D. Little, the consultant is hekping TISCO to strength its marketing and slash cost. The target-to cut cost by 25%.

According to J.J.Ieani, the managing director of the company, " The challenge to TATA STEEL will not only come from imported steel, but also from local players. The ways to combat that it has to become a low cost manufacturer of high quality products." In order to achieve this objective, the company has undertaken several organisational restructuring programmes as follows::

Organizational Restructuring: Case of Essar Steel

From a modest beginning in 1969 in marine and construction business the Ruia have today built asset valued Rs. 17000 Crore including a fleet of modern ships, a state of the art of 2 million tonne hot-rolled steel mill and a 500 MW power plant. The Essar steel plant commissioned in 1996. (*B.T.* July 1999, P-44). It is perhaps the only producer of its kind , with more than 1650 mm and 2000 mm width respectively, coil gauges from 1.6mm to 2.5mm; and plat gauge upto 20mm (*B.T.* Jan 7,1999, P-352). The Indian Economy went into slump andthe cash rich Essar Steel was sueezed between declining steel prices and not availability of Funds (*B.T.* Nov, 1999. The Ruia's Essar steel has been facing trouble in repaying its huge debts to the financial institutions. In order to find out alternative cash source and concentrate upon their core business:

The group is spinning.off its various divisions into separate vèntures, which will eventually lead to improve cash flows.

The Pellestisation unit is planned as a division of Essar steel is likely to be hived off as a separate company.

A joint venture with Air liquid of France, which will takeover the assets of oxygen unit-a division of Essar steel.

Recently the company has launched its 24-carrat steel programme along with the appointment of retailers to increased domestic market share and increasing realization per tone.

Conclusions

All the companies in steel industry today is facing competition. The competition has affected each company to such an extent, that no one is a casual spectator. In order to meet the challenges of competition each company in Indian steel industry has started some restructuring exercise. The favourable results are expected. In fact steel is not a sunrise sector. The setting sun has been casting long shadows over the industry. In order to survive this volatile environment each company in the steel industry has to make very calculative move. It is evident that corporate restructuring is complex and heterogeneous phenomenon, but they have to cut cost and go for more and more value added products. The old companies like SAIL, TISCO have also to further change the mindset of their employees. They should withdraw from businesses that do not add value to their core activity of making steel. This is what J.J. Irani says, "What does it mean when TISCO's slogan is "we also make steel." The truth is we make steel. Now faced with nimble footed competitors and global pressures, the old giant has been shacked into releasing that it too has to learn new tricks. (B.T. April 7,1999 P-31).

Section - IV

CORPORATE GOVERNANCE

22

RESTRUCTURING OF COMPANY LIQUIDATION PROCESS IN EMERGING DIMENSIONS OF CORPORATE GOVERNANCE

*S.P. Kala**

Due to globalization of markets and rapid growth of cross-border transactions, the dimensions of trade, industry, commerce and even services have undergone perceptible and drastic changes. These changes and developments have forced changes in the way of thinking and ideologies of the people who govern them. The Indian corporate governors have realized that their companies cannot participate and compete with their counterparts elsewhere in the world by continuing with their outdated traditional culture and system of control and strategies which might have been successful in the past. One of the effective tools which the Indian corporaters have started relying upon is to adopt principles of good corporate governance while governing the organization under their domain.

The term corporate governance is much in use since last five-six years. The term corporate governance is receiving everybody's and anybody's attention who are in any way concerned with the management of the Indian corporate world may it be the Government, Professional bodies like Institute of Char-

* Professor & Chairman, Department of Business Management, H.N.B. University, Garhwal.

tered Accountants of India, Institute of Company Secretaries of India, Institute of Cost and Works Accountants of India. The prestigious bodies like CII, ASSOCHEM, FICCI and others are also keen to evolve a suitable uniform code of corporate governance which could easily be followed by the India corporaters and the corporate world. Corporate governance in simple terminology is a collection of complimentary business processes essentially determined by the system under which corporations operate and function. These processes are highly influenced by factors such as internal and external environment, the stage of development of economy and sophistication of capital markets. The concept of corporate governance planks around the central theme of disclosures, ethical values and corporate best practices. In India the corporations are governed by many laws like Income Tax Act, Laws related to Excise and Customs, Labor Laws, Consumer Protection Act, MRTP Act and so on but more prominent among all is the Indian Companies Act, 1956 within fourwalls of which the corporations take birth, operate and die. During last five-six years efforts to liberalize the economies and to integrate them with global and cross border markets have led all the corporaters to seriously consider and review the role of corporate governance. In fact throughout the world the Regulating Agencies and the Government Authorities have also taken a lead in streamlining the corporate laws in respective countries so as to simplify various critical issues related to corporate control. The concept of investor's protection and public interest have become the top priority areas in the agenda of Government governance so as to match corporate regulations and the regulatory mechanism with good corporate governance universally. To ensure good corporate governance the corporaters expect good Government governance as both are two sides of a single coin and contemporary to each other. Good corporate governance is not possible unless there is encouragement from the Government by providing conducive environment to corporations where they could function smoothly, efficiently and effectively. One of the priority area which needs urgent attention of the Government of India is to modernize the law related to corporate insolvency or company liquidation which is one of the important part of the corporate exit policy. Indian Companies Act is three dimensional in nature as it deals with registration of the companies, functioning of companies and liquidation of companies. In this article an effort has been made to show the path for contemplating the changes in the third dimension of the Indian Companies Act which deals with the corporate insolvency or the company liquidation.

The Department of Company Affairs under the Ministry of Law, Justice and Company Affairs, Government of India, is the nodal agency for administration of the Companies Act, 1956.To administer the Companies Act, the Department has three tier set up namely, the secretariat at New-Delhi, the Regional Directors at four Regions at Kanpur, Mumbai, Calcutta and Chennai and the Registrar of Companies in States and Union Territories, the Official Liquidators attached to various High Courts.

The Official Liquidators attached to various High Courts are the officers from one of the wing of central civil services namely Indian Company Law Service and are appointed under the provisions of section 448 of the Companies Act, 1956. The Head Quarter Secretariat through four Regional Directors exercise administrative control over the Official Liquidators though they function under the direct supervision and control of the respective High Courts where they are attached . The primary duty of these Official Liquidators is to conduct the winding up of the affairs of the companies under the Companies Act. Presently there are eighteen offices of the Official Liquidators in India in different States and Union Territories.

The company liquidation which may also be termed as corporate insolvency is governed by the Indian Companies Act under the provisions laid down in Part VII – sections 425 to 560 thereof. The Act recognizes three types of winding up or insolveny of companies namely, (i) compulsory winding up (ii) voluntary winding up – creditors or shareholders and (iii) voluntary winding up under the supervision of the Court. The compulsory winding up is also known as company liquidation by the order of the court. The post liquidation legal procedure to be adopted in each type of liquidation differs but the manner in which liquidation takes place and is conducted more or less the same and is known as Company liquidation proceedings.

There are very few cases of liquidation under the category of voluntary liquidation and none under third category and almost ninety nine per cent cases are of first category i.e. winding up or liquidation by the order of the Court. In this type of cases when a company is put under liquidation by the order of the Court, the Official Liquidator is appointed by the Court as the Liquidator of the company which has been ordered to be wound up. The Official Liquidator in that capacity steps into the shoes of the management of the company and functions under the direct control and supervision of the respective High Court. The primary duty of the Official Liquidator as the liquidator of the company is to realize the assets and properties of the company and to disburse the proceeds among the creditors and the contributories or the shareholders of the company as quickly as possible. He is duty bound to conduct the liquidation proceedings and process effectively and efficiently so that the company could be dissolved expeditiously. Here like the other corporaters or the governors of the corporations the Official Liquidator is required to follow the norms of good corporate governess and for that he is required to act smartly and efficiently so that the company liquidation process could be handled effectively and expeditiously.But is he able to do it. The simple answer to this question is no under the present circumstances because of the fact that the provisions and the mechanism provided under the existing Companies Act have gone out-dated and needs to be changed and restructured.

Normally in India when a company is ordered to be wound up by the High Court, it takes minimum five to ten years to get it dissolved and conclude the liquidation process. In one of the study conducted by the Author of this article in 1995 it has been found that there were certain cases where the winding up order were issued thirty years back and the companies were still to be dissolved. In U.K. and U.S.A. it takes six months to one year to get a company dissolved.

The Government of India has been very much concerned of this matter since long and the major event happened in this field in 1977-78 when vide Resolution dated the 23rd June, 1977 a High Powered Expert Committee under the chairmanship of Justice Rajender Sachar, the then sitting Judge of the Delhi High Court was constituted for review of Indian Companies Act, 1956 and the Monopolies And Restrictive Trade Practices Act, 1969. The Committee submitted its report to the Government of India on 29th August, 1978. In that report while making recommendations for certain changes and amendments in the Companies Act, in regard to the time consuming winding up procedure, the committee observed:

"Provisions dealing with winding up procedures have long remained neglected area in the Act. Delay in termination of winding up proceedings and blocking of corporate assets is injurious both to the shareholders and to the economy in general."

" The winding up process is a long drawn affair and before the companies are finally wound up, it takes years for settlement of various matters viz. filling of statement of affairs, realization of assets, finalization of list of contributories etc. and obtaining a final order of dissolution."

The Administrative Reforms Commission of India at one time while touching upon this subject also said that " the longer the winding up proceedings, the greater is the loss to the community since defunct companies control and conceal corporate wealth which is a national waste."

These observations made by the above prestigious bodies support the truth that the liquidation of companies or say corporate insolvency in India had been a neglected area of corporate laws. The corporate insolvency or company liquidation is a part of the Indian Companies Act,1956. This Act repealed the original Act of 1913, which had been in force for 43 years. Act of 1956 is in force since last 45 years or so. During these long years great many changes of far reaching consequences have taken place but the procedure and mechanism for company liquidation in India remain unchanged.

The Justice Sachar Committee made several positive and radical suggestions to improve and modify the existing Companies Act. One of the significant suggestion, first time in the history of the Indian Companies Act, was simplifying the procedure for liquidation of companies besides, in that direction providing for enabling provisions in the Act for appointment of professionally qualified persons as "Liquidators- Private Company Liquidators" on the lines of Insolvency Practitioners in U.K. for expeditious completion of winding up proceedings. The recommendations and suggestions made by Justice Sachar Committee which were dynamic and radical remained a glorified piece of master work, hotly debated and admired but so far the recommendations for changes relating to the company liquidations have not been the part of the amendment in the Companies Act, because no effort was made by the Government of India to introduce changes as suggested in that part of the Companies Act which deals with company liquidation. However, realizing the seriousness of the situation late, a working group comprising of persons from corporate world and the professional bodies with sound knowledge of law, economics and company affairs was constituted by the Government of India in August, 1996 to suggest a new Companies Act which presented its report to the Government in February, 1997. Based on this report the said working group submitted to the Government a working draft of Companies Bill which was debated and discussed at various seminars, symposium and workshops organized by the professional bodies like Institute of Company Secretaries of India, Institute of Chartered Accountants of India, CII, ASSOCHAM, FICCI and other organizations and agencies concerned with corporate world and industry. Finally the Companies Bill 1997 was introduced in the Rajya Sabha on 14th August, 1997. This Bill contained 458 clauses and 3 schedules and sought to facilitate healthy growth of the Indian corporate sector under liberalized dynamic and highly competitive environment. It is not possible to highlight all the features of the Bill here which certainly made an effort to rationalize procedure, process and mechanism of company liquidation, specially by underlining the proposed introduction of a concept of appointment of Private Company Liquidators alongwith the Official Liquidators to conduct the liquidation proceedings in the Companies Act through amendment in the Act for making the law of Corporate Insolvency or the Company liquidation more effective and efficient thus making it a model tool for corporate exit policy supporting the fundamentals of good corporate governance. Due to development in the political scenario the Bill did not see the light of the day and had to be withdrawn. It is now the high time when the Government of India should reform the law relating to the corporate insolvency or company liquidation.

There are two main reasons why India needs reform in corporate insolvency process, one is that till 1980s India was not only more protected from competitive forces than many other countries but has also started late. As markets continued to open up, we started talking global and good corporate governance. Indian corporations have to simultaneously look behind their inertia and to face a big technical gap in products as well in the process. Another factor is that in India too much bank and institutional credit is locked up in inefficiently organized and financially distressed companies. Industrial sickness in India mainly arises out of bad financial structure and or chronically inefficient use of factors of production and or poor marketing positioning. The Indian corporations are at times under threat of their very existence and survival for which a clear cut exit policy and mechanism should be in readiness to bail them out so that the corporate wealth which is under threat could be shifted to other lucrative and profitable ventures. There is thus a need for revamping our company liquidation process and mechanism by its restructuring making it conducive to the changing business environment and result oriented.

There are certain barriers and bottlenecks because of which the law relating to the company liquidation under the existing Companies Act is not sufficient to meet the expectations of the emerging dimension of the corporate world and intern not coming up to the expectations of the good corporate governance. Some of these barriers and bottlenecks are insufficient staff and lack of qualified staff, lack of proper space, lack of proper infrastructural facilities in the offices of the Official Liquidators. Some of the problems are out house problems like non cooperation on the part of the directors of the companies under liquidation, specially in case of filing of statement of affairs and sizable time and energy of the office of the Official Liquidators is wasted in identifying and locating and taking into possession the records and assets of the companies. The professionals of repute from legal, chartered accountants are not generally volunteering their expert services to the Official Liquidators for the reasons that the fees paid to them is meager in comparison to the fees and remuneration paid to these experts outside. This has resulted into a situation of helplessness for the Official Liquidators as he is left with no option other than either to rely on his available staff or to do the job himself particularly when it comes to plead the matters before different courts. For want of expert legal services from the Legal Luminaries in important areas sizable time and energy of the officers and the staff of the Official Liquidators is consumed in dealing with the court cases and other legal matters with the result other equally important areas of the work in these offices connected with the liquidation of the companies is neglected or omitted to be attended properly. Under the existing process, for each and every act of the Official Liquidators they have to approach the respective High Courts, seeking orders and directions which is certainly a time consuming factor since the

Hon'ble Company Judges in respective High Courts, apart from the liquidation matters, also look after the other matters under the Companies Act and so. Unlike in USA and UK there is no system in India to consider liquidation matters on special footing or top priority. The realization and disposal of assets in most of the cases results into long litigation and sometimes with no results. This situation ultimately results in unreasonable delay in finalization of liquidation proceedings. It adversely affects the interests of the poor public whose funds are blocked in the companies under liquidation. From the date of filing of winding up petition, on an average two to three years of time is taken by the Courts for putting the company into liquidation. During this period the persons in the management of the concerned companies do not take any interest in managing the company well and sometime try to dispose of the valuable assets for ulterior gain. The books of accounts in case of some companies are not audited for long years which makes it difficult for the Official Liquidators to take immediate action to realize the funds or dues of the companies until the books of accounts are completed and updated which is a taxing and time consuming job. Frequent rotation of the Company Judges and the transfers of the Official Liquidators is also responsible for making the liquidation process a long drawn affairs as it affects the continuity and results in to vacuum at times. There is no interaction between the Judiciary and the Department of Company Affairs in liquidation matters though both are equally concerned and responsible for expeditious completion of liquidation of the companies concerned. In this situation sometime the Official Liquidators find themselves landing and then standing in no man's land neither owned by the Department of Company Affairs nor by the High Courts. There are some more problems being faced by the Official Liquidators in discharge of their duties efficiently and effectively but it is not possible to mention all of them here.

Herein before an effort has been made to throw some light on the causes which has resulted in hampering the efficiency and effectiveness of corporate insolvency or company liquidation which is a unique example of improper corporate governance. Based on these barriers and bottlenecks highlighted above certain suggestions are pointed out below to make the whole process efficient and effective. The law of liquidation relating to companies is presently part of Indian Companies Act, which is the biggest piece of legislation in India, should be removed and may be incorporated under a separate enactment which shall exclusively be dealing with the law of corporate insolvency or company liquidation in India. The concept of appointing professionals as private Company Liquidators on the lines of the system being followed in UK and USA should also be introduced in India as recommended by Justice Sachar Committee and further by the Working group and which find a place in Companies Act Amendment Bill 1997. A separate Agency by restructuring the existing one is also suggested to handle corporate insolvency which should be under the direct control of a Governing body within the Department of Company Affairs under the name and style of " Board of Corporate Insolvency ". The job of this Body will be to supervise the functioning of the Official Liquidators including the Private Company liquidators in the country. For day to day supervision at the four Regions there may be appointed the Chief Official Liquidators to assist the Board and to keep a watch on the functioning of the Official Liquidators including Private Company Liquidators.

It is learnt that the Department of Company Affairs has set up a Committee for drafting an appropriate law for winding up of companies and for restructuring the existing mechanism by setting up of a tribunal to ensure speedy winding up of companies.The Committee will certainly go in to the details of the problems and come up with the suggestions which could make our corporate insolvency law more efficient and effective at par with the laws of other countries with whom we have economic and corporate links like UK and USA.

REFERENCES

1. High Powered Committee Report on the Review of The Companies Act And MRTP Act (Justice Sachar Committee Report), 1978.
2. Report of the Committee On Industrial Sickness And Restructuring (Goswami Committee Report), 1993.
3. Industrial Sickness In India – T.C.A. Anant and Others, 1995.
4. Working Draft of the Companies Bill, 1997.
5. Indian Companies Act, 1956.
6. A Guide To Insolvency—A Bulletin Published by Insolvency Service of U.K.

23

THE CHANGING HORIZONS OF CORPORATE GOVERNANCE

S. L. Gupta & M. K. Sehgal***

Corporate Governors play a significant role because top management teams around the world face a period of unprecedented business opportunities and threats. The top management must recognize, grasp and achieve five fundamental objectives to secure a firm basis for competitive success: Achievement of sound business performance standards and concurrent strategic development in a highly competitive international scene; creation of committed strategic relationships with key customers; effective use of technology to satisfy customer's strategic needs; development and maintenance of a pro-active and dynamic role for top management and effective use and development of people. Even for today's successful management teams these represent substantial additional workload for the less successful companies, the tasks represent a substantial corporate development challenge and also present areas of significant rise.

Companies having some part time Directors on the Board are called board-managed companies by the department of company Affairs.On the other hand where the board has one whole time

* Chairman, Deptt. of Management, Kurukshetra University, Kurukshetra.

** Associate Professor cum Dy. Director, S.A. Jain Institute of Mgt. & Technology, Ambala City.

employee MD and a few more whole time Directors, besides part-time Directors the firm is viewed as a 'MD Managed Company.' The external directors are expected to initiate in the board meetings, discussion on environmental developments and their implications for the organisation. The organisation would immensely benefit if people from the following walks of life can make significant contribution to the effectiveness of the board; outstanding technologists with considerable experience in a related field; renowed management consultants/academicians, who can contribute innovative ideas or generate fresh thinking distinguished administrators with useful innings in government administration.

Like democratic governments businesses must be governed by a set of rules that reflect the interests of their shareholders and the public at large. These 'rules of the game 'for business are an important dimension of reform efforts in developed and transition economics alike. Countries that ignore or lag behind in corporate governance reform will rapidly find themselves at a competitive disadvantage in attracting long term capital for development.

In a global conference on corporate governance held at New Delhi during February 1999, delegates from 80 nations concurred that the following efforts must be undertaken in their countries: public education efforts are needed to promote better understanding of essential corporate governance principles and their relationship to democratic development.

* Companies need to undertake voluntary reforms by developing codes of conduct and best practices guidelines. Business association can facilitate this process by developing model corporate governance programs.
* Independent, non-executive company directors with diverse talents and experience need to be appointed to corporate boards in larger numbers.
* Legislation needs to be passed to put in place internation-

ally accepted accounting principles, standards of financial disclosure, conflict of interest disclosure, anti-trust laws, bankruptcy laws, and prohibitions on insider trading.

Motorola, a U.S. based multinational, evaluates its board by asking questions about:

The level of involvement of the board in CEO succession.

Sufficiency of information for CEO evaluation.

Appropriate processes to assess the CEO.

CEO's commitment in time spent with regard to company regard to company direction.

Changes proposed by the CEO with regard to company direction.

The CEO's capabilities to formulate vision and mission

The CEO's efforts to put in place appropriate structures to evaluate the company's strategy and objectives and resolve to effectively inquire into major performance deficiencies.

The CEO's capability to deal with unforeseen corporate crisis.

Conclusion

Corporate governance is highly essential for corporate success. The specific issues which are significant in Public service management are: building accountability in government within the organisation; public service management, performance appraisal, sanctions and incentives; moulding bureaucracy for results and customer orientation; removing constraints for reform; evolving a character of values in civil service and combating corruption. Most large, publicly owned corporations probably have boards that operate at some point between nominal and active prticipation. In an indicative study ranging from hospitals to Fortune 500 firms found that:

* 30% of the boards actively worked with management to

develop strategic direction (active Governance).

* 30% worked to revise as well as ratify managements proposals (nominal Governance).
* 40% merely ratified managements strategic proposals (phantom Governance).

The boards of most publicly owned corporations are composed of both inside and outside directors. Inside directors/ management directors are typically officers or executives employed by the companies. Outside directors may be executives of other firms but are not employees of the board Although there is no clear evidence indicating that a high proportions of outsiders on a board results in improved corporate performance, there is a trend in the U.S.A. to increase the number of outsiders on boards. The typical large U.S.corporation has an average of eleven directors, of whom two are insiders. People who favour high proportion of outsiders state that outside directors are less biased and more likely to evaluate managements performance objectively than are inside directors. This is the main reason why the New York Stock Exchange requires that all companies listed on the exchange have an audit committee composed entirely of independent, outside mambers.

In contrast, those who prefer inside over outside directors contend that outside directors are less effective than are insiders because the outsiders are likely to have the necessary interest, avalibility, or, competency. Directors may sometimes serve on so many boards that they spread their time and interest too thin to actively fulfill their resposibilities. They could also point out that the term outsider is too simplistic some outsiders are not truly objective and should be considered more as insiders than as outsiders, they suggest like this:

Affiliated directors who though not really employed by the company, handle the legal or insurance work for the company and dependent on the current management for a key part of their business.

Retired directors who used to work for the company, such as the past CEO and they are partly responsible for much of the corporation's current strategy and probably groomed the current CEO.

Family directors who are desendents of the founder and own significant blocks of stock and have personals agendas based on a family relationship with the current CEO.

The majority of outside directors are active or retired CEOs of other corporations. Others are academicians, attroneys, consultants, former government officials,major shareholders and bankers. In Germany, bankers are re preseneted on almosst every board-primarily lblecause they own large blocks of stock in German corporations, in Denmark, Sweden, Belgium and Italy however investment companies assume this role. The investment company investor AB casts 42.5% of the Electrolux board. 1995 surveys of large U.S. corporations found that 69% of the boards had at least one woman director up from 60% in 1992 and only 11% in 1972 with ones third now having two female directors. Boards having at least one monority member increased from 9% in 1973 to 47% in 1995 (African American 34% Latino 9% Asian 4%).

The globalization of business has not yet had much impact on board membership. One study of U.S. boards found 37 international (non-U.S.) directors on only 30 out of 100 boards surveyed. Of these, 5 were insiders and 32 were outsiders. The scarcity of international directors may be changing as more corporations increase their operations around the world.

The role of the board of directors in the strategic management of the corporation is likely to be more active in the future. The change will probably be more evolutionary, however, rather than radical or revolutionary. Different boards are at different levels of maturity and will not be changing in the same direction or at the same speed.

Some of today's trend in corporation governance that are

likely to continue include:

* Institutional investors, such as pension funds, mutual funds, and insurance companies, are becoming active on boards and are putting increasing preesure on top management to improve corporate performance.
* As corporations become more global that they will increasingly and international directors to their boards.
* Shareholders are demanding that directors and top managers own more than token amounts of stock in the corporation stock increasingly being used as per of a directors competition.
* Outside or nonmanagement directors are increasing their numbers and power in publicly held corporations as CEOs loosen their grip on boards.Outsiders are now taking charge of annual CEO evaluations.
* Boards will continue to take more control of board functions by either spiliting the combined Chair/CEO into two seprate positions or establishing a lead outside director position.
* Society, in the form of special interest groups, increasingly expects boards of directors to balance the economic goal of profitability with the social needs of society. Issues dealing with force diversity and the environment are now reaching the board level.

How do we rate the behavior and performance of boards in the Indian private sector? Let me take a recent example to get on to the subject. There are reasons to believe that in the first half of the nineties the boards of many of the public companies approved massive investment in certain manufacturing sectors, ignoring the changes that were waiting to happen in the marketplace. We know the consequences, the loss of shareholder value in the capital market and the fallout on banks and financial institutions in the form of non- performing assets(NPA). All this can be attributed-and Moody's has done so in their periodic assessments- to the 'corporate governance' problems of the Indian corporate sector.

Clearly in hindsight, the concerned management(S) may be viewed as wanting in strategic foresight. But what about their respective boards? Are they not to be equally blamed for being passive onlookers boarding on being negligent in some instances; they had signally failed in their oversight responsibilities. While many boards have woken up now to their deficiency, have they really learned their lessons? I somehow doubt it .Company management(s) are , as always, populated by people and advised by organizations who are all certain that they have just the right strategies. Some come up with technology driven solutions to what they think are their problems, some talk of transforming the organisation through a process akin to genetic engineering, grafting and revitalizing corporate genes, some want to work with them as substitutes mangers. There are all kinds of wise strategists, waiting to relieve the company of the burden of thinking- a new kind of division of labour, along the lines of comparative advantage of strategic and operational intellect.

If the board has to develop and enforce an effective mechanism for supervision and control, it must then learn to grapple with the complex problems of governance. If the top management or the managers at the senior levels do not perform, the board has the power of removal, but on occasions when this power is exercise, it may, more often than not, turn out to be too little or too late. As the board has the final responsibility, it must, therefore as a deliberate policy initiate the requisite steps to guard against any likely shortcomings and failings in its oversight functions. Also in all of the three areas that I have referred to earlier, the board must, consistently and critically, undertake a kind of directorial due diligence' to satisfy itself that it is geared to meet the demands of its responsibility mandate. What then are the issues of priority for the board?

Issues of Priority

First, is information: The board should empower itself to have access to information that focuses attention on problems which may need intervention or on potential intervention pertaining to its oversight responsibility relating to strategic, regulatory and stakeholder concerns. The board may have its own view as to how it wishes to go about its task of understanding and decision-making and therefore it is essential that it is directly involved in determining the content of such information. It cannot meaningfully delegate the function to the management.

Second, the board and its directors must be willing to give time and resources to engage the management team in a serious dialogue on strategic direction and issues of importance that may come up from time to time. In the world of uncertainty and change, business issues are becoming increasingly complex and the board must enforce discipline on itself as well on the management, in order to ensure that a given situation is being analyzed fully, truthfully, honestly and transparently.

Third Is expertise. In some sectors the absence of requisite may catch the board quite unawares. In the financial services sector, in particular., there is a growing realisation that there is an acute gap between how the market operators behave and knowledge and understanding of the implications and ramifications of their behavior. On occasions the consequences can be disastrous.

Fourth, is the issue of education for outside board members, an outside board members needs to be prepared thoroughly before sitting down for his or her first board meeting. The financial institution should provide a comprehensive orientation program, one that includes(among other things) a detailed presentation of the firm's activities, advance copies of all reports to be discuses, guidance about how to judge the parameters of risk-taking (including a comprehensive review of the quantitative risk modeling used by the institution), and a review of the institution's accounting procedures.

Fifth, is the splitting up of the post of Chairman and the Chief Executive Officer(CEO), which the Global Advisory Board regards as a fundamental principle. The underlying premise is that without the direction of an independent leader, it may be normally very difficult for the Board to perform its critical oversight function. The independent Chairman should have the right to initiate board appointments, board committee assignments, and the setting of the board agenda and all other matter that have a bearing on the fiduciary responsibility of the board of directors.

Sixth, is in the matter of business ethics. The board has to ensure that a management is observing the ground rule of ethics, transparency and disclosure. It is not unusual to find that in their drive for profit and growth mangers are tempted to subvert the market process. There is always an in built tension between ethical practice and a deviant practice or malpractice not specially prohibited by the regulatory authority. It has to be the responsibility of the board to ensure that market rules and the behavior pattern approved by the regulatory authority are respected in letter and spirit. The moral strength of independent directors is derived from the public trust they enjoy and the board as the collective body must consistently strive to treasure this. In the financial services industry, there is also the onerous responsibility that the board has namely to be aware of the systematic consequences of their failure in supervisory and control responsibilities.

Seventh, is the question of seeking a balance amongst the interests of the different stakeholders. The primary market discipline comes from the capital market and the perspective of the top management is generally to enhance shareholder value. There are differences between academics as to the best means of seeking a convergence of interests. However, the fact remains that the interests of the shareholders and the interests of other stake holders—customers, employees, suppliers and local communities—will rarely converge. There is now an increasing realisation that the board has to work towards some approximations that balances these often competing interests format the standpoint of the larger social interest.

Eighth, is the issue of short and long term objectives. Over the past two decades stock price appreciation has been a very effective measure to exert market discipline on corporate. The board has used quite often this same measure to finally judge the performance of the incumbent management. With top managers' compensation also incentives by stock price appreciation, there appeared to have arisen a virtuous companionship of corporate knighthood in constant search of the Holy Grail of ever—appreciating stock prices. This instrument has worked well in squeezing out the flab in US corporate, debunking old ideas, idiosyncrasies and hobby horses, forcing corporate—management and board alike—to think along new lines more in tune with the music of new technologies and global opportunities. However, the time has possibly come when the instrument - like all manmade ones-faces obsolescence. Inflated CEO pay-packets - including astronomical severance packages for non-performing personages - a possible attenuation of corporate flab, and a need to reclaim visionary long-term strategic thinking have a set in motion the drive to institutionalize a commitment to long-term objectives. Pension fund managers are often being viewed as the custodians of the long-term.

Ninth is the question of the board culture. Mere compliance with a dry code of corporate governance model is no guarantee of the quality of corporate governance inside the boardroom. How good are we as a board? How good am I as a board member? How well does the chairman perform? There are the questions the board and its members must learn to ask . A code of governance is the architecture. It is the people who live and operate inside of the structure that gives life to it. A company may well comply with all mandatory and optional requirements and may make all that is required to be disclosed in the annual reports of the companies. But such compliance does not necessarily provide the assurance that the company is adhering to the true spirit of corporate governance. These disclosures are snapshots and do not capture the process. In evaluating whether a company has compiled with corporate governance codes or not, one must look, as one does in a due diligence scrutiny , for 'off-balance-sheet' practices.

Tenth and finally is the issue of self - evaluation of the board. There is a strong body of opinion that urges a process of self-evaluation by the board and the establishment of standards of performance.

Boardroom self-evaluation schemes under which the competence of the directors is reviewed annually by fellow board members are making rapid headway in the US. The Washington DC based National Association of Corporate Directors sets out five elements for discussion: personal characteristics, core competencies, independence, level of commitment and team and company consideration. A convention is developing where directors are clearly told that re-nomination is not automatic and that poor evaluation will lead to a request for resignation. It postulates a boardroom culture that encourages constructive evaluation, clarity of goals and processes in the specific circumstances of the company and full disclosure of the procedures and criteria to the shareholders. We have a long way to go before we can set appropriate assessment criteria.

How does one see the future? There can be no clear cut answers but I would make the following observations on the emerging trends.

1. General acceptance of the corporate governance code is a welcome development. This may, however, tend to lapse into a mechanical adherence to a few formal requirements such as the constitution of board committees and their composition and the categorization of existing non-executive directors intake independent categories. One can see signs of smug self satis-

faction among corporate bodies for technical alliance with governance code, but, hopefully, there are visible signs of societal pressures on the functioning of the boards. The principal of 'accountability through disclosure' which is the foundation of corporate governance codes is gradually triggering off investor pressures and greater media scrutiny helping develop, accept and publicize new standards of openness. It is instructive to note how things have started changing in Germany; old habits of secretiveness are wilting under pressure of public scrutiny. Five years ago, at a shareholder meeting of Hoechst, some shareholders asked how management plans to revive the business's dismally performing share price. Company officials were stunned. Putting questions directly to management at shareholder meetings was regarded as tantamount to breaking a fundamental code of German corporate conduct. Today in Germany such sessions can become grueling. Some while back, the chairman of Daimler-Chrysler had to sit through 14 hours of non-stop and intensive questioning from shareholders and rapid and extensive dissemination of information are putting mounting procure on the boards to perform. In the process it is piercing the corporate veil on the performance of the carmine and the non-executive directors. These are encouraging market developments.

2. The market for corporate control can have a disciplining impact. It is interesting to note what happened in the US during the 1980's. A keen observer of that period has described the late sixties and seventies as a period where a typical mindset of top management could be easily summarized-introverted, corporate centered view of business mission focused on growth, diversification and opportunity for the 'corporate family'. What are the prospects for development of the market for corporate control that can put inefficient management on notice and with it the passive and negligent boards? In the Indian private sector, with the global inflow of capital, a market for corporate control is fast developing and we are likely to witness sea changes in the different sectors.

3. There is also a contrary trend. An attempt to insulate oneself from the discipline of the market. The management belonging to a strong promoter group, if it is not allowed to have its way may try to overcome the problem by changing the character of the company itself. In the US where CEO's have been traditionally powerful there is a trend to take public corporations private finance by private equity funds many of which have their roots in the leveraged buyout take-over of the 1980s. Having at their command huge liquid funds they advance the cash needed to buy out the public shareholders and the compliance costs of being a public limited company disappear. The 'independent board' is then replaced with an interested board of direct owners. In the US there are reportedly three such 'privatization's' every week; in Europe it is still not such a regular occurrence, but the trend is rising. The first quarter of 2000 saw a record of 49 privatization's deals valued at $6.9 billion in the US. The value of companies being taken private now exceeds the value of public companies being floated. I foresee this development in the corporate sector in India too. With direct foreign investment inflows in the new technologies areas and multinational corporations becoming more active in taking stakes in the Indian corporate sector, a large segment of our corporate sector is likely to increasingly prefer to function as private limited companies.

REFERENCES

1. Warren J.Keegan, *Global Marketing Management*, 5th Edition, Prentice Hall of India, New Delhi, pp. No. 18

2. *The Management Accountant*, Oct. 2000, Vol. 35 No. 10

3. Davis, Stelhen M. (1999), "*The Race for Global Corporate Governance, Economic Reforms Today*, No. 1

4. Satya Raju, R. (1999), "*Corporate Governance in a Changing Environment*"

5. Mishra, R.K. (1998), "Corporate Governance in Public Enterprises; a New Framework", ASCI Formal of Management.

6. Human Development in South Asia - Report - (1999)

7. *Productivity,* Jan. - Mar. 2000 (vol. 40, No. 4)

8. OECD code of Corporate Governance.

9. Supplement on Corporate Governance, *Financial Lines,* (March 19, 1999)

10. Report of the Kumar Manglam Birla Committee on Corporate Governance appointed in SEBI.

11. The Corporate Restructuring of the 1980s and Its Import for the 1990s by Gorden Doneldson in Donald H. Chew.

24

RESTRUCTURING CORPORATE GOVERNANCE IN INDIA

Sujit Sikidar & Santosh Kumar Mahapatra***

Introduction

Of late there has been a long debate for corporate governance. The concept of corporate governance is not new but has drawn attention at the instance of various scams and irregularities in the early nineties that shook the confidence of investors. The whole concept of corporate governance gained recognition when Sir Andrian Cadbury was invited by the London Stock Exchange in the year 1991 to look into financial aspects of corporate governance. With the liberalization of econonmy and international capital movements, companies are finding that high standards of governance are increasingly important factor.

This has made the corporate governance a global issue.

Meaning and Significance

In the corporate philosophy, shareholders are having equity stake in the company and responsibility of shareholders lies in selecting a few shareholders amongst themselves and often from

* Professor in the Department of Commerce, Gauhati University, Guwahati - 781 014

** Senior Lecturer in the Department of Commerce, Gauhati University, Guwahati- 781 014.

outside to constitute a committee to manage the affairs known as 'board of directors'. Board of directors is therfore, a formal body responsible for governance of corporate functions as collective wisdom to give appropriate directions to the entity in order to achieve the group objective in the most efficient manner. Corporate governance is the system by which affairs of the company are reviewed and directed furthur (Bhowmik,1998) (1). Thus, corporate governance in its usual sense refers to the accountability relationship among the shareholders, directors and managers. It is also argued that a firm is also accountable to all its shareholders and society in general. Some even recommend that accountability should be to the most important stakeholders group and not necessarily to shareholders. Sen (1999) is of the view that a company is a legal entity and is subject to all laws of the land as a citizen. It therefore, has to discharge the obligations to all other stakeholders by paying taxes, complying with environmental and safety regulations as well as adhering to labour laws, contract regulation laws, consumer protection laws and all other laws. It is only after every body's dues are paid off, the residual amount belongs to the shareholders as the reward to the risk bearers. It is thus primacy of the shareholders value and supremacy of stakeholders that are important for economic efficiency, social justice and national wealth creation.

If one goes deep inito the corporate governance, one can find that it primarily involves company's board, shareholders and auditors role in management practices. There may be conflict of interests of management and shareholders. But in a good corporate governance each group understands and exercises its rights, duties and responsibilities. The shareholders have pressure on the management to get better value of their shares while management should see that how shareholders and stakeholders both can be satisfied. Auditors job is to see the interest of the shareholders and stakeholders so that management can not go scot free.

Role of Boards

In India, there are three kind of directors: promoters, nominees of financial institutions (Fis) and professionals who are experts in certain fields. Promoters and nominees of the Fis are the executive directors while the professionals act as non-executive directors. The law has not differentiated between 'executive' and 'non-executive' directors. It only provides for rotational and wholetime or managing director. Every rotational director automatically retires after a period of three years and seeks his re-election. A managing director can be appointed for a term of five years only concurrent with his continuing as a director only and must seek reappointment thereafter. The executive control is in the hand of managing director.

Under company law, it is manadatory for the Board of directors to present to report the shareholders on their stewardship at regular interval. A good corporate governance looks into review of operation at board level at a regular interval. It should look into periodical statements on financial performance, production and service obligations to shareholders as well as other stakeholders. The board should ensure the compliance of various statutory regulations besides taking care of image building that adds to the shareholders value in the long run.

The dominance of family control over business has made corporate governance more complex as compared to US or UK. Controlling families are usually in a position to strongly resist to the changes required, because such families often have voting control in their hands (Gupta, 1996). The minimum public offer as required by law has been reduced to 25 percent from 60 per cent and this has provided better scope on the part of family controlled business to retain a greater control by means of voting power. It has created a situation that the family controlled companies are immune to controlling interest from outside shareholders. Even Bhagwati Committee on takeover code has proposed to allow promoters to increase their voting control to a level of above 50 per cent. Such a proposal may protect the promoters for all the times but small investors from public may be helpless as they will be unable to vote out the non-performing and dishonestt controlling groups.

The nominee directors who are nominee of banks or financial institutions should not only take care of their interest in the company but also play a constructive role for all the shareholders. Though the company law has no mention about non-executive directors, the term refers to those directors who do not have executive responsibilities in functional operation. They are professionals having expertise and experience in any particular discipline and can be drawn from banks, financial institutions, public sector undertakings, private sector companies, chartered accountants, engineers etc. The problem in corporate governance arises when such professionals are brought to the board by the promoters and they may influenced by and obliged to them. Good corporate governance always depends on the independence of non-executive directors. The Cadbury committee (1991) has recommended that, "non-executive directors should be selected through a formal process and nomination should be a matter of board as a whole". The 'code of best practices' set by the committee also states that non-executive directors should bring an independent judgement to bear on issues of strategy, performance, resources including key appointments and standards of conduct.

Non-executive directors as members of 'audit committee' can provide constructive services in improving the standards of corporate governance. Although the concept of audit committee is new to India, its role in upgrading the standard of corporate governance has been recognised in the USA and UK. In order to provide statutory status to the audit committee, government has made suitable provisions in the Companies Bill, 1997 and made it mandatory for all public limited companies with a paid-up capital of Rs. 5 crore and above to set an audit committee. Audit committe have the potential to improve financial reporting, check fraud, increase efficeincy of the directors and strenghten the position of external auditor as well as internal control system. The effectiveness of the audit committee depends on competence, commitment and independence of its members.

Role of Auditors

Auditors are playing an important role by providing constructive services in improving the standards of corporate governance. Cadbury Committee, in its report, had re-inforced the role and responsibility of auditors by mentioning "the centeral issue is to ensure that an appropriate relationship exists between the auditors and the management whose financial statements they are auditing. Shareholders require auditor to work with and not against management, while always remaining professionally objective is to say, applying their professional skills impartially and retaining a critical detachment and consciousness of their accountability to those who formally appoint them".

Auditors are often criticised that they work more for managers than shareholders. In this regard RBI has black listed some of the auditors of banks when Indian Bank incurred huge loss in 1995-96. Such cases may be rare but clearly indicates the huge loss to be suffered by shareholders in case of negligence by the auditors. Therefore, in improving the standards of corporate goverance, auditors should assume more responsibility and sincerity. To make audit more effective a system where audit firms can be changed every three or four years may be adopted by corporates. The companies should also disclose all the relationship with their auditors including consultancy. Malegam (1998) rightfully remarked that, 'we can not say that as one profession, we will both audit and supply and advise on the business needs in a total situation and we will, therefore, have to have very effective standards to ensure that audit independence is not sacrificed at the alter of business expediency.'

Role of Shareholders

Good corporate governance is possible when shareholders

assume their responsibility to elect directors, appoint auditors and express views or anxiety on the affairs of the company. Individual shareholders, because of their holdings too small, can not provide any worthwhile support to corporate governance except showing concern and raising certain questions. However, financial institutions and institutional investors holding block of shares are n better position to contribute towards better governance. Fis should take active participation and act in the interest of general shareholders to improve the standard of corporate governance. To cite an example, the decision of FIs to ascertain details from the Tatas on their move to levy a charge on group companies for the use of Tata brand name and the recent creation of holdings between the holding company Tata Sons and other groups has set a trend. Gupta (1999) is of the opinion that, 'institutional shareholder activism is the only hope and practical way for securing improvement in corporate governance in India'. Therefore, FIs must take the lead and play the role of a 'watch dog'.

Restructuring Corporare Governance

The history of corporate governance is not new and good is its essential feature. A good corporate governance calls for an accountability of all concerned shareholders' responsibility to elect directors, appoint auditors and express their veiws or anxiety on the affairs of the company, directors' responsibility to keep shareholders informed, auditors' certifying that accounts prepared exhibits a true and fair view of the state of affairs, accountability by executives, advisors and other staff on whose judgement and advises the management relies and finally the chairman who gives direction to the board (Bhowmik, 1998) (2). Therefore, there is a need to restructure corporate governance. Restructuring corporate governance means redesigning the governance principles, structure of board, audit committeee to improve the standards of governance and meet the expectations of interest groups or stakeholders including shareholders. The recommendations made by Cadbury Committee are mainly targetting corporate as an individual, the responsibility is largely bestowed upon board and auditors. Shareholders, no doubt play an important role in upgrading the corporate governance standards, and so in restructuring a company board, enough opportunity should be provided to enable them to safeguard their interest.

There is a need of operational code of corporate governance for effective corporate governance. The Confederation of Indian Industry (CII) has drafted a list of codes for corporate governance, which may be kept in mind while restructuring a company to upgrade the corporate governance standards. Some of the important features of CII's code on corporate governance are:

1. The Board should be single tiered and meet at interval of two months and atleast six times a year.
2. The non-executive directors should comprise 30 percent of the board if one of them is Chairman otherwise it should be atleast 50 percent of the Board.
3. No. individual should be a director on Boards for more than 10 companies at any given time and should be present for atleast 50 percent of the Board meetings, failing which he should not be re appointed.
4. Non-executive directors must be active, have defined responsibility and should be paid commission and offered with stock options for their professional inputs besides sitting fees.
5. An audit committee comprising atleast three non-executive directors should be set-up and given access to all financial information.
6. There should be transparency and corporate disclosure norms should be at par with international standards for GDR issues. Additional information on monthly average stock prices, value addition and segment-wise performance should be disclosed in annual reports.

7. The Board should be informed of the operating plans, budgets, periodical results, details of defaults, payments made for intangibles and foreign exchange exposure.

Epilogue

The concept of corporate governance is not new but has gained recognition after the Cadbury Committee (1991) expressed its view on various issues of corporate governance. With the liberalization of economy, companies are finding that high standard of corporate governance has become a neccesity. The CII has also recommended a list of codes for corporate governance that may bring qualitative changes in the corporate governance practices prevailing in India. A good corporate governance calls for an accountability of all concerned- shareholders, directors and auditors. A strong desire, presence of contestability among various interest groups and acceptance of responsibility can upgrade the governance standards. Now, it is high time that companies should come forward to restructure their companies to improve the corporate governance standards and prove their worth.

REFERENCES

Bhattacharyya, A.K. (1996), 'Corporate Governance', *The Chartered Accountant,* Vol. XLV, No. 5, November

Bhowmik, T.R. (1998) (1), 'Corporate Governance and its Relevance', *Financial Express,* May 15.

____________ (1998) (2), 'Good Governance Calls for Accountability', *Financial Express,* May 19.

Gupta, L.C. (1996), 'Corporate Governance in India', *The Economic Times,* November 16.

_________ (1999), 'Reforming Corporate Governance', *The Economics Times,* April 14.

Malegam, Y. H. (1998), 'The Role of Accounting Professionals', *The Chartered Accountant,* Vol. XLVI, No. 7, January.

Sen B. (1999), ' Principles of Corporate Governance', *Business Standard,* May 12.

25

INTERNAL RESTRUCTURING AND CORPORATE GOVERNANCE

M.K. Sehgal & Veneet Kohli***

At the dawn of a new century and third millennium, India and the world are at the threshold of opportunities as never before. The last two centuries of the second millennium had been tumultous both in terms of the magnitude of the change and the profound effect it had on the life of mankind. Rapid industrialization and an explosive growth in technology in the era of e-commerce brought the world almost to the near edge of self-annihilation. As we come to grips with the strategies to survive in this competitive world, a phase of uncertainty being the only constant across borders, industries and markets. India is not isolated from feeling the world-wide impact. The imperative for business enterprise all over the globe and in India in particular is to understand and nature of this change and leverage it effectively to achieve corporate goals of profitability and growth. Even the Indian organization displays, a mixed set of values, characteristics of both western and eastern societies like nurturing and task obsessiveness, collectiveness and individualness, humanism Vs power orientation.

* Director(Dy.) cum Associate Professor, S.A. Jain Institute of Mgt. & Technology (AIMT), Ambala City

** Asst. Prof. S.A. Jain Institute of Mgt. & Technology (AIMT), Ambala City.

The concept of corporate governance relates to how effectively organizations are managed? There is going to be a greater realizations that good governance is a must not only to gain credibility and trust but also as a part of strategic management for survival , consolidation and growth. There is a great demand for simplification, greater accountability and transparency necessitated by increasing investor awareness and competitive market forces. There has also been a pressure on the financial institutions since they nominate their members on the boards of different companies and also underwrite their issues. These financial institutions face problems of NPA,s and defaults on payments. There has been a greater of these organizations more closely.

Company act has provided a framework for corporate Governance and have detail about the powers, duties and responsibilities of the board, Instituted system of checks and balance with punishment for transgression of law, still it is not sufficient for effective corporate Governance. India Industry Association has taken the initiative in framing such a code. CADBURY COMMITTEE on corporate Governance has framed a similar code. Professional body for promoting the Industries affairs (Confederation of Indian Industry, CII) published a code of corporate Governance and has made 17 specific recommendations. The Cadbury Committee on corporate Governance was set up in May 1991 specifically for Internal Restructuring matters and recommended 19 standards related to Internal Auditing, Financial responsibilities and level of co-ordination and confidence, Internal control System, Ethical corporate Citizenship shareholders values.

Internal Restructuring is very suitable way for Good corporate Governance and suited to present corporate scenario internal Restructuring includes Industry structure and development, change in organization Outlook, change in segment wise or product wise performance, Internal control system and their adequacy, discussion on financial performance and operational performance, Development in Human Resources through organization Development intervention and Industrial Psychology \ Behaviour science techniques therefore in view of the above facts a good Governance requires intelligent Internal Restructuring with full disclosure and efficiency. Internal restructuring minimize. Different Risks like Legal and statutory Risk. Financial risk Business Portfolio Risk and Internal Process Risks, Political Risk and effective Internal Restructuring minimize a business risk coping with demand of corporate world otherwise business cannot be compete without proper Risk management system in this Globalizes competitive corporate world. In a recent study, concerning 50 manufacturing organization both in the public and private sector, covering 3378 supervisors, first line and second line managers finally reached the following conclusion to know organizational climate for internal restructuring.

INTERNAL RESTRUCTURING THROUGH CHANGE IN ORGANISATIONAL CLIMATE

S.No.	*Characteristics*	*Low (16%-40%)*	*Medium (41%-60%)*	*High (61%-85%)*	*All-India Average*
1.	Superintendent –	0(-)	19(38%)	31(62%)	63.21%
2.	Safety & Security	4(8%)	19(38%)	27(54%)	60.30%
3.	Monetary Benefits	3(6%)	30(60%)	17(34%)	56.12%
4.	Objectivity & Rationality	4(8%)	34(68%)	12(24%)	52.43%
5.	Recognition & Appreciation	11(22%)	26(52%)	13(26%)	51.32%
6.	Welfare Facilities	11(22%)	31(62%)	8(16%)	48.39%
7.	Scope for Advancement	11(22%)	35(70%)	4(8%)	47.32%
8.	Grievance Handling	17(34%)	27(54%)	6(12%)	45.83%
9.	Training & Education	21(42%)	25(50%)	4(8%)	43.46%
10.	Participative Management	30(60%)	18(36%)	2(4%)	39.68%

Source: Personnel Management, C.B. Memor, p. 674.

Those organizations which can forecast technology are going

to survive and others will perish. Raising venture capital, addressing the issues of corporate governance, bringing about a change organization structure, people orientation, implementation of IT strategy, leveraging production systems for productivity would all be sensitive issues which need to be addressed by the organization in this new millennium.

Corporate governance is not a legislation or set of rules, which compels manager subservience to its dictate. It seeks to lay down norms and ethical practices for running the business ethics and value systems with organizational structure strategy, compensation strategy, and succession strategy and with transparency. Change is inevitable because of the economic liberalization and global communication and competitiveness which demanding greater transparency and accountability by bench marking in different field. Human resources should be treated as human potential for making it enthusiastic and dedicated. Lack of proper utilization of human resources lead towards unproductive expenditure and deficits in public sector enterprises. The over accumulated deficits were RS. 10522 crore at the end of 1987-88. By the end of 2000 the deficit will be more than 10 lakh crore. Privatization of AIR India and Indian airlines is on the time of restructuring

India today is a society in transition. The nation is witnessing unprecedenting changes in the economic, political and social environment. There is an upsurge in the desire of people to catch up with the world. Our capacity to meet the challenge will depend on how best and fast we respond to these changes. This is both an opportunity and a challenge. It could spell doom if we don't respond positively. And the next decade will be the most crucial in more ways than one.

Strategies and development policies will have to be interwoven into a pattern, which fits into the world trends, to meet the emerging needs and tackle problems unique to this country. We can no more afford to be isolated from the world. The expansion of the telecommunication network-AT & T, Motorola, Telestra,

NPP (Nippon telephone & telegraph), CNN, Skynet, skumar.com etc. leading to the emergence of the global village , will not allow us to live in our town world . We will be forced to take not of what is happening around us and prepare ourselves our institutions, businesses, farmers, bureaucracies- to play a more interactive role. Simply put, we must be proactive.

Though the decisions regarding organizational Restructuring are taken by the top management, yet it is more or less a democratic endeavor. For its smooth implementation, commitment and participation are required from all quarters and at all levels. The first and foremost task of a HR manager is to see that efficient and skilled manpower is retained and given proper training so that they can successfully work on new projects and jobs. It is essential to critically examine the utility of available manpower and only then a proper way can be suggested.

"Expertise in the human resources area" has been ranked as second in importance next only to "expertise in strategy formulation clearly the competitive advantages of an organizations in global economy depends primarily on how well its human resources are managed undoubtly the financial technological and other material resources are critical to the organization success. But it is the peoples industriousness, talents, creativity and above all. Commitment and involvement that generate and effectively deploy these resources. Total employee involvement really necessary for the internal restructuring. It involve recognition of employee contribution, holesome involvement development techniques like transitional analysis, T-group training, sensitive training and other internal restructuring program and only possible through total employees commitment and involvement which create real worth of restructuring and helpful for effective corporate governance voluntary retirement schemes are live example of corporate internal restructuring in last decade that are predicted changes due to fast changing scenario of corporate world and corporate governance.

The human resource development (H.R.D.) has to demonstrate a sense of strong business orientation. The major should be on the rationalization of human efforts. There are many organizations which have several sub units doing the same kind or related work there by generating duplicacy in efforts. This affects the efficiency as well as productivity of the organization. Open communication is an integral part of restructuring exercise. The management should, therefore, share business information with all executive and employees to seek there co-operation in achieving the goals and objectives of the restructuring.

If we analyse the Mega–trends which affected the corporate restructuring worldwide include following:

The Global Economic Boom of the 1990s,

The emergence of free market socialism,

Global lifestyles and culture nationalism,

The privatization of the Welfare State,

The rise of the Pacific Rim,

The Decade of Women in Leadership,

Of particular relevance to organisational restructuring, are the following trends:

1 Economic considerations transcending political considerations.

2 The Movement to Worldwide Free Trade.

3 The powerful Drive of Telecommunication .

4 The Relative Abundance of Natural Resources.

5 Inflation and Interest Containment.

6 The Asian consumer Boom

7 The advancement of democracy and spread of free enterprises.

8 New attentiveness to the Environment.

Since Independence the state has been the major player and agent of economic growth in India. It promoted and developed the public sector to the commanding heights of the economy covering practically all facts of economic activities. Our organization is protected by high tariffs and other instruments of economic policy. Recent changes including the break up of the socialist economy coupled with the faster development of the so-called free market economy, forced our policy makers to redesign economic policies. The economy policy in China, Russia, Asian Tigers and other parts of the world are indicative of the future scenario. This redesign had to be done quickly in order to respond positively to the crisis situation created by the adverse balance of payments and the slowing down of the economic activity in the recent past. The government of India initiated changes on the exchange rates, foreign trade investment, fiscal, monetary and industrial fronts.

The concept of business without boundaries is gaining momentum. This will have significant bearing on the productivity movement in the next decade or so. The most likely changes in this decade (2000-2010) are:

A. A qualitative shift in the role of the government.

B. Economic consideration and the liberalization will become stronger.

C. Increasing sensitivity to the social needs and the environment.

D. Extraordinary expansion in the services sectors.

E. Intense competition with in the country and globally.

F. Fastest Technological advances (High obsolescence rate).

G. These will be a decade of the entrepreneurship and business alliances.

H. A shift towards a more transparent, free and equal society.

I. The integration of our economy with the world economy will gain momentum.

J. Productivity will emerge as the main issue.

K. The export will be burdened with heavy pressure.

THE NEW NATIONAL AGENDA

The most important aspect in the coming years will undoubtedly be the productivity. The rising expectations of people can be met only through increased productive utilization of the resources, which in its turn will be instrumental in improving the quality of goods and services produced by the country. In this fiercely competitive world business organizations are left with no other alternative but to improve their performance if they have to survive and performance can be improved only if these are able to produce quality goods in a cost-effective manner. It should be a continuous process.

Michael porter has rightly pointed out that the only meaningful concept of competitiveness at the national level is productivity. An important aspect of raising operational restructuring at all the level of the organizations is being increasingly exercised by the different corporate. MNCs are centralizing their R&D operations to rationalize the cost of R&D. Major pharmaceuticals corporations have rationalized their R&D efforts across the globe.

INTEGRATED STRATEGY FOR INTERNAL RESTRUCTURING

These everyone talks about improvement in each and every thing and it should start from the scratch. Various names as TQM, Kaizen, strategic management by objectives etc. has been assigned to such improvements as the tool of internal restructuring. The following key aspects should be considered in this regard. These are:

Workers participation

Customer perception and needs

Sharing gains of productivity

Flexible manufacturing system

Motivation

Technology and product developments

The above aspects should be combined together to form a strategy that can be pursued by the organization to attain the success in the competitive environment of the new millennium.

Human resource management is replaced by human potential management. HRD strategies are playing vital role for formulation of vision; mission, goals and objectives shared values and action through long term organizational development interventions. Internal Restructuring through human resource development by improving and retaining a strong talent base strategy for human talent, by performance management by fixing the standards or bench marks for everyone, training and development focus on the behavioral/ physiological aspect which leads to healthy interpersonal relationship. Internal restructuring through the proper reward / compensation system, reward mechanism options are key to motivated talented employees, Instantaneous performance reward quarterly bonuses and quality of life enhanancers is also ways to recognize performance. Employees retaining and separation in proper systematic way is also burning issue for internal Restructuring point of view and leads towards good corporate Governance. Voluntary retirement schemes were in existence in the last decade as a weapon of internal Restructuring and here is a practical example of public sector unit :

Today corporate have to take care of quality of life of workers and their work environment. The management cannot afford to be selfish. No productivity improvement movement can survive unless and until it leads to some benefit to the workers. Management has continuously evolved the policies for redesigning the work, improving working conditions, jobs enrichment and

INTERNAL RESTRUCTURING THROUGH VRS IN NTC (National Textile Corporation)

Number of workers Retired Under VRS

STATE	*1992-93*	*1993-94*	*1994-95*	*TOTAL (UPTO APRIL 1995)*
Andhra Pradesh	735	260	62	1057
Karnataka	558	347	166	1071
Mehe	38	---	---	38
Delhi	324	196	85	605
Punjab	189	44	3	236
Rajasthan	710	291	163	1164
Gujarat	5318	1229	628	7175
Maharashtra	6551	3077	1328	10901
Madhya Pradesh	3396	740	137	4281
Tamil Nadu	83	41	127	251
Pondicherry	60	----	38	98
Uttar Pradesh	4021	1292	590	5903
West Bengal	2013	165	321	2499
Assam	47	---	6	53
Bihar	335	6	39	380
Orrisa	---	----	4	4
Total :	24378	7641	3697	35716

so on so forth. ***Organization when they are properly rewarded and they feel that they are really achieving something by working in Managers should believe that people work when they work they become loyal to the organization when they are properly rewarded and they feel that they are really achieving something by working in the organization.***

Though the decisions regarding organizational Restructuring are taken by the top management, yet it is more or less a democratic endeavor. For its smooth implementation, commitment and participation are required from all quarters and at all levels. The first and foremost task of a HR manager is to see that efficient and skilled manpower is retained and given proper training so that they can successfully work on new projects and jobs. It is essential to critically examine the utility of available manpower and only then a proper way can be suggested.

The Human Resource Development (HRD) has to demonstrate a sense of strong business orientation. The major focus should be on the rationalization of human efforts. There are many organizations which have several sub units doing the same kind or related work thereby generation duplicacy in efforts. This affects the efficiency as well as productivity of the organization. Open communication is an integral part of restructuring exercise. The management should, therefore, share business information with all executives and employees to seek their co-operation in achieving the goals and objectives of restructuring.

Globalization of workers and rapid growth cross border transaction the dimension of trade industry commerce and even services have undergone perceptible and drastic changes. These changes and developments have forced changes in the way of the thinking and ideologies of the people who govern them. Need of corporate restructuring for effective corporate governess needed from last 6-8 years. Professional bodies like institute of charted accountants of India, Institute of company secretaries of India, Institute of cost &works accountants of India. The prestigious bodies like CII and others are also involved for framing suitable uniform cord of corporate governess which can easily applicable and followed by India corporate and corporate world. To ensure good corporate governess the corporate expect good government governance. The department of company affairs under the ministry of law, justice and company affairs government of India, is the nodal agency for administration of companies' act 1956. Many legal implications are in the way of corporate governance in the process of corporate restructuring like 1. Mergers and takeovers

–excise Duty implications 2. Income tax implications of demergers 3. SEBI (Substantial acquisition of shares and take overs) Regulation.4. Provision of Companies Acts 1956 like section 390 to 394 securities regulations.

Stamp duty on transfer of assets as corporate restructuring mainly consist of mergers demergers and slump sale. With the above legal issues implications have to deal with very careful manner to achieve excellence corporate governance through internal and external corporate restructuring process in the era of change and development.

On the basis of recommendations of various committees like Cadbury committee Greenbury committee Organization for Economic Corporation and Development (Europe) and World Bank Kumar Mangalam, Birla committee, The Associated Chambers of Commerce for two Internal restructuring matters related to Corporate Governance. Some of the issues relate directly with, like the board should consist of 50% executives and 50% non executives professional for governance, as its board of directors, the board should meet at least 4 times in an year with a gap of not more than 4 months, 50% non executives, in grievance handling committee, audit committee, remuneration committee and grievance redressal committee. Quarterly and half-yearly results shall be provided to share holders, companies shall provide "shareholders charter" listing out significant developments about the performance. If the company, all the categories of shareholders shall be treated equally. On the light of above all recommendations is very much true. That internal restructuring effects the over all operations of the corporate, whether it is related to Human Resources restructuring, Marketing restructuring, Product Internal restructuring. Recommendations of the various above-mentioned committees and code of conduct suggested by them leads to Excellent Corporate Governance through right and appropriate Internal Restructuring Strategy.

REFERENCES

The Cadbury Committee, *Financial Aspects of Corporate Governance,* Dec 1992

Confederation of Indian Industry, *Desirable Corporate Governance—A Codes,* New Delhi, April 1998.

Gosh, Dutta, S. and Padamnabhan V. Corporate restructuring- A Case Study of Eveready Industries India Ltd, in *Restructuring to Change,* Excel Books New Delhi.

Nand Kumar D.V.human resource management in organisational restructurings.

Indian Management, Vol. 34 No.1, Feb 1995 Study Report On VRS, CII Eastern Region Jan 1990

C.B.Mamoria and Dr. Udai Pareek, *Personnel Management,* Himalya Publishing House, 2000, pp. 674.

Arun Monappa & Mahrukh Engineer, *Liberalization and Human Resource Management,* Response Books, New Delhi, 1999.

Rao, T.V. (1996) *Human Resource Development Experiences Interventions–* Sage Publications, New Delhi.

Bhattacharya, A.K. (1996) "Corporate Governance, *The Chartered Accountant,* Vol. XLV No. 5. November.

"Reforming Corporate Governance" (1999), *The Economic Times,* April 14.

Shiva Ramu, S. *Restructuring and Break-ups,* Response Book, New Delhi, 1999, p. 175.

26

CORPORATE RESTRUCTURING VIS-A-VIS CORPORATE GOVERNANCE: Contemporary Issues in Corporate Restructuring in the New Millennium

S.L. Gupta & Rakesh Kumar***

Over the last decades, industrialization and technological revolution have changed the nature of business enterprises from family owned organization to corporate entities. The modern corporations are owned by a large body of widely dispersed shareholders and are run by managers who may not own stake in the business. Unless the board of directors is efficient and vigilant, managers may not show necessary commitment to shareholder's interest on their own. Apart from shareholders, there are other stakeholders like creditors, employees, customers, suppliers and the society whose fates are interwoven with business corporations. India has been witnessing hostile takeovers, leveraged by outs and corporate restructuring on a large scale particularly since 1990. It is well known that takeovers are the result of short-term pressures from financial markets at the cost of long term performance. There is another school of thought, according to which takeovers are the financial market's way of disciplining inefficient managements. This has necessi-

* Chairman, Dept. of Management, Kurukshetra University Kurukshetra.

** Manager, National SC & ST Finance Corporation of India, New Delhi.

tated a suitable framework for corporate governance. Corporate governance is nothing but a set of structural arrangements with a view to aligning management of companies with the interests of its shareholders. Corporate governance domain extends to the interest of other stakeholders and eventually to society at large. In a tune sense, corporate governance is needed for creating an outperforming organization, which should be responsible to increasing customer satisfaction and shareholders value. In the absence of effective corporate goverance, the objectives of long term shareholder value, corporate democracy transparency in operations and reporting and internationally acceptable standards of performance remain illusory. In India, corporate governance has acquired a new urgency due to ever changing profiles of corporate ownership's preferential allotment of shares to promoters, inflow of foreign capital, and deliberate dismantling of control mechanism that had hitherto provided protective cover to every poorly managed corporate with economic liberalization.

A Company is an enterprise authorized by law to conduct business. Some control, so to say, the governance is required by the representative of key stakeholders for furtherance of corporate growth and protection of their interests. As shareholder's democracy is of paramount importance, companies shall have to expose their policies to shareholders. In the area of financial decision making it is obvious on the part of all shareholders and other stakeholders to judge whether the company's management has the ability to undertake various projects with high growth potentials. In this context, the Board of Directors is to determine corporate purpose and set broad directions for their achievements by executive directors and managers. Corporate governance ensures how effectively the board of directors and management is discharging their functions in building and satisfying stakeholder's confidence. According to CIT's draft corporate governance deals with the laws, procedures practices and implicit rules that determine a company's ability to take managerial decisions vis-a-vis its claimants. There is a global consensus about the objective of good corporate governance as essentially the one, which maximizes long term shareholders value. Since shareholder value must necessarily maximizes corporate value and best satisfy the claims of creditors, employees and the state.

In order to protect and promote the interests of all stakeholders corporate governance should cover well-defined systems and processes as has been said earlier also. There is a need to consider structural and organizational aspects like constitution of board of directors, their optimum size, composition, qualifications, role and competencies, frequency of changing board members and nominee directors. The organization of different committees by board members such as management committee, investment committee audit committee, etc., forms in integral part of the system for sound corporate goverance. While the main board of the company would deal with major policy decisions and strategic directions that the company should take the constitution of these committees makes focussed attention on various aspects of company's working. The board along with different committees and chief executive officers should devise right kind of management process for organizational effectiveness. The management include performance management systems, periodic business review, environmental audit, secretarial and legal audit, bench marking customer satisfaction, bench marking employees satisfaction, having surveys about them and so on. Evidently the efficacy of corporate goverance hinges on these well-defined system and processes.

In the international arena studies reveal the at sound and effective corporate governance enhances corporate dynamism and flexibility minimizes overall cost of economic adjustment and changes and improves global economic performance. Good governance practices entail active participation of shareholders in the direct and indirect management of corporation. Sound corporate decision making has emerged as the direct and positive outcome of good corporate governance system. One would hardly deny that the high standard of living enjoyed by the people of the developed countries is due to phenomenal success of their business. Reasons attributed to the business success are sound top management decisions, meaningful roles and functions played by directors and corporate officers like CEOs, and well designed legal and institutional settings. Hence, in the global scene, good corporate governance remains the key to business success and prosperity of the society.

A significant development in the later part of the century is the growing role of market in both industrialized and developing world. This growing importance of market and consequent premium on competitiveness is related to global integration of product, capital and labor market. Hence the spread of capitalism and concomitant globalisation demand efficiency, corporations in the world market place. Investors today are demanding more transparency in business operations, adequate and qualitative financial and non-financial information, and more accountability of company's board and management than ever before. Good corporate governance must address these issues.

In the words of Cadbury, as the world has shrunk, major institutional investors have moved beyond their domestic markets in search of attractive investment opportunities abroad and also look to spread their risks geographically. As they do so, they demand high and consistent standard in terms of both financial reporting and treatment of shareholders interests, making board room accountability and standards of corporate governance a global issue. Furthermore, today there is an increasing need among growing companies to tap international capital markets for funds. As they compete to attract investments and raise capital world wide, high standards of governance of companies is demanded by investors. Hence corporate governance is emerging as an important issue in the international business.

India has been in the process of adopting a policy of liberalization of markets, provocations of ownership and globalization of the economy. The changing needs and ever growing expectations of the information by rich customers, fast growing competition, governments policy on exports, etc., are cumulatively forcing the top management of the corporate world to be on their toes for anew paradigm. The governance of companies in India today requires high degree of professionalism of the board, transparent operations and disclosures through fairness in accounting and reporting of business operations. This will certainly attract both domestic and foreign investors for financial and technological resources required for development.

Public sector in India was established with an objective to promote equitable distribution of goods and maintain quality and quantity of goods and services in a manner suited to the Indian people. Even though private sector has also grown phenomenally, but the public sector still dominates the economy. The performance of this sector continues to bother the Govt. Each time when its objectives are revisited. The public sector companies have failed to increase the shareholder value and now the expectations are built on private sector. This would again continue to suffer for want of prevailing relationships of between the politico-bureaucratic system and industry as it is against corrective mechanism of market forces. It is seen that most public enterprise boards do not contribute to business strategy development. A number of enterprises have been taken by surprise by the process adopted by the government in liberating the Indian economy from the shackles of controls, quotas, embargoes and protection. Many public enterprises have turned sick, as their products have no appeal left for consumers.

Public enterprise boards have been an utter failure with regard to succession planning. No effort is made to groom people internally to succeed the CEO. Sometimes, boards just do not have an idea as to who would succeed in CEO in the event of his/her retirement or resignation and they have virtually no opportunity to observe the style and functioning of the CEO's immediate junior colleagues. Most boards do not even recommend the names of insiders to their administrative ministry or to the public enterprises selection boards nor lobby the case of insiders. On the information side public enterprise board falls short of expectations drastically. Whereas in the case of private sector, a number of sub committees of the board are appointed to look into major issues of audit, purchases, recruitment, export, performance evaluation, joint ventures, etc., through consultants, data bases and special studies, public enterprises boards have failed to notice this trend. Public enterprise boards have spared little time for developing the enterprise business strategy. This has happened primarily because no clear vision exists. Therefore, boards have failed to comprehend changes in direction of the organization nor critically observed the contribution of CEO in changing such direction. The contribution of boards in resolving corporate crisis is equally unsatisfactory as members are indifferent and do not feel the urgency to come forward and contribute mite because they are neither brought to book nor punished.

Despite nonperformance on financial and physical fronts by public enterprise boards where such entities have conceptualized schemes of their assessment and brought these schemes to the notice of their administrative ministries. Pubiic enterprises boards have to play a critical role to fulfil conditions of sound corporate governance vis-a-vis creditors as they are very important stake holders. Creditors need financial information on the operations of the enterprise on a continuous basis. Such information could be any or all of the following liquidity, solvency debt paying capacity, debt service coverage ratio, interest coverage ratio, value added, turnover, market share growth etc. By installing an effective system of financial disclosure, boards can ensure effective corporate governance. Corporate governance is needed in respect of suppliers. Here also it is important because about 60% of the cost are due to materials. As the quality of raw material and other spares have got vital role to play in sale of public goods, it is the duty of management to see that nothing is compromised with quality. It is also required to be seen that smooth supply of the material is maintained. The suppliers also expect to have good repaying capacity of the public enterprises.

So far we have made the broad contours of the corporate governance. There are varied norms adopted for the corporate governance depending upon the stages of development of different countries across the world.

The developed countries have gone much forward in revolutionizing the technological efficiency. It would be too difficult to adopt the same modes in developing countries because the process of liberation has not yet been complete and then there would be inherent weaknesses in the system as a whole. Nevertheless, efforts would be made to highlight some of the most pragmatic features of corporate governance as needed for the development and growth as has been needed for the satisfaction of all those entities associated either directly or indirectly with the corporate in India. The essentialities on the basis of which corporate governance has been thought of are as follows:

Promoters who belong to business houses control a very large proportion of the corporate sector. Their attitude are predominantly feudalistic and they tend to create an impression about their products among the customers and shareholders as if their depend on them for their benevolence to get value addition. This continues to be the general attitude barring few that have pledged for quality management and pleasing the consumers. It is a state of dilemma as to whether continue with the practices as have been adopted in the developed world or engross in the culture left behind be British Raj and still the facts remains that their exploitative manifestations persist even today.

The second aspect worth considering is that the multinational corporations manage significant proportion of the corporate sector. They are exploitative and insensitive to value addition doesn't matter what has been their reputation in their countries of origination. No political intervention is possible to mend such corporate because of the excessive amount of protection given due to labor union pressure. There is a heavy dependence on the corporate sector to get finances. During the process small shareholders continue to be exploited at the pretext of giving protection to the them.

The third important feature is that a significant part of share capital of quoted companies is held by domestic institutions most of which are government-owned. In a sense, till recently, the Indian corporate sector seriously looked after by the numerous regulating agencies from beginning to dissolution. Investment had to have been sanctioned to license holders, project finance used to be provided by multiple lending institutions, the need for working capital was met by applying standard rules and also the price of issue had been determined in a most rigid manner. The corporate were responsible for providing bit by bit informulation in respect of their operation to government agencies and other lending individuals or institutions. The obsessive government control did not provide any leeway and hence power and undue privilege continued to affect the corporate sector in variety of ways.

The need for impressive corporate governance was felt at the time of introduction of reform in 1991. The lethargic managers suffered defeat in the product market. There was scant regard to quality and when force competition emerged in liberalization era, the Indian companies started talking about quality innovation in the product market, reduction in the cost, technological changes etc. There was an another setback when companies were sold to foreign institutional investors. There after their moral demanded them to show and take into confidence the investors in regard to disclosures and boosting up of performance.

The lending institutions that were quite liberal in their approach as they continued to consider waiver and allowed capital restructuring now expected them to behave in a rational manner. This attitude paved way for adoption of revised standards of accountability. The lending institutions further became responsible to their own shareholders as entry to public in shareholding in financial institution became imperative. The advent of regulatory authorities desired for stringent accounting and disclosure policies. Capital market started demanding the model approach to corporate governance. The capital market witnessed the drastic reform with the setting up of Securities Exchange Board of India (SEBI). The corporate governance required improvement in the area of disclosures, widening of scope of information, quality of disclosures and so on.

Despite the developments taken place so far in the matters of corporate governance the impact is too little in the overall environment. Some companies have constituted corporate governance committees and at the instance of financial institutions, the borrowing companies have set up audit committees but without any surprise they are no where near to code of developed countries. Another set of efforts in the direction is in regard to nomination and compensation which is yet to be fully implemented. Stock options and performance linked compensation are yet to be founded. Sporadically code of codex has come to be seen in lines with the recommendation of Cadbury committee but wishfully, market pressure regulatory measures and enthusiastic executive management would push the process forward.

The importance of corporate governance lies in the fact that information status about company's performance and overall decision making should get to be improved. Entire onus lies on Board and hence toning up of board constitution is of utmost importance. The standard of corporate governance will stand automatically improved once a task of selecting right kind of people for board is undertaken. It is worth mentioning here the role-played by auditors in contrast to what has been played by the board. In this case quality of information and audit would enhance the competitiveness and capability of the board. There is a strong belief that good corporate governance rest with ethical and professional qualities of the auditors.

The next important aspect of the corporate governance is due to the presence of large investors and giant financial institutions. It is virtually impossible to meet the power and resource requirement of management of large companies by small investors. These large companies enjoy the best legal opportunities and exhibit strong muscle power. There is an easy way to involve small investor indirectly in the affairs while institutional investors like mutual fund etc. are coming at interface with these large companies. The corporate governance is further weakened by the non-executive directors who are foul in managing the affairs, and reckless talk under risk with public capital. Whereas fact remains that some of the observers have gone on to recommend the number of such directors to an extent of two thirds of the total strength of the board. The limitation is due to their involvement in so many boards. The companies act has increased their involvement upto the maximum of twenty-five boards.

The law has widened the empowerment and responsibilities of the board in regard to diversification of the business, merger and reconstruction, takeovers and buy back of shares. However, they are supposed to get approved the appointment of sole selling agent and also buying agent, a register of contract and agreement in which directors have an interest, ratification of the decision regarding new issues, preferential allotments and their objectives, use and so on from the shareholders in annual general meeting. But in reality shareholders never insist for taking their consent during decision making. They get to be cheated. To utter surprise, board has been made competent to exercise their power in the accounting practices of the firm but they never wish to do it theoretically. It is obligatory on the part of the management to disclose and justify the use of accounting practices, which are not in accordance with approved standards. They have followed several non-prudent practices like keeping an inadequate provision for potential liabilities and the many financial leasing practice to suit the whims of promoters and management.

The corporate governance is expected to deliver its worth as to reflected in value maximization and protection of the interest of small shareholders. The results are yet to be achieved and tremendous amount of efforts are needed on the part of law and regulations enforcement institutions. No laxity has been observed to be given even in the developed countries where most of the shareholders are knowledgeable, the systems and procedure are streamlined, the management and boards are loyal to their duties, the approach is democratic and law enforcement is also stringement. The effect of climatic conditions, level of advancement and geographical spread etc., can never be same for any two countries and its shall be unwise to repeat the experiences of developed countries in developing countries. But nonetheless. CII has evolved a code for corporate governance, which can be put in the form of following points:

(i) As the key to good corporate governance lies with the well functioning board of directors, the full board which is single fiered, should meet at intervals of two months and at least six times a year.

(ii) The Non-executive directors should comprise 30 per cent of the board, if one of them is the chairman.

(iii) The Non-executive directors should compromise at least 50% of the board if the chairman and the managing director are the same person.

(iv) No individual should be director on the board for more than ten companies at any given time.

(v) Non-executive directors must be active, have defined responsibility and be conversant with profit and loose account, balance sheet, cash flow statement, financial ratios and have some knowledge of company laws.

(vi) Non-executive directors should be paid commissions and offered with stock options for their professional inputs, besides their sitting fees etc.

(vii) Directors who have not been present for at least fifty per cent of the board meetings should not be reappointed.

(viii) The board should be informed of the operating plans and budget, long terms' plans quarterly divisional results and internal audit reports.

(ix) details of defaults, payments for intangibles and foreign exchange exposures should be reported to the board.

(x) An audit committee comprising at least three non-executive directors should be set up and given access to all financial information.

While accepting corporate disclosure norms, as recommended by the working group on companies act regarding financial and non-financial information, draft code recommended for disclosure of additional information in the annual report on the monthly average share prices, value added and financial performance of divisions and segments should be adopted.

(x) Disclosure norms and levels followed at home should be the same, as those required for GDR issues.

(xi) Major Indian stock exchanges should gradually insist upon compliance certificates signed by the CEO and CFO clearly starting that accounting policies and standard have been followed. Management is also responsible for preparation, integrity and fair presentation of financial statement and the board has been the company's system of internal accounting and administrative control through audit committee or directly.

(xii) The government must allow for reducing the number of companies having nominee directors, the draft envisages that financial institutions should withdraw from company boards where there individual share holding is 5% or less or the total FI holding is under 10%.

(xiv) Companies that default on fixed deposits should not be permitted to accept further deposits, make inter-corporate loans or investments and declare dividends until the default is made good.

What actually happens in India is very much different from the developed countries

The average shareholders do not have much expertise and they are being exposed to the risks of dealing with corporate in a big way only recently. The mutual fund and the other debt instruments deploying the money of small investors are not operating in an accountable manner.

The change taking place is fast but the potential and capability of managers and experts on the board and law enforcement agencies are no where near to expected level.

The problems are not properly examined in the academic circle and hence what ever is thought for corporate governance by committees and other who have been entrusted the task to evolve the corporate governance had to be accepted. Let the problem be given research orientation.

It may be presumptuous to expect that good governance will emerge if suitable incentives are offered and ground rules for good practices are laid down clearly. Fundamental changes in attitudes, commitment and respect for democratic norms must emerge before claim of the corporate sector coming of age can be sustained. The first fundamental principle of corporate governance should be to implement punishment sufficiently severely and in proportion to the nature of the corporate crime. This is a precondition for generating respect for law and institutions of corporate governance. Throughout the industrial world, it is well known that strikes are far more effective than carrots in obtaining the desired level of compliance.

27

CORPORATE GOVERNANCE AND RESTRUCTURING

M.Manickam & M. Manuneethi Cholan***

Corporate governance is a part of corporate ethics and value system. The term corporate governance has emerged on the Indian scenario recently. Only during the last few years, the need for improvement in governance is attracting the attention of Indian industries. Good corporate governance is the key to ensure that the competitiveness of the Indian industry is maintained and further strengthened. There appears to be very little in India by way of meaningful corporate governance.

Concept of corporate governance in its true sense has still not been fully evolved. Corporate governance can be defined from several angles. It is not capable of being precisely defined. Corporate governance can be defined as a system of structuring, operating and controlling a company with the specific aim of fulfilling the long-term strategic goal of the owners. The takeover boom, entry of multinational corporations and foreign institutional investors after the announcement of new economic policy had brought the concept of corporate governance to prominence. The recent mergers, acquisitions and other leveraged restructur-

* Professor & Head, Department of Commerce, Bharathiar University, Coimbatore-641046

** Deputy Director (Inspection), Department of Company Affairs, Shastri Bhavan, Chennai-600006

ing have added a new dimension to the concept of corporate governance.

Significance of Corporate Governance

Of several aspects of corporate governance, financial aspects of corporate governance are the most important because the ultimate objective of a business is to maximize the wealth of the shareholders. The increasingly institution dominated and performance driven investors are putting enormous pressure on corporate management for delivering unfailing financial performance. Good corporate governance leads to the growth in sales, profits, assets and market value of shares. Overall growth leads to growth in shareholders' wealth. From financial Institutions point of view, corporate governance is a philosophy by which owners and managers are expected to be perennially responsive to other entities such as shareholders, promoters, institutional shareholders, deposit holders, creditors, consumers and finally to institutional lenders.

The dominant players are the financial institutions. The public on an average is the second largest equity holders in companies. The third and fourth are the promoters and foreign institutional investors respectively. A vital element of corporate governance lies in the management, which is answerable to the shareholders as to the custody and conduct of company's business activities and the commercial exploitation and preservation of assets. Corporate governance is a concern of great importance to shareholders because shareholders' wealth depends in large part up on the goals the people who set the strategy of the company. All the reports on corporate governance have emphasized that the basic objective of a corporation is to maximize shareholder value. Hence it is generally considered that the sole responsibility of any business is to its shareholders and the business is expected to maximize the value of the shareholders.

With the growth of corporate form of organisation, management and ownership have been considerably distanced from each other. A number of company failures have been reported and several instances of mismanagement have been alleged, with some well known and senior corporate executives being hauled up for non-performance and non-compliance with the country's legal requirements. In all such instances common investors have lost out, either through repayment defaults or by erosion of market value of their holdings.

Many of the developing countries including India have moved in varying degrees in the direction of an open market driven economy, which is an essential ingredient of capitalist societies. Globalisation of markets calls for a correspondingly improving compliance with global practices in all spheres of corporate activity. An apparent linkage exists between a company's governance standards and its market value. Shareholder activism is driving more and more companies towards better governance.

Committees on corporate governance

A brief summary of reports of various committees on corporate governance is presented in this section. A comparative summary of the recommendations of all the committees on corporate governance is also presented at the end. Based on the discussion in this paper, a code of governance that is most appropriate for Indian corporate sector developed by the authors has also been given. The reports of the following committees have been examined in this paper.

1. Cadbury committee.
2. Greenbury committee.
3. Organization for Economic Cooperation & Development (Europe).
4. World Bank.
5. Confederation of Indian Industry.
6. The Associated Chambers of Commerce and Industry of India and
7. Kumar Mangalam Birla Committee.

In England Cadbury committee presented a report on financial aspects of corporate governance in December 1992. It formulated the rules and procedures to enhance the effectiveness of the board. It emphasized the need to maximize the shareholders value by a good corporate governance system. Subsequently, Greenbury committee was appointed to bring out the best practices in determining and accounting for directors' remuneration. All listed companies registered in United Kingdom comply with the code to the fullest extent practicable and include a statement about their compliance in the annual reports to shareholders by their remuneration committees. Any areas of non-compliance should be explained and justified. The Cadbury committee report has formed the basis for a debate on code of corporate governance in India. The report hence has drawn a worldwide attention.

The Organization for Economic Co-operation and Development (OECD) in its ministerial level meeting on 27-28 April, 1998 had established an ad-hoc task force on corporate governance with an objective to develop a set of non-binding principles that embody the views of member countries on corporate governance. The principles contained in its report were: 1. protection of shareholders' rights 2. the role of stakeholders 3. need for disclosures and transparency and 4. responsibility of the board for better corporate governance. In September 1999, the World Bank published a report on corporate governance and presented a framework for implementation. It has observed that globalization would bring uniformity in corporate governance system.

The Confederation of Indian Industry's (CII) Desirable Corporate Governance is the first major functional exercise on corporate governance in Indian Industry. It is expected that the code for corporate governance be followed uniformly by Indian companies in private and public sectors. The code of governance is applicable to banks and financial institutions also. The code of governance emphasizes protection of investors' interest and developing high level of confidence in business and industry.

There are 17 recommendations to be followed by companies in reporting corporate governance. It also emphasizes the global concerns about the objectives of 'good' corporate governance: maximizing long-term shareholders' value.

Consequent to the CII publication on code of corporate governance, Indian companies have started reporting details of future investments, expansion, diversification plans, intellectual capital valuation, brand value, economic value added, financial ratios etc. The recent annual reports of companies contained a report on corporate governance. Economic value added signifies the effort of the company towards reporting shareholder enrichment. Quantifiable measures like economic value added and market value added have started appearing in annual reports. Disclosure of these information provide shareholders an understanding of the direction in which a company is moving. Recognizing the importance of good corporate governance the Indian Companies Act has also been modified to provide considerable importance to the role of board of directors in corporate governance.

Consequent to the appointment of Kumar Mangalam Birla committee on corporate governance, a draft report was submitted to The Securities and Exchange Board of India (SEBI) recently. It agreed that the fundamental objective of corporate governance is the enhancement of the long-term shareholder value, while at the same time protecting the interests of other stakeholders. It set out a time limit for implementing the recommendations.

The Associated Chambers of Commerce and Industry of India has also published a report on corporate governance. It emphasized that care should be taken in appointing directors, particularly in listed companies for better corporate governance.

The above reports emphasize the importance of a code of good corporate governance for Indian corporate sector. These concepts also led to the emergence of code of governance in

Government and code of electronic governance due to the introduction of electronic commerce in India.

Findings from analysis of recommendations of various committees on corporate governance

The Cadbury committee states that board of directors is responsible for the governance of their companies. It insists that the boards should pay particular attention to their duty to present a balanced and understandable assessment of their company's position. Financial reporting should be true and fair. The committee further recommends that the board should also ensure the integrity and consistency of their reports.

Kumar Mangalam Birla Committee recommends that board meetings should be held at least four times in a year, with a maximum time gap of four months between any two meetings. The committee further recommends that the members of the board give due importance and commitment to the meetings of the board and its committees. The committee insists that there should be a ceiling on the maximum number of committees across all companies in which a director could be a member or act as chairman.

Organization for Economic Co-operation and Development (Europe) and Cadbury committee emphasize the need to protect the rights of shareholders and they recommend that all shareholders should be treated equally. Kumar Mangalam Birla committee recommend that a director should not be a member in more than ten committees or act as chairman of more than five committees across all companies in which he is a director.

Confederation of Indian Industry and Kumar Mangalam Birla committee insist that the disclosure of financial statements should be accurate and regular. They further insist that financial statements should reveal timely, accurate, substantive and material information. Organization for Economic Co-operation and Development (Europe) recommend that any material interest in transactions or matters affecting the corporation should be disclosed by board of directors of the company.

All committees invariably recommend setting up of audit committees. Confederation of Indian Industry insist that listed companies with either a turnover of over Rs.100 Crores or a paid up capital of Rs.20 Crores should set up audit committees within two years. Both Kumar Mangalam Birla committee and Confederation of Indian Industry recommend that the audit committee should have maximum non-executive members, who should have adequate knowledge of finance, accounts and basic elements of company law. Cadbury committee recommends that the audit committee should have minimum of three members. Membership should be confined to the non-executive directors of the company and a majority of the non-executive directors serving on the committee should be independent. Membership of the committee should be disclosed in the annual report.

The Associated Chambers of Commerce and Industry recommend that the board of directors, when they find themselves unable to accept the advice of audit committees on any issue, the board should be competent to overrule the advice but should be required to report the facts fully to the general body of shareholders at the next annual general meeting for their information.

However, in India audit committees do not exist except in few well-managed companies. It is expected that with the implementation of the recommendations of various committees audit committees would be set up in all the listed companies in future.

Cadbury committee, Confederation of Indian Industry and Kumar Mangalam Birla committee recommend that non-executive directors should be included in board of directors to bring an independent judgement to bear on issues of strategy, resources including key appointments and standards of conduct. Confederation of Indian Industry recommends that in order to secure better effort from non-executive directors, companies should pay a commission over and above the sitting fees and consider offering stock options for the use of professional inputs. It further recommends that independent directors should have clearly defined responsibilities within the board and become active participants in boards, not passive advisors

In England Greenbury committee was especially setup to report on remuneration policy. It recommends that the remuneration committee should be setup by the board of directors. The remuneration committee should consist of only non-executive directors. It further recommends that remuneration committees must provide the packages needed to attract, retain and motivate directors of the quality required but should avoid paying more than is necessary for this purpose

Kumar Mangalam Birla committee recommends that the remuneration committee should comprise minimum of three non-executive directors, the chairman of the committee being an independent director. The committee also recommends that the chairman of remuneration committee should be present at annual general body meetings to answer the shareholder queries.

All committees invariably emphasize the need for increasing shareholder value by good corporate governance. The Associated Chamber of Commerce and Industry recommends that companies should concentrate not only on wealth maximization of the shareholders but also on the social responsibility and the accountability to its other stakeholders.

SUGGESTIONS FOR BETTER CORPORATE GOVERNANCE IN INDIA

The authors suggest the following specific recommendations for policy makers, with a view to further strengthen an effective corporate governance system in India.

1. The Board

A. The board should consist of 50 percent executive and 50 percent non-executive professional as its Board of directors.

B. The chief- executive should not be the chairman of the board. A professional non-executive chairman should head the board.

C. A person should not hold directorship in more than 10 companies and the chairman of a committee of directors in not more than 5 committees across all companies in which he is adviser

D. The board should meet at least 4 times in a year with a gap of not more than 4 months

E. Financial institution should not have nominee directors form the institution itself. However the institution can nominate outside professionals with rich experience.

F. Informal outside directors shall be well remunerated to enable them to attend to the board work seriously.

II. Committees of the Board of Directors

A. The following three committees of the board are recommended.

i) Audit committee,

ii) Remuneration committee and

iii) Grievance redressal committee

B. The audit committee shall consist of at least 3 non-executive directors with at least one director having accounts financial knowledge. The chairman of the audit committee shall be present at the Annual general meeting to answer shareholders' queries.

C. The remuneration committee and grievance redressal committee shall have 50 percent non-executive directors.

Transparency and Disclosure of Information

A. Key information, operating plans and budgets together with long term plans shall be disclosed in the Annual report.

B. Quarterly and half yearly results shall be provided to the shareholders.

C. Shareholders shall be informed of any transaction involving substantial payments.

D. Companies shall provide "shareholders' charter" listing out significant developments about the performance of the company.

E. The annual report shall contain details of Economic value added, Market value added, Total shareholders return, Brand value and Human assets value.

IV. Rights of Shareholders

A. All categories of shareholders shall be treated equally.

B. Shareholders shall be entitled to postal ballot voting

C. Shareholders shall be provided with the data of new directors and they shall also be informed of any pending legal proceedings against any director.

V. Implementation of the Suggested Code of Corporate Governance

A. The code suggested above shall be incorporated in the listing agreement with the stock exchanges where the stock is listed for trading.

B. All listed companies with a paid up capital Rs 10 crores and above and a market capitalization of Rs.50 crores and above shall implement the above codes from 1st April 2001, and

C. There shall be a separate section on corporate governance in the annual report with a detailed compliance report of code of corporate governance.

Conclusion

The implementation of New Economic Policy and the

introduction of corporate governance have taken place in India only during the end of the 20th century. However, it is an accepted fact that the strategies incorporated have started functioning in the right direction. The ongoing economic reforms initiated have created a conducive environment and has started yielding expected gains. Optimistically, it can be viewed that the establishment and growth of corporate governance in the expected lines will definitely bring a stable and steady economic development in India. It is expected that the implementation of corporate governance code suggested by the authors will help to achieve the goal of good corporate governance in India.

REFERENCES

1. The Cadbury Committee, *Financial Aspect of Corporate Governance*, December 1992.
2. Greenbury Committee, *Recommendations on Corporate Governance*.
3. Organization for Economic Corporation & Development (Europe), *OECD Principles of Corporate Governance*, April 1998.
4. World Bank, *Corporate Governance: A Framework for Implementation*, September 1999.
5. *Confederation of Indian Industry,* Desirable Coporate Governance—A Code, New Delhi, April 1998.
6. *The Associated Chambers of Commerce and Industry of India.* Corporate Governance.
8. Securities and Exchange Board of India. Draft Report of the Kumar Mangalam Birla Committee on Corporate Governance, May 1999.

28

MERGER AND ACQUISITION: A STRATEGY FOR CORPORATE RESTRUCTURING

Dr. V.S. Garg & Mukesh Sehgal***

Only recently unfettered from the rigid shackles of government control and exposed to market forces, corporate India will now have to chalk out and carry through long-term corporate strategies to enhance competitiveness and subtainability. They will have to index internal ability, and react to changes in their industries and in the overall economy to best avail the opportunity available.

With 40 years of over-regulation resulting in deep distortions in the economy, there is an acute need for business to embark on a pragmatic approach to restructuring. Corporate Restructuring offers an obvious strategy for correcting the flaws of decades of a command economy.

The compulsion to become world-size because of the globalisation of the economy, requiring corporations to focus their efforts on their areas of core competence, and to form alliances with global players. The whole purpose of a restructuring today is to withstand growing competition within and outside the country and to keep the company floating profitably

* Director, MAIMT, Jagadhri (Haryana)

** Director, (Dy) cum Associate Professor, S.A. Jain Institute of Mgt. & Tech., Ambala City.

against all those risks and threats which the top management anticipates and prepares itself to face those probable challenges by restructuring suitably.

Business Organisations engaged in a broad range of activities including expanding, shrinking and otherwise restructuring asset and/or ownership structures. There has been a marked increase in the nature, scope and variety of these activities, motivated either by purely financial considerations or by long-term strategic perspective. These raise more fundamental issues than the previous merger waves. The daily newspapers are awash with details of mergers and acquisitions, tender offers (both friendly and hostile), spin-offs and divestitures, changes in the ownership structures, and struggle for the corporate control. If we talk about latest one Tata Tea is going to buy Tetly for 271 million pounds. Chairman Rattan Tata says it *is a great signal for global industry by Indian Industry.* Similarly corporate India's two largest business houses, the Tatas, AV Birla group and the US Based AT&T are joining hands to emerge as one of the major cellular telephoney player in the country. The wave is on full swing for achieving excellence.

Introduction

Restructuring has raised important issues both for business decisions and for public policy formulating. No firm is regarded safe from a takeover possibility. Restructuring may be critical to the healthy expansion of business firms as they evolve through successive stages of growth and development. Both internal and external growth may be complementary in the long-range evolution of firms. Successful entry into new product markets and into new geographical markets by a firm may require restructuring at some stage in the firms development. Successful competition in international markets may depend on capabilities obtained in a timely and efficient fashion through this exercise.

Present Status of Corporate Restructuring in India

In the liberalised but developing economies like India corporate restructuring is regarded as an important instrument whereby the free play of market forces lead to the removal of structural imbalances or economic inefficiencies and the current recession. Even among the developed economies there is a wide diversity in the scope and extent of legislation and regulation. The existence of such diversities in many developed western economies pose a threat of duplicating the western models in countries like India without a realistic appraisal of realities to determine the extent to which these should be adopted. *The success or failure of measures adopted to restructure any company or organisation depends upon how realistic an appraisal was carried out.*

In India corporate restructuring is still in its adolescent stage and so is the status of regulatory framework which has not yet completely evolved and is characterised by fragmentation, where several status and regulatory bodies have a role to play in the regulation of corporate restructuring. Most recently we have seen many internal and external type of restructuring in almost all the sectors of industrial world which indicate the real impact of it.

The past experience has shown that the companies are willing to adopt unfair and hostile approach in takeovers and acquisitions. Even at the cost of their corporate image. *The capital market at present is in the doldrums.* Therefore, the the supply of the companies vulnerable to takeover is on the rise. In such scenario, characterised by survival of the fittest the takeovers and acquisitions are a direct threat to the inefficiently run businesses. The takeovers are presently regulated by SEBI and stock exchange listing rules, which suffer from certain flaws. In order to remove the so called flaws in the regulations, SEBI appointed a committee to recommend changes in the existing laws governing takeovers.

In developed free economies corporate mergers and amalgamations are a regular feature. *In Japan, USA and European nations hundred of mergers and amalgamations take place every year as a regular phenomena of combination and reconstruction of the business enterprises.* Across-the-border merger and takeovers of multinational companies are the usual phenomenon in the developed nations.

Is Corporate India prepared for restructuring through mergers and acquisitions?

Business organisations engaged in a broad range of activities including expanding, shrinking and otherwise restructuring asset and/or ownership structures.

There has been a marked increase in the nature, scope and variety of these activities, motivated either by purely financial considerations or my long-term strategic perspective. These raise more fundamental issues than the previous merger waves. *The daily newspapers are awash with details of mergers and acquisitions, tender offers (both friendly and hostile), spin-offs and divestitures, changes in the ownership structures, and struggle for the corporate control.*

Recent big cross-border and in-country deals - to name a few random examples, Chrysler and Daimler-Benz. Vodafone and Airouch. British Petroleum and Amoco, Exxon and Mobil, and our Hindustan Lever/Tata Oil Mills, KEC and SAE, Electrolux acquisition of Intron and Maharaja, GE Capital/SRF Finance, Ranbaxy and Crossland, suggested a seismic shift in structure of the global economy, which can profoundly impact the Indian economy in its efforts to seamlessly integrate with the global economy.

Financial fluctuations have a similar catalytic effect. A low market, with low interest rates can have an especially strong effect after a period of high inflation, in which the cost of hard assets have increased more rapidly than stock prices.

Witness the efforts of India's leading business houses to systematically revert to core businesses. For example, TISCO has divested its cement business to Lefarge of France: TELCO has spun of its construction equipment business into a separate company, and so on. In the two wheeler industry, after Piaggiio LML notwithstanding their differences raised their market share with four stroke engines. Rahul Bajaj has been forced to become more aggressive. Pharmaceuticals and the automobile will also witness a new process of consolidation. Big concerns too are likely to sell their stakes to foreign partners like Siddarth Shriram to Honda and Anand Mahindra to Ford.

Highlights

- Corporate restructuring is creating a market for both acquisition and disposal of business units.
- Three years of economic slowdown are causing shake outs in many sectors, forcing losses to exit.
- Share prices have been low enough to make acquisitions of large equity stages feasible in terms of price.
- A formal takeover code has laid out the mechanism for both hostile and negotiated takeovers.
- The financial institutions are, for the first time, willing to help the M & A game by selling their holdings. Since Financial institutions have large exposures in terms of equity holdings in the cement companies, a uniform policy would facilitate smooth takeovers and mergers. *IDBI has prepared a study on the cement industry covering almost every type of information like regional demand, distribution of supply, performance, problems and prospects. FI want the cement industry to adopt suitable restructuring strategies to improve technology, reduce cost and achieve economies of scale. So far FIs have played an important role in six mergers over past two years including the Rs. 450 crore acquisition of Rassi Cement Ltd.*

Adding to the ammunition, the financial institutions are signalling, for the first time ever, that they will no longer protect existing owners of companies from take over bids. Thus, despite sharing the aggressive intent behind the first two waves—dating back to the mid-1980s and the early 1990s respectively—the third M & A wave is also dramatically different in terms of the extent of firepower it has armed both the battlers with. The predator lurking within the Rs. 8,342.75 crore Hindustan Lever resurfaced with the negotiated acquisition of the Rs. 59.11 crore Lakme from the Rs. 35,000 cror Tata Group. A potent takeover Scud, targettign a 20 per cent stake, was fired at the Rs.1,162.72 crore Indian Aluminium by the Rs. 1,146.72 crore Sterlite Industries. Alarmed by the prospects of consolidation in the aluminium industry, the Rs. 1,457.15 crore Hindalco immediately launched a broad-side against the Rs. 162.28 crore Pennar Aluminium, bidding for a 13 per cent chunk of the company. Simultaneously, acquisitions resurfaced in the Pharmaceuticals sector. With the Rs. 400 crore Wockhardt snapping up the Rs. 200 crore Merind. And the troubled cement industry saw a major restructuring bid as the Rs. 832.49 crore India cements mounted a raid on the Rs. 349.64 crore Raasi Cement—aiming to increase its holdings from 18.03 per cent by another 26.78 per cent.

The compulsion to become world-size because of the globalisation of the economy, requiring corporations to focus their efforts on their areas of core competence, and to form alliances with global players.

The need to take advantage of the relaxation in government policy, which is allowing companies to take decisions that are based on economic realities. The Government is chalking out a fresh agenda for corporate restructuring. Department of Company Affairs secretary T.S. Krishnamurthy has advocated setting up of a separate authority to deal with the mergers, demergers, and corporate restructuring matters in order to expedite approvals and decisions and improving the corporate efficiency. A separate entity to deal with the mergers and acquisitions is required because the laws related to these issues are very complicated and processing procedure is very time consuming.

Analysis of Restructuring

The use of M&A as corporate strategy raises important issues. On the positive side, M&A may be critical to the healthy expansion of businesses as they evolve through successive states of growth and development. For, both internal and external growth may be compatible with the long-range evolution of a company. Successful entry into new geographic and product markets often requires the speed, accompanied by an existing infrastructural frramework, that only M&A can give access to. For these, as well as other reasons, some economists argue that M&As increase value through efficiency gains, and move resources to their best users.

Others are more sceptical, however, and claim that M&As are frequently descriptive, rarely resulting in efficiency gains. At best, they allow a redistribution of wealth, but generate no real economic benefits. Further, at the macro level, they affect investment, R & D, and employment-generation adversely, often bringing financial ruin upon companies that have been unable to bear the high costs of M & A, and have been forced to close down. There is, therefore, a real fear that Indian companies will over-react to their new freedom, and indulge in speculative and harmful M & A.

For, in their quest for what they fondly imagined as invincible proportions and market domination, they engendered cropping handicaps for themselves: directionless, diversified conglomerates instead of sharply-focused corporations. Unanticipated added costs instead of anticipated economies of scale. Paralysing cultural mismatch instead of energy-enhancing managerial synergy.

On the contrary, the benefits of a successful acquisition are powerful, offering as they do dominant market shares, the strength of sheer size, and unique competitive advantages. The swelling of the M & A wave has created a critical historical juncture, when this question must be answered if the entire process of restructuring through acquisitions and sellouts is to generate real benefits for the participants.

The solution: identifying possible ways of improving future gains by carefully selecting the type of mergers, the target company, the anticipated efficiencies, and a management strategy that will maximise potential synergy. This method will allow managers to practise a more realistic pricing policy, counter assimilation problems, and benchmark synergy expectations—all of which will, ultimately, lead to more value-creating M & A.

The Strategy. Empirical evidence suggests that in most cases of conglomerate mergers, capital expenditure is the only function that is brought under the supervision of the new management. This is probably because companies believe in their ability to induce financial synergy through M & A, which will decrease the cost of capital.

Cash-Flow/Investment Opportunities (Strategic Realignment). When companies feel that there are few investment opportunities, either within themselves or in the same industry, they look to redeploy their capital in a more attractive industry. This logic is similar to the BCG product Matrix, which recommends the companies milk their cash cows to fund the question marks in the hope that they become stars. Thus, the company turns itself into miniature capital market, allocating cash from low growth areas to fields of higher return.

Tax Savings. Tax laws distinguish between internally and externally-generated funds, offering tax benefits to acquiring companies. To exploit these benefits, companies might opt not to return money to shareholders and, instead, acquire other companies. Acquisition can also help utilise unused tax-credits.

The problems: Many pure conglomerate mergers can be explained by the desire to improve the rate of ROI. But several roadblocks remain.

There is little economic logic to the belief that post-acquisition companies are able to borrow more cheaply. For, there is no net reduction in the risk from a situation where these companies remain separate but guarantee the debt.

The notion that the diversified predator can generate larger returns—through increased earnings and capital appreciation—for its shareholders than non-diversified predators is a misconception. On the contrary, there is more uncertainty about the side and variability of future cash-flows as overall risk for diversified companies is higher.

Individual shareholders are as capable of investing in attractive sectors as companies. Thus M&A may not be the only means for creating value for them.

Reducing Company -Specific Risk to Lower the Discount Rate

The Value Driver: M &A strategies that reduce unsystematic (company specific risk) will lower the discount rate (beta) of the company. Specialised diversification can stabilise cash-flows in relation to market fluctuations.

The Strategy: Using the DCF method of calculating the present value of future earnings, it is clear that to increase valuation, one can either increase earnings or reduce risk. There are two kinds of risk that a company is exposed to: systemic (common to the universe to investable assets), and unsystematic (company-specific). Most forms of reducing systematic risk are equally available to the individual investor.

However, company-specific risk-reduction is a function of diversification strategy, and hence, can not be achieved by individual investors. It needs to dampen the company-strategy hinges on extending reputations capital-through brand extensions, for instance-developing critical mass in buying and selling, reducing technological and marketing risks, and reinforcing managerial skills. Moreover, mutual forbearance reduces competition as it leads to tacit collusion. Companies buy into their rivals industries in order to threaten a retaliatory strike on their competitors' main markets.

The Problems. Investors can reduce risk by diversifying within the market basket more cheaply than a company can through M& A. That's not all.

There may be cases of over-extension into unrelated product areas or product-lines that dilute the original brand image.

Often, the motivation to merge is to protect cash-flows by investing in counter-cyclical businesses. This risk-pooling concept is weak since several counter-cyclical industries have been known to nose-dive in unison. Further, companies may have no competency for managing such unrelated business.

Summary

Restructuring is a wider concept which includes mergers, acquisition, diversification, spin-offs etc. In the present era of liberalization, globalizaton and privatization - the competition is becoming stiff. In the recessionary phases, as one going on presently, and to cope with the competition a corporate body needs strong financial muscles as well as complete acquisitions, whereby the main objective of the acquirer is to grow larger so as to crush the smaller fishes in the pond. Spin-offs are generally resorted to concentrate on one particular area and specialize. Due to legal complications and lack of support from the financial institutions (in completing mergers), such type of practices were not popular in the past. However, with the change inthe outlook of the Government and FIs the number of acquisition cases are increasing and in the next two years we can see more activity in this area.

REFERENCES

Globe, Devra L., and Lawerance J. White, "A Time-Series Analysis of Mergers and Acquisitions in the US Economy," Chapter 9 in Alan J. Auerbach, ed., *Corporate Takeovers: Causes and Consequences.* Chicago Press, 1988, pp. 265-309.

Jensen, Michael C., "Takeovers: Folklore and Science." *Harvard Business Review*. 62, November-December 1984, pp. 109-120.

Rohatyn, Flex G., "Needed: Restraints on the Takeover Mania." *Challenge*. 29, May-June 1986, p. 30.

J. Fred Weston, Kwany S. Chung & Susan E. Hoag. "*Mergers, Restructuring & Corporate Control*, pp. 2-6.

W.T. Grimm, *Mergerstat Review*, 1987, and previous years.

Financial Analyst, April 1999 pp. 29.

Business Today, Dec 7-21, 1998.

Business Today, March 7-21, 1998, pp 61-64.

The Hindustan Times, 12-6-99.

The Economic Times, 12-7-99 & 21-5-99.

The Financial Express, 5-6-99 & 27-4-1999.

The Tribune, 23-5-99.